NOT FOR GLORY—

Who are today's great teachers?

By WILLIAM JEREMIAH BURKE

A COWLES BOOK

TO BLANCHE CRIPPEN

PREFACE

How do you find *the* National Teacher of the Year? There is no simple answer. I have helped search for this teacher each year since 1960, when LOOK Magazine first became co-sponsor of the National Teacher of the Year Award, along with the U.S. Office of Education and the Council of Chief State School Officers.

My odyssey began when Patricia Carbine, LOOK's managing editor, called me into her office. "Pack your bag, Jerry," she cheered, "you're going to Honolulu." This had to be a joke. As director of LOOK's editorial research department, I generally kept close to my desk. Long trips were just for writers and photographers. The date was Nov. 3, 1960. The assignment was for real.

Each year since I have traveled on this assignment. It begins when each chief state school officer submits his nominee for the award and a committee of educators, approved by the co-sponsors, meets in Washington, D.C., to screen the candidates and select from five to ten for interviews. I have observed each teacher in his classroom, talked to school officials, students and townsfolk. I have also made full reports to the committee to help them in their selection. I often wrote them in longhand on planes, in airports, in hotels, and in motels. Much of the material for this book comes from these reports.

This search has made me intimately aware of the lives of scores of teachers throughout the United States. Each finalist has had a valid claim to the award, the most coveted honor in education. All stand as worthy representatives of the teaching profession. Many of them were born on farms, in poor families. They had to work harder than most children to get ahead. Some were orphans. Many of them were born before World War I, when American life was home-centered, church-centered, and simple. This book pays tribute to them and to all teachers, who are fighting the battle of education in classrooms from Maine to Hawaii.

Much of the credit for the continued success of the National Teacher of the Year Award goes to Dr. Edgar Fuller, Executive Secretary of the Council of Chief State School Officers, and to Miss Blanche Crippen, Assistant Executive Secretary of the council. They were among the first to see in my reports the germ of a book, and to encourage me to write it.

WILLIAM JEREMIAH BURKE

CHAPTER ONE

"... The basis of all good teaching is a genuine love for children. All teachers should have that. With many, many persons, teaching is just another job. With some it is a profession. With me it is more than just another job, more than a profession—it is a way of life...."

HELEN ADAMS

1

1961 NATIONAL TEACHER OF THE YEAR

HELEN "MISSY" ADAMS
Kindergarten
Cumberland Elementary School
Cumberland, Wisconsin

RUNNERS-UP

ADELINE BABBITT
Remedial Reading
Kamehameha School for Girls
Honolulu, Hawaii

MRS. SHERMAN LEE, JR.
Mathematics
Marietta High School
Marietta, Georgia

JAMES DeROSE
Science
Marple-Newtown Senior High School
Newtown Square, Pennsylvania

HELEN MANEY
History
Geneva High School
Geneva, New York

KENNETH EASTER
Vocational Agriculture
Dos Palos Junior-Senior High School
Dos Palos, California

MRS. ISABELLE MATTSON
Fifth Grade
Union City Community Schools
Union City, Michigan

RUTH LEE
Home Economics
Teague High School
Teague, Texas

BROOK PETERSON
English and Social Studies
Waconia High School
Waconia, Minnesota

2

1961

President Kennedy, smiling and relaxed, walked easily and gracefully from his office into the White House Rose Garden. The day was May 2, 1961. The ceremony about to take place in the garden—honoring the National Teacher of the Year—appealed to his sense of dedication to education. He exuded boyish charm and wit, obviously getting a big kick out of bringing to the nation's attention the classroom teacher who had been chosen to represent the highest ideals and practices of education.

As I stood in the early spring sunshine, my thoughts turned back to the nine wonderful teachers I had met during the past winter as I gathered reports to help our committee choose from among the finalists for the award. This was my first assignment; it was LOOK Magazine's first National Teacher of the Year ceremony. During my nine weeks of travel, searching for the award winner, I had learned that teachers come in all sizes and shapes of commitments and abilities. But I had learned too that they have one thing in common—a deep belief that by helping children they are helping the future of this country. Each came to that belief by a different path—a path I was asked to trace.

* *

My first stop had been Marietta, Ga., on the morning of Nov. 9, 1960. The Presidential election was still in doubt, and I thought about the changes that might come if John F. Kennedy were elected. As my car sped past landmarks of the Civil War, I thought, too, about new changes coming to the South after 100 years, with education feeling that change first. I would have to measure all this. It made me nervous.

3

There were adjustments I would have to make. My own school experience rested far behind me. Since my school days there had been two World Wars, a Depression and a scientific revolution. Did I have the perception to measure that distance?

My first adjustment came quickly, physically. I was suddenly in a traffic jam on Winn Street, a snarl produced each school day by the cars of Marietta High School students. Here I was in the middle of part of this young, mobile generation of kids growing up in an age that applauds speed and comfort. These are kids learning more in a short time than I have in my entire life. I felt like an artifact.

Mrs. Sherman Lee, Jr., a mathematics teacher at Marietta High, put me at ease. She was my first interview, the first candidate, and her soft southern drawl drained away my nervousness.

"What made you become a teacher?" I asked, the stock but basic question sounding a bit hollow.

"One of my relatives was a teacher," Edna Lee said. "He was a cripple and taught sitting in a wheelchair. He often called on me to recite, and was so pleased when I did well. He was an inspiration to me. He asked me to take up teaching, and I made up my mind that I would never do anything to disappoint him."

She never did.

Mrs. Lee had a way of putting her hand on my shoulder as she confided in me. It was an instinctive gesture of friendliness and understanding. Her face was serious, determined and a little sad, but her quick smile gave it a candlelight softness. She was tall, five feet, seven inches, slim with jet black hair and sea-green eyes. In her large, capable, work-hardened hands one saw the story of her life. We talked about it.

"I was born on a farm near Homer, Georgia," she told me. That was Sept. 23, 1921. "Even though we owned our own small farm, it was hard to make a comfortable living. How rich I felt making $1.00 a day for picking two hundred pounds of cotton, or 75 cents for pulling fodder. My mother was in poor health so my father, my two younger brothers and I had to run the farm. I did much of the housework. Each summer I canned about 500 jars of fruit and vegetables for the family." Edna Poole walked about four miles a day to school. Her parents had never graduated from high school, but they wanted more for their children. They sacrificed for this hope. Edna's school paper and supplies were purchased with egg

4

money. She helped pay for her own clothes by sweeping classroom floors. "By the time I was a senior I knew I wanted to go to college and I knew that I wanted to teach school," she said. "I had enjoyed helping others with their school work all through my school days."

But getting to college was another matter. "When I graduated from high school, my father and mother were so proud! I'll never forget my father and brothers cutting enough cord wood to sell to get money for my graduation clothes. This was my graduation gift from them." Edna had to work at every odd job she could find to get to college. She picked berries for 10 cents a gallon, kept house two weeks for a neighbor and made $6. She got into Piedmont College. She had missed only one day in high school.

Edna Poole worked her way through Piedmont, and during summers between teaching jobs she later earned a master's degree at the University of Georgia. She also went back to school at Emory University to study child development and new methods of teaching—just to keep her teaching fresh.

When Edna arrived at Marietta High to teach, only eight students showed up for her math class. Seven years later, at the time of my interview, she was teaching geometry to a merit group, college algebra and trigonometry to another merit class, and review algebra and trig to two other groups. Each class averaged 30 students. She was also a guidance counselor.

Henry Kemp, superintendent, told me, "Mrs. Lee's classes are so well organized they operate on schedule whether she's in the room or not. Once or twice she has been out of town attending conferences, and the class officers put the day's problems on the blackboard and the session begins promptly without wisecracks or horseplay. To take advantage of Mrs Lee's absence would be letting her down.

"Take a look at the textbooks they are using. They are the same textbooks used at Georgia Tech. College teachers tell me they love to have students in their classes who have been taught by Mrs. Lee."

Mrs. Lee's nomination for the National Teacher of the Year Award was based on more than simply her ability to teach mathematics. She worked hard to get scholarships for her college-bound students. Without her help, many of her pupils wouldn't get to college. Marietta High graduates in 1959 were awarded more than

$200,000 in scholarships; 78 percent of the seniors went to college. In 1957, only 56 percent had gone on. Much of the credit for the increase must go to Edna Lee.

But perhaps her best and most creative work was done with students who had little chance, who couldn't qualify for college. She told me many heartbreaking stories about "dropouts" and about her efforts to get them back in school. For example, an older boy had dropped out of school. He wanted to become a mechanic. "Can you fix my car?" Mrs. Lee asked him. He tried, and failed. "How would you like to go to a school where they could teach you all about engines?" she asked. "Then you could become a master mechanic and earn good money." He took her advice and went back to school.

Mr. Kemp, the superintendent, recalled that a Marietta citizen asked him, "How much do you pay Mrs. Lee? Whatever it is, it isn't enough. I have a boy no one could handle or teach and your Mrs. Lee took hold of him and now he has a scholarship."

Grateful parents abound in Marietta. Once, one of her friends had a small boy with a large problem. No one could make headway with him. He hated school and he hated teachers. Mrs. Lee drove by the boy's home and said, "How about going swimming with me this afternoon?" They went. School wasn't mentioned. The next day they picked blueberries in the woods. They waded in a creek. On the third day, Mrs. Lee brought along a book. They sat down and read from it. The boy's interest was kindled.

"Kids are easy to discourage," she believed. "Don't tell them they can't make good."

I watched her conduct an advanced math class. She had one group go to the blackboard and write out the problem to be solved. Then she called on others to go to the board and explain what the problem was and give the right answers. She was never satisfied with approximations. She cut the wordy ones down. She made each student give precise definitions by drawing him out and making him think. She could have called on her best pupils, but instead she asked the slower ones to explain the problems. She was very patient and helpful, waiting for the right answers. The brighter pupils enjoyed the exchange.

A good teacher has a well-thought-out philosophy. I wanted to know Mrs. Lee's. "Education is the exciting process of becom-

6

ing acquainted with the world, and finding one's place in it," she argued. "It is my belief that a student will take much of the responsibility for his own education if the teacher can only stir his curiosity, help him experience the joy of mental awakening, and discover with him the possibilities that lie within his own personality. I have never had a discipline problem in my classes. I attribute this to the fact that my students and I are so concerned about our joint discoveries we are never bored.

"Finding a way to reach each student takes much thought. You have to have a warm interest in each, and the student must feel this. Attention to the individual takes much time, much energy. But it is worth it to awaken minds so that they will have more depth and dimension."

Mrs. Lee felt close to her students. She knew them well. "A teacher must demonstrate to her pupils, in her own life, her profound beliefs, not piously, but quietly and sincerely," she said. "It is futile to preach to students that moral values and concern for others are important unless they can see the teacher adapt them into her personal life. It is a mockery to stress good citizenship if the teacher neither votes nor respects the dignity of the people around her who may have political views different from her own. If democracy is to live,it has to be built into the classroom.

"Teaching must not be haphazard. The teacher must plan carefully, taking each student from where he is to where she wants him to be. The pursuit of knowledge is not enough. There must be compassion. There must be character development. As far as human relations are concerned, the classroom is the world in miniature."

Edna Lee didn't limit her world of experience to the classroom. She and her husband, a clerk in the local postoffice, worked a small farm, which she bought with her first savings from teaching. Mrs. Lee also helped direct the Girl Scouts, organized adult education classes. Once, after she gave an experimental mathematics lesson on Atlanta television, the station offered her a lot of money to conduct a regular televised class. "I turned it down immediately," she said, "because I love the personal contact with young minds; I love the give and take of the classroom." She brought talent to that give and take. One of her hobbies was spelling, and she kept lists of spelling words. Each year Mrs. Lee coached the spelling contestants for the Southeastern Fair's Annual Spelling Contest. The year I visited her, Mrs. Lee had coached a pupil who won first place for the state of Georgia.

Hard work hurts few souls. Mrs. Lee was a good example of this. Her life was marked by hard work: she had taught for 18 years, never missing a day of school.

Before leaving I asked Edna Lee to reflect for a moment: "What are the rewards of teaching?" I asked.

Her simple reply was: "You don't ask for glory."

* *

I rented a car in Waco, Texas, for the second leg of my journey. Driving east along Route 84 for about 50 miles, I watched the right-hand side of the road for the sign pointing to Teague, Pop. 2,725. I was on my way to meet Alice Ruth Lee, "Miss Ruth" to the townsfolk. Although not related, she and Mrs. Sherman Lee shared much in common: both grew up on small farms; both had never missed a day of teaching.

I made the turn and drove into Teague. It was once a small railroad town, and the superintendent of railroads, when he married, had the name of the little way station changed from Brewer Prairie to Teague, his bride's maiden name. In those days, cotton was king in Teague, and farmers even let it grow in their yards instead of flowers. There wasn't any money in flowers. Now the town prospers on cattle, poultry and fat Texas hogs.

Leo Stuver, superintendent of schools, greeted me first. He was a hearty, 240-pound Texan, reared in nearby Mexia, moved with the heavy grace of a college tackle, a position he played for Sam Houston State Teachers College. He chuckled and winked: "Miss Ruth is at the hairdressers. She expected you tomorrow, and she wanted to look real nice." Leo Stuver took me to his house for a home-cooked meal, topped off with fresh pecans from his backyard, and talk about education and Ruth Lee.

Just about everyone in Freestone County knew "Miss Ruth." She had been teaching in Teague for 37 years when I visited her. Mothers and fathers who had gone to her classes now sent their children to her. When not teaching, she worked with civic clubs, sang in the church choir, or hunted deer with the town's best deer hunters. She could have any job in town. Offers from schools in

8

big cities did not interest her. Like Leo Stuver, she believed that education began at the grassroots level. Stuver put it this way: "Men and women of attainment should till the educational soil wherever they find it."

Miss Ruth was such a tiller. The Rev. Elwood Birklebach, pastor of the Methodist Church where Ruth Lee soloed in her fine soprano voice, told me, "When she sees a need she acts upon it. She is a pragmatist. No ivory tower education for her. She represents a complete integration of spiritual life with her profession. All her students recognize her leadership. Our tendency of late is to berate our negative side. This was most evident right after Sputnik. Miss Ruth inspires us more to a positive faith in our potentialities."

I first met Ruth Lee in the living room of her cottage on the Teague High School campus. She taught home economics, and the cottage (her own idea) was her classroom. The pupils designed it and built it for her. She wanted a classroom that had the earmarks of a real home—kitchen, living room, sewing room, bedroom and bath. Here her students learned to cook, sew, buy furniture, choose drapes and wallpaper and draw up a family budget.

At first there were only girls in her classes, but soon there were almost as many boys. Several members of the football team were in the cooking class I attended. Their work for the day was food preparation for the team, which was driving 60 miles for a game that night. They prepared the oven, cooked the rib roast. Miss Lee asked them the reasons for each move, told them what distinguished cuts, what meat cost per pound, how best to slice it for sandwiches. Then she gave a brief lesson in table manners and the duties of host and hostess.

Miss Ruth pairs the students off, one boy to each girl when possible, and teaches them both to be homemakers. She may have foreseen the results. Many of her students who pair off in home economics cook up something more, go steady and eventually marry. Moreover, not one of these marriages has wound up in the divorce courts. Most males have a distorted view of household management and shun the responsibilities that go with it. No boy trained by Miss Ruth ever fell into that error.

Miss Ruth holds the attention of her boys with classes that

discuss topics like, "Rent a House or Buy—Which?" She also sponsors the school's cheerleaders; many of the girls in her classes help mend ripped uniforms.

I sat through two of her classes, one in cooking and another in sewing. She walked around the room giving friendly advice—but always explaining why she suggested changes. She used her small-town, homey vernacular, and acted like a member of the family. She had a good sense of humor. She made the boys wash their hands "clean as an anchor" before preparing the food for cooking. She reviewed each class and asked for an oral summary from each student.

Later, as we chatted in her cottage's living room, Miss Lee's students served us tea and cookies. She talked about her life: "I was born Sept. 14, 1903, in a small, five-room frame house in the little central Texas town of Groesbeck. I went to Texas Woman's University at Denton, and later I studied at Sam Houston State Teacher's College at Huntsville. I earned my master's there. My parents were poor and I remember how hard my brothers and sisters and I worked growing vegetables and fruits. We took them to town to exchange for staples and dress goods. There was love and understanding in my family. We worked together, played together, prayed together. Grace before meals and family prayer before retiring for the night were as much a part of our daily routine as pumping water from the cistern into the 'No. 3' washtub, which we left in the sun until the water was warm enough for the daily bath."

She also went to school in Teague. I asked her how this came about.

"When the town of Teague was incorporated in 1907, the Lee family moved into it from Groesbeck. Our house in Teague was still unfinished. Sheets and old dresses were tacked over the windows for privacy. The first few nights we threw mattresses on the floor and slept in one room.

"I enrolled in the first grade in the O. M. Roberts Elementary School. Later, as my interests widened, I studied music and drama. I had private lessons in public speaking, piano and voice. When quite young I was a soloist for community affairs, weddings and funerals. I still am. I began teaching in Teague as soon as I graduated from college, and have been here for 37 years."

10

Who are today's great teachers?

She had not missed a day of teaching since she started, per- haps because she loved it so much. "When I was a child," she recalled to me, "I liked 'to play school' and every time we played school I wanted to be the teacher. It is as simple as that. I just think I was cut out to be one."

Miss Ruth got a lot from teaching, and gave it a great deal in return. Her days often stretched from 8 a.m. to midnight. She was perceptive. I asked her what makes a good teacher. "You must enjoy teaching," she answered. "You have to make others happy in order to be happy yourself. A teacher must be a leader, must develop leadership in others. I make it a point to visit every student's home. I have two conference periods a week, and I in- vite the parents of my pupils to attend them. Most of them went to school to me anyway. Every Friday, we have what we call Goodwill Day. My students are asked to prepare lunches for the civic clubs, make sandwiches for the football team, or do some other useful thing. Selfishness retards mental growth. You have to be a good listener. Don't do all the talking. Don't pretend that you know everything. Admit you don't know. You can't fool your students. If you are unsure of yourself, they quickly sense it." She was right, of course.

I met other people in Teague, and went to a pit barbecue at the Teague Veterans of Foreign Wars. Miss Ruth was a strong part of the fiber and fact of that town. Her sphere of influence didn't end at the school door, or with the school day. "Every- one in this town is indebted to Miss Ruth," said Leo Stuver. "You may wonder if a teacher who is in the same school for so many years can avoid getting in a rut. Miss Ruth keeps abreast of things. She is willing to try something new. She is creative, but she is also practical. She can distinguish between a fad and a genuine breakthrough. She has zest for life. She owns a cabin out at Red's Lake some 20 miles from here, and every chance she gets she goes out there and fishes—takes some of the kids with her. She has a boat, and the students use it all the time. Down here in this part of Texas we hunt deer from a platform we build in trees. From them we can see the deer and they can't smell us. You have to be agile to climb up into one of these trees, but Miss Ruth is right up there with the rest of us. I've known her to start at four o'clock in the morning to go deer hunting."

11

Miss Ruth kept close to her boys and girls. She understood them, and worked to help them over those rough patches of adolescent growth some adults never seem to remember. She had this advice for teachers: "At sometime in her career every teacher experiences the call for help from some student with a personal problem. The call is not always a direct request; in fact, it is usually not voiced at all. But a perceptive teacher recognizes the unexpressed need and tries to give the necessary help in the most acceptable manner in her power."

This, Ruth Lee did daily.

Before I left Teague, Leo Stuver wanted me to take some bags of pecans, and a man I had met at the barbecue offered to drive me all the way to Dallas to catch my plane for Honolulu. The friendliness of Teague ran deep. Reluctantly, I headed my rented car for Waco.

As I drove away I suddenly remembered a painting that hung back of Leo Stuver's desk. It was no Rembrandt, but it told a story. It was a crude painting of a sheep barn. In that barn, years ago, was held the first school in Teague. There are old folks still living there who can remember going to school in that barn. From this came the passionate desire for higher things, a way of life, and Ruth Lee was its finest expression.

I turned my head quickly to catch a last look at Teague. The softness of pin oaks and pecan and sweet gum trees faded from view. I thought, how pleasant it would be to return one spring day and sit under a sweet gum tree with Miss Ruth, eat some of her sandwiches and swap yarns about our rural childhood days.

I felt in my pocket for the crumpled letter that had been sent to me before I started my assignment. It was an endorsement telling me what a wonderful person Alice Ruth Lee was. The letter was signed—Lyndon B. Johnson.

*　*

No place in the world welcomes visitors with more warmth and hospitality than Hawaii. The first whiff of tropical air after a flight from winter relaxes body and soul, and you feel a rebirth of pagan instincts as old as the race.

I met Dr. Adeline Babbitt in the lobby of the Surf Rider

Who are today's great teachers?

Hotel on Waikiki Beach. She placed a lei of small, fragrant orchids around my neck, kissed me on the cheek and said, "Aloha." In one moment we were friends. We sat on the terrace of the hotel and she pointed to an orchid in my plate. "Where but in Hawaii would a chef garnish a plate of food with an orchid?" she remarked. Dr. Babbitt knew the islands well, and loved them. She had lived there more than 30 years. Under the table and around our feet, small doves picked up stray crumbs, making a throaty sound. There must be something special about people who inhabit islands where birds are not afraid of them.

Adeline Babbitt was tall and looked like Bette Davis, with the same small mouth. She carried the mark of New England and Meriden, Conn., where she was born on Oct. 8, 1894. But she was more worldly, than simply New England. She spoke four foreign languages—Spanish, Italian, Arabic, French—and pidgin English, the *lingua franca* of the Pacific islands. She seemed a character out of Somerset Maugham's tales of Oceania. She collected Japanese prints. When I met her she wore a Burmese sapphire ring, a silver bracelet from Italy, and her mother's diamond wedding ring. She dressed conservatively, eschewing the ubiquitous muumuu and other bits of commercialized native attire so readily donned by tourists.

Adeline Babbitt's life had been an international amalgam. She started kindergarten in Connecticut at age two, and, after the seventh grade, moved with her family to the Canal Zone in Panama. She graduated from Canal Zone High School in 1914, and began attending a round of small New England colleges, summering at Columbia University Teachers College. She studied under John Dewey and learned his "method" teaching. She also had as her mentor at Teachers College, William H. Kilpatrick, who taught her that the method was not an end in itself, but a beginning toward better teaching.

During these years, Adeline Babbitt organized kindergartens in Bristol, Conn., and Charleston, S.C. Her work in Charleston included training classes for kindergarten teachers in the schools for Negro children.

In 1925, she got her B.S. degree from Columbia. She began to study clinical psychology.

Teachers College asked her, in 1926, to go to Hawaii to be

the principal of the Henry and Dorothy Castle Memorial Kindergarten. She went, and immediately began organizing the first nursery school on the islands, training her own teachers. In a year this grew into an all-island training school. Ten years later, the school Dr. Babbitt started became part of the University of Hawaii's preschool unit. Adeline Babbitt began teaching methods of child development at the university, and helped organize the school anew. She worked closely with the architect, designing mezzanine observation balconies for student teachers, ramps leading to the playground, a child's-size kitchen and library. In her free time, she returned to Teachers College to continue toward her doctorate. (She took her master's at the University of Hawaii in 1934.) She got her doctorate in 1946.

Since then, Dr. Babbitt had been an island-wide and world-wide worker. She organized and opened the first child care center in Hawaii, in Honolulu. She put into operation seven model schools in Libya, five in and around Tripoli and two in Benghazi. She also trained teachers in five other schools in Benghazi, which helped polish her Arabic.

In 1937, she founded the International Association for Childhood Education, and was its first president.

Dr. Babbitt retired in June, 1960, in Hawaii. When I met her later that year, she had been "unretired" and held a full-time job teaching remedial reading at the Kamehameha School for Girls, a private school founded by Princess Bernice Pauahi Bishop. On the adjoining campus is a similar school for boys. These twin schools, situated on a high hill overlooking Honolulu, have a combined campus that any college would envy. The buildings are large and handsome, the grounds filled with every variety of tree, shrub and flower. There is a pink garden, a white garden, a red one and a yellow one—each cared for by a separate gardener, all watched by the master gardener, Sam Yee.

No student may be admitted to the schools unless he or she has some Hawaiian blood, since the Bishop family established the schools to insure the education of all native children. The Kamehameha Schools had 55 ethnic groups when I was there. Hawaii's admixture of racial strains has produced some of the most beautiful girls in the world, and it seemed several hundred of them were in the girl's mess hall to welcome me. They sang the doxology in

14

the Hawaiian language just before I sat down at Dr. Babbitt's table. When the meal was finished, all the girls sang the "Hilo March" in liquid, vowel-laden Hawaiian. "This is in your honor," whispered Dr. Babbitt. "This kind of welcome is reserved for dignitaries." I was touched by it, and I patted the hand of little Eleana Fojas, one of Dr. Babbitt's pupils who had been designated as the hostess for our special table.

Harold W. Kent, a retired Army colonel, administers the school's funds and is its president. "I brought Dr. Babbitt out of retirement," he reported, "because of her extraordinary qualifications. Many of the younger teachers lacked the kind of experience we felt we needed. Most school administrators would envy me my job. They have trouble raising enough money to keep their schools going and their teachers paid. My school is so richly endowed I have trouble finding worthwhile ways of spending the money that piles up."

I visited the Hawaiian State Department of Education in its brand new Queen Liliuokalani building near the Governor's mansion, and talked to Lawrence M. Kasdon. "Half the pleasure of my job is working with teachers like Adeline Babbitt," he told me. "Her mastery of child psychology is well known. But being a great teacher instead of just a good teacher involves a sort of mystical quality, that extra touch. It is almost like the Biblical laying on of hands, and Dr. Babbitt has this gift to an extraordinary degree."

Dr. Babbitt was well known in Hawaii. It is interesting, yet of the tradition, that teachers are popular in the communities they serve. We drove out to Pali one day in Dr. Babbitt's little red Nash Rambler, taking the old road and avoiding the crowded highway. From the delicately gowned mountains, in wispy unreality, flowed a waterfall that fell upward, not downward, the wind catching and holding the spray and tossing it toward heaven. Dr. Babbitt knew many native families along the old road and we stopped often. We never stopped talking. I asked about education. "Every teacher must have an understanding heart—maybe the word for it is empathy," she said. "You must admit to your students that you don't know everything. You must be honest with them. They know when you are telling the truth. You can read it in their faces."

15

I was surprised. This was almost word for word what Miss Ruth Lee had told me just over 24 hours earlier back in Texas. No two women could have had backgrounds farther apart, and yet they had the same philosophy. Educators must share a common insight.

Dr. Babbitt was deeply religious. She told me she had searched all her life for a religion she could feel at home with. She said we must all seek that part of every human being which is Christ-like.

During my visit I went out to Dr. Babbitt's home. It rested on a hill, large and graceful, filled with art objects from Japan, China, Burma, Thailand, Bali, the Philippines and other distant places she has visited. She lived alone; she had no family. She had come to Hawaii originally on the condition that she be allowed to bring her mother with her. Her mother loved Hawaii, and remained there until her death.

I asked her if she regretted not having children of her own. "You're throwing me a curve, but I can answer you. I think I have done more for humanity playing the role I was cast in. I paid my own way to California a few years ago to attend a UNESCO conference. Everyone was talking about programs for Europe and the Middle East. I got up before all those people and shouted, 'Do you know there is a Pacific Ocean?' I asked them what they planned to do for the millions of people in that vast area of the world. My outburst won me a Fulbright grant to Burma. I went to Libya later. When I built the school in Benghazi, parents came from miles around to offer me their children. I told them we only had room for a certain number of children, that we only had a certain number of chairs. The next day these same parents would come back carrying chairs. Sometimes they would shove a child through the door and run, hoping I would find a place for it. The day I left Burma a school holiday was proclaimed and buses were hired to take all my pupils to the airport to see me off. I have had the unique good fortune to be teaching in three countries when they gained independence—Hawaii, Burma and Libya. The school children in Burma always called me 'Bomayi'— meaning 'Big Chief.' They would come running to me and would shout, 'Bomayi! Bomayi!'

"Does that answer your question?"

16

Who are today's great teachers?

The world is Dr. Babbitt's classroom, its ignorant children her family. Part of it educates her; she teaches parts of it. Not long after I left her, fresh lei around my neck, I received a letter. Dr. Babbitt had sold her house, gone to Bangkok, Thailand, for a two-year experiment in the use of reading labs, teaching in the English Department of Chulalongkorn University. She would return to Hawaii, but I, too, could almost hear that distant cry calling her out to her teaching:

"Bomayi! Bomayi!"

* *

Kenneth Easter surprised me.

I thought about him as I rode in a rumbling clankety-bang taxi from the little airport at Merced, Calif., to Dos Palos. This is the new land of cotton. The highway was flecked with it, blown from trucks on the way to the cotton gins.

Ken Easter, I found out later, required each boy in his agriculture class to pick a minimum of 100 pounds of cotton each season to qualify for the annual class field trip. Dos Palos High School, where he taught, is on the line between Merced and Fresno counties, two of the richest agricultural counties in the world, with a total annual agricultural income of more than $300,000,000. His students came from, and returned to, some of the finest farms in the nation.

Ken surprised me because I expected him to be an extrovert with a flair for showmanship, a gentleman farmer type. But when I met him, he was modest and unassuming to the point of shyness. He weighed about 190 pounds, stood six feet tall and had blue-gray eyes. His hair was thinning into baldness. His cheeks were hectic with tiny blood vessels showing through his fair skin. He wore slacks and a sports coat, his teaching uniform. I got the immediate impression that here was a down-to-earth human being with lots of common sense and character. I was right.

Ken Easter headed the large vocational agriculture department in Dos Palos High. His job seemed simple: train young men to be excellent farmers. But it was not easy work. Most schools delight in winning one American Farmer award in national competition. It is a rare distinction. But Ken can spot a good student as quickly as he spots prize sheep or cows. In 1960, the Dos Palos

17

Future Farmer Chapter (which Ken had advised since 1933) won *three* American Farmer awards, the highest national honor given. Only one boy in every 1,000 membership can win the award. In the years Ken Easter had been adviser, the Future Farmer Chapter at Dos Palos had 47 State Farmers (highest state honor), 11 American Farmers, two Star State Farmers, five regional Star State Farmers, four state officers. In fact, the year the club won the three national awards, Ken Easter was one of 25 teachers in the nation given the Honorary American Farmer degree at the National FFA Convention. At the same time, his son Steve got one of the three American Farmer awards.

Ken Easter, surprisingly, had also trained state championship parliamentary procedure teams, three regional public speaking winners, one state runner-up, two state winners in co-operative marketing operations. He knew his stuff.

Farmers for miles around sought Ken Easter for advice. He was a farmer at heart. So were his sons. Both were American Farmer winners. Ken and his family lived in a ranch-style home just outside of town, filled with trophies and blue ribbons won at county and state agricultural fairs. Ken was also a judge at these fairs, and had been a member of the California Fair Board's committees. He was a respected judge at livestock contests.

What was Ken Easter like? Lionel Tocher, his assistant, who came to Dos Palos in 1931, a year after Ken's arrival, knew him better than anyone else, and said: "Ken is basically a good organizer. With a minimum of confusion, he gets things done. He brings out the best in each boy. He is purposeful, but not demanding. He ties things together. He has a flexible mind and a modern one. He reads a lot, keeps up with the current scientific literature covering his special fields. When he started this school we had only horse and mule power. Now the San Joaquin Valley is one of the most highly mechanized areas in California."

Easter showed me through the vast building used for his department. It was the largest on the high school's campus devoted to one department. In its 9,800 square feet were two shops, two classrooms, a library, an office and a laboratory. Here kids could tear down and put together tractors and cars, and learn the mechanical as well as theoretical side of farming. Ken Easter's school at Dos Palos was one of the first in California. Most of

18

Who are today's great teachers?

Ken's students went to work on family farms and ranches as soon as they finished high school. Few seniors went on to college. Many of Ken's former students were wealthy, occupying places high up in local government, and fraternal or civic organizations. Several taught high school agriculture, one managed a 10,000-head beef-feed yard, another was president of the American Dairy Association in California. They all had prospered from Ken's courses in scientific farming and business accounting.

I saw dozens of boys in Ken's workshop tearing down cars, tractors and trucks and putting them back together again. They have to know how to make instant repairs on farm machinery. And, with an eye to the future, Ken even had them working on a small airplane engine. Most of these kids will own private airplanes when they become big ranchers.

The school didn't spring from nothing. Ken Easter helped build it year by year. And he built with it his own philosophy. He explained: "You have to be interested in your product—in my case, youth. The student is the spark that ignites the good teacher, not the other way around, for your exceptional student acquires his knowledge in many ways and moves toward his goal under almost any kind of teacher. It is the slow learner who needs to lean on the teacher for direction and reassurance. My disappointment comes when a student does not realize his potential. You can't fool students, and you can't fight them. You have to get them on your side, and you have to keep them there. Your side, if you are a good teacher, is the right side. You teach from the strength of maturity and experience, some of that experience being nothing more than trial and error."

There had been grumblings about Ken Easter pushing his students to win awards. "I try to get my boys into contests," he replied, "but I also try to teach them to be gracious in victory and good sports in defeat. I want them to be useful citizens, to get into local, perhaps statewide politics, and to prepare them for this I teach parliamentary procedures and public speaking. Ignorance and apathy hold people back. One must have the intelligence to take the right side on public issues. What is the aim of education if it is not to develop the superior citizen? A good citizen earns his way through his own efforts."

Ken Easter's efforts brought him up from modest beginnings.

19

He was born on Oct. 3, 1907, in Ashland, Oregon. His grandfather was a teacher, doctor and preacher; his father a teacher and farmer. Ken followed the tradition. His family moved to California by wagon when he was a boy. In 1913, his father died, and Ken and his brother had to earn their educations. He worked his way through the University of California at Berkeley, wrote for the college agricultural magazine and joined Alpha Zeta, an agricultural honor fraternity. He graduated in 1929, got on the Dos Palos staff in 1930 as a student teacher, and became a regular in 1931. He was chosen head of the agricultural department in 1933, with an enrollment of 25 in the field; in 1960, 157 boys studied vocational agriculture.

Ken Easter kept up. He did graduate work at Fresno State College, the University of California at Davis, and received a Master's Degree in Education from California State Polytechnic College in 1964.

I received a letter from Ken in May, 1966. "I am now almost out of classroom teaching. A new department has been given to me. I initiated and now direct the Work Experience Program at Dos Palos, as well as continue to supervise the Agricultural Department. The Work Experience Program places students in business firms throughout the district for actual on-the-job training. I have 53 students in the field and have a large waiting list. Our daughter Ellen is now a sophomore at the University of California at Davis. Steven, our youngest son, is a lieutenant in the Army and is serving in Viet Nam. Bill, the oldest, has completed his Doctorate at Michigan State and accepted a position with the Bureau of the Budget.

"As to education, I miss the more relaxed era where pressures for grades and achievements were a little less taxing on the student. I believe we can get a job done without subjecting the young to such competitive pressure for grades. We enjoy youth only once, and I'm afraid the modern system is taking the joy out of youth. I also believe that education for the local level suffers from a lack of competent leadership from administrators and from school board members. It has been my observation that many physical education majors become administrators and are inadequate in the roll of leadership. School board members as a rule seem to lack any understanding of education, and only consider ways to save money rather than improve education.

"I completed my work for the Master's just ahead of my youngest son. I'll never catch up to Bill with his Doctorate!"

Perhaps not, but Ken Easter planned to continue his own education—and that of others. When I was in Dos Palos, the total enrollment of the high school was 850, and 315 of these students took courses under Ken and his staff. The population of Dos Palos is 2,000. It's plain to see that a good many of these people and their sons owe their education to Kenneth Easter.

* *

I entered the classroom quietly, unannounced. Brook Peterson, 25, and his students were listening to a Joan Baez record, "All My Trials." It was a good theme song for this young teacher. He had only begun to experience the trials and tribulations of teaching. He wasn't bitter; he was creatively militant.

Brook Peterson grew up under hard-working, conservative parents in a small Iowa town. His father was a chiropractor; his mother kept active in youth work, civic affairs and state politics. After high school, Brook went to Grinnell College and majored in history, minoring in English and philosophy. He held a scholarship and worked part time and stretched himself into athletics and school activities. During summer vacations, he worked and traveled, finding jobs in a steel mill, on a railroad freight dock and with construction companies. He met his wife Rosemary at Grinnell; they were married at the beginning of their senior year and graduated together in 1958. That summer, Brook got a graduate assistantship in the department of educational administration at the University of Minnesota. His test record was so high, and he so impressed the faculty selection committee, that he got the assistantship without any work completed on his M.A. But, after a year, lack of money forced him out of the university and into the ninth grade at Waconia, Minnesota, where he taught social studies and English. That's where I found him, sensitive, bright, dynamic, in his second year.

Brook, slim and crew-cut, with glasses, dressed like an Ivy Leaguer and looked almost as young as his students. He thought as they did. Even in 1960, Brook Peterson had been impressed with the style and message of Joan Baez. I thought, "What a pleasant way to conduct a class." While Brook changed the records, he talked about the traditions and origins of folk music. In his classroom, playing Joan's recordings that later became widely popular, Brook demonstrated the importance of folklore and balladry in early America. He let his students hear—then learn to listen for—the relationship between ballad singing and poetry.

Waconia, Minn., is a bedroom community in the suburbs of Minneapolis, close enough to feel its effect, distant enough to avoid strong orbital pull. Waconia High School is almost shabby, its oldest sections going back to 1918. The senior high school had 409 pupils. The building, like the teaching methods Brook Peterson rebeled against, is an anachronism in today's modern, accelerated education.

During class, Peterson paid no attention to me. For a teacher with only two years experience, he seemed remarkably well poised and assured. He talked in an easy un-selfconscious manner. He was in control. When the bell rang and the students bolted for the door, he raised his voice with authority and commanded, "Remain seated." They froze in their tracks. You knew then that he could be firm, even though the classroom atmosphere had been friendly and informal.

Peterson never told his class who I was or why I was there. He didn't want his students to know. He later told me he was honored at being nominated as a Teacher of the Year candidate, but he didn't think he had earned it in just two years.

Armin C. Block, the school superintendent, thought otherwise. "Brook Peterson is the finest teacher I have ever known. He is constantly alert to the desires and needs of his students. He comes to me quite often to obtain permission to try some new theory or approach or tactic that will make his teaching more meaningful. He also has compassion. He spends a lot of time after classes visiting a girl who is dying of cancer. We know she hasn't a chance. She was a good student when she was able to attend classes, but since her confinement to bed Brook goes to her home several times a week to give her private lessons. He won't take

22

pay; he does it to make her happy. He knows she will never get well."

I sat through other classes. In social studies, Brook talked about capitalism and communism. He listed the various forms of government and economic systems, showed how citizens fared under each, and wrote notes on the blackboard. The class also studied the large map of Russia on the wall. After class, Peterson handed each pupil a copy of "You and American Competitive Private Enterprise," a booklet put out by the National Association of Manufacturers. I recalled, with a smile, the oft-repeated charge that our high schools are using "Leftist" literature.

Waconia is conservative. It was once run almost like a feudal barony, the domain of a multimillionaire banker who fancied himself a benevolent despot. The town had been settled by German families, some Catholic, some Lutheran. As a result, Waconia, population 2,500, has three competing school systems: the Catholic parochial school; the Lutheran parochial school; the regular public schools. This means a costly duplication of buildings and facilities. It disturbed Brook Peterson; it jarred his independent mind. He was a young and often courageous liberal in an ultra-conservative environment. He thrived.

Peterson wasn't sure that teachers' unions were good. "Teachers are to blame for their own troubles," he insisted. "In some ways the teaching profession is standing still. I don't like committees and overworked administrators. I suppose I am a foolish idealist, but I would like to see a child-centered school system and not a textbook-centered system. There must be a warm personal relationship between teacher and pupil, and it is essential that a teacher know each pupil's parents and home life. There are still people in Waconia who are suspicious of education and educators. As one old German farmer put it: 'Vot can you teach Karl to do mit his hands?' Anything you could do with Karl's mind would be superfluous in this old farmer's opinion."

Young teachers like Brook Peterson have a hard time making ends meet. I met his attractive wife, Rosemary, in a modest little house, and Kristen Anne cried for me convincingly in her crib. Rosemary had to put in odd hours teaching music to help out with the mortgage and taxes and other expenses. Brook spoke for the

23

new teacher. "We ought to go to college in the summer, but we young teachers have to sell insurance or take some other job during our vacations," he argued. "I want to go to the University of Minnesota during the summer to earn my master of arts degree, but I really can't afford it right now. Why did I go into a profession like this? Not because I am dedicated. I hate that word. Dedication is a euphemism for poor pay. I teach because I think there is a job to be done with the youth of this country, and because teaching offers such a challenge. I am not a great teacher. I'm just learning, I make mistakes. There is a lot I don't know about teaching, but I'm going to find out. If necessary I'll find out the hard way. I think most teaching today is slipshod."

Brook fought against the shoddy teacher. He had already won state-wide recognition for his attempts to win better accreditation for schools and teachers. He wanted to raise the salary and standards of teaching to the levels of other professions. "How many school administrators know what kinds of teachers they have under contract? Most administrators are too busy with business matters to know what is going on down the hall in the classrooms. My own 'super' knows about these things, but he's an exception. He gives me free time to work with the North Central Association. The best schools in our area are accredited by this association. These schools have a scientific checking system whereby each teacher's classroom performance is observed and evaluated. The observers come from outside the school. I could be an observer at the nearby Robinsdale School, for instance."

"Do the teachers resent your checking up on them?" I asked.

"Not at all. There is nothing punitive about this. We do not fire teachers who make a poor showing in the tests. They thank us for pointing out some mistakes they may be making inadvertently. They correct these mistakes. I wish some observer would run a check on me. I'm not perfect. Who is?"

Brook Peterson had a simple message for young people attracted to teaching: If you *want* to teach—do it.

But if you want to make a lot of money fast, pursue the dollar, lose your identity to an amorphous, impersonal organization—go elsewhere. Teaching calls for something deeper.

Today's youth shouts for its role in the world of tomorrow. It has tossed in its challenge to the older generation—by demon-

24

strations, protest, hard work, example. Young men and women, like Brook Peterson, carry the protest of youth into teaching every year, and better the profession. They come from the best campuses, from government programs like VISTA and the Peace Corps. They have experienced much; they bring a wide perspective into the classroom. Our children benefit.

Yet we still face a crisis. Without good teachers, without young teachers like Brook Peterson, protesting, honing, changing our educational process, we will fail. Quantitative improvement, which we are getting, means little without qualitative improvement. The real crisis in education is not today, despite the signs, but tomorrow. Young teachers, well-paid, highly-trained, motivated, must save our schools. To ignore this need is to condemn us to mediocrity.

Brook Peterson summed up: "I hope graduate training will increase my competence in the service of the public school child and the local community. May God guide all of us charged with the serious business of providing educational opportunities for curious, energetic youth."

Teaching need not be all heartaches, tired feet and mortgages. There's a joy in it, too. Chaucer hinted of this in his *Canterbury Tales:* "And gladly wolde he lerne, and gladly teche." Brook Peterson, and others like him, soon find that joy in teaching.

* *

Four-year-olds in Cumberland, Wisconsin (population 1,872) get excited about education when they're told, "Next year, you'll go to school—to Missy." They know—and love—the town's only kindergarten teacher, Helen "Missy" Adams. She's an institution.

Helen Adams almost didn't become a teacher. The odds seemed against her. At one time, even a high school diploma was out of her reach. But Helen Adams fought the odds, and won.

She was born into a poor farm family in Shell Lake, Wisconsin, not far from Cumberland, on June 11, 1917. She always knew what she wanted, and what she wanted most, since the age of six, was to teach. She played teacher to her two older sisters, using apple boxes and orange crates as desks. Poverty forced her to stop her formal education after grade school. And her dream faded. For five years she worked at various domestic jobs. "Deep inside," she recalled, "I so wanted to go to school." She started back to the classroom. She entered Shell Lake High School, overcoming embarrassment about her age. "All of the strange feelings I had anticipated," she said, "were lost in the excitement and joy of being in a classroom again." Then, in her senior year, Helen Adams suffered a ruptured appendix that kept her out of school half the year. Her teachers gave her special tutoring, and she graduated with her class. Their help made a lasting impression and influenced her when she began teaching.

She enrolled in the kindergarten-primary department at Wisconsin State College in Superior and worked her way as a waitress and baby sitter. Often she had no money for her own meals. In her junior year, in 1944, she filled a mid-year vacancy in the kindergarten of the Cumberland Elementary School, and stayed on.

That first year was a tough one. She was afraid she might fail. "I used to go home from school every night and cry," she told me. But out of those trying days began the charming nickname "Missy," given by her children. Helen Adams tells the story: "Some of the projects I assigned in those first months had a degree of difficulty many of the children could not overcome. 'Miss Adams, please help me!' became a frequent cry. 'Miss' in the mouths of children soon became 'Missy.' All the children began to call me that, and they still do." Now, even the teachers call her Missy, and few of the townsfolk know her real first name is Helen.

Tragedy struck at Missy once more. In mid-afternoon, at school, in January, 1949, she got an upset stomach and headache. She began to drop everything she picked up with her right hand. The next day her legs began to ache; the back of her legs seemed to pull. She lost most of the feeling in her right arm and hand. She had polio.

For a while it seemed that she might be permanently crippled. Her right hand and arms were in complete paralysis; her legs useless. For two hours in the morning and two again each afternoon, she had her mother massage her legs, bake them in a "health oven" (which took the place of hot packs). She also did 12 specific exercises. She had to train her left hand to write and do the work of both hands. She stayed out of school a month, and started back a few days at a time. In the kindergarten each day, Missy got help from a senior high school girl. Missy sat in a chair; the school custodian made a special stool so she could elevate her legs. It was an ordeal.

One little old lady, remembering those days, told me, "It broke your heart to see that brave girl inching her way to the classroom, her little jaw set, her head held high. No one knows what she went through."

For more than a year, Missy re-educated the muscles of her hand and arm by clutching a rubber ball and squeezing it. She even took the ball to bed with her, so if she couldn't sleep she could work with the ball and not waste precious moments to recovery.

Full recovery was slow in coming. It took Missy from January, 1949 to the summer of 1951 before she had control of her right arm and hand again. When I met her there was no trace of the affliction that might have ended another's career. Missy carried a heavy work load.

Missy was 5 feet, 3½ inches tall, and weighed 103 pounds when I met her. She was strong, agile, athletic. She had dark-brown hair and her eyes sparkled, fed by some inner light of affirmation. It was a light that negated all the setbacks of her life. She had a gypsy's love of rings and bracelets and vivid colors. She eschewed earrings. Her mobile face acted as a barometer of her moods. Her voice was a fine instrument. When she talked to her pupils she achieved the most astonishing reactions from them just by the inflection of her voice. She handled her class like a conductor handles an orchestra—every word and gesture exactly tuned to the evocation of the mood or reaction she sought. The children adored her.

Missy said, "I feel at home with children at the first stage of mental curiosity—the most formative and receptive age of all— and I think I'll always be more at home with children of kindergarten age." She believed that some traits are formed in the prenatal stage, that some kindergarten children arrive in school with a complex of built-in faults and virtues, strengths and weaknesses. A kindergarten teacher needs patience and understanding to shape weakness into strength, fault to virtue. Missy Adams had that and more.

I went to some of her classes. The kindergarten rooms formed a new annex to the old elementary and junior high school building built in 1924. Missy made the original designs for the annex. The

27

rooms were bright and cheerful with lots of windows and gay child-art, lots of little people's toys and picture books. There was a piano in one room and a phonograph and several home-made drums and other instruments. With these, the children learned to keep time to the records and Missy's baton. They reflected Missy's sense of rhythm.

At nap time, on Missy's order, they would all lie down on their brightly-colored mats, each with a child's name on it. Later, they all drank milk together, orderly and politely; drew pictures, tried out new skills, heard records and finally sat entranced while Missy read a story. In all my experience I have never seen such responsive children. Their expressions evoked by Missy's magic begged for a camera.

Missy was a good psychologist. She had outlined the activities in her classes, and the problems, in her own well-written brochure, "Living in the Kindergarten." As Missy proved, it needn't be all naps and noise.

She was sensitive to the shaping of a child's attitude toward school. She protected this trust well. She had discovered that in rural Cumberland, children from the farms were shyer than children who lived in town. She also knew that four-year-olds got intimidated by six-year-olds. Her formula: start the term by forming groups of 12 children each, representing farm groups, town groups, or personality and age groups. In the beginning she staggered the groups. Then she combined one group with another. In short order she had them all integrated and meeting together as a class in one room in perfect harmony—well, almost perfect— and adjustment.

She was a wizard at handling a small child's large problems. One boy in her class would lie down by the door and cower like a frightened animal until his parents came for him at the end of the day. Missy tried everything. Nothing worked. Then she gave him a Halloween mask to wear. The mask gave the boy security. He began to mingle with the other children. He cooperated in class.

She told about another boy: "Many children are very shy in the beginning of school. I never force them, but just let them stand on the side and work themselves into the situation. One little boy was so shy he couldn't make himself join in games. Whenever we played circle games I would explain to him how much we needed every child, especially him, to make the circle 'BIG.' I would make sure the circle wasn't closed and a space left for him. He finally felt the need to close the circle. After that, he suggested we play a circle game over and over again, day after day, because now he knew how important he was—he was needed to make the circle BIG."

There were other low hurdles. Each fall the kindergarten had its immunization program. To prepare the children, Missy dramatized getting shots the day before the doctor came. She told them it would hurt, just a little, but no more than if they had pricked their fingers when changing the doll's clothes. They knew what to expect. And the doctor joked, "What do you do to those kids, threaten them if they cry?"

The other teachers I visited in the Cumberland school told me they loved to have Missy's kindergarten children move up to their classes. They are well-trained, have respect and love for teachers. They need little discipline. This Missy-stamp remains on them for life—a fact we forget about kindergarten teachers. They are the molders who reach a child at his most curious, most receptive time. Many, like Helen Adams, are and must be our best teachers.

We also overlook the humor in the kindergarten. It is there, and Missy often found it, enjoyed it and related the stories with glee:

* "One day we were all sitting on the square—here we are very quiet because we are listening to stories, records or planning our work. This particular day, they couldn't sit still, wiggling like worms on hot ashes, so I told them how proud I had always been when I called them to the square for a story and they had listened so well, but today they had disappointed me. One boy then looked at his playmates and said, 'Don't you know you're not suppose to disappoint Missy or God!' "

* "We were working on vocabulary enrichment and I was trying to challenge them with new words. So I asked if anyone knew another word for *big* and another for *little?* No one thought of the words *large* or *small*, but after a minute of real concentration one little boy brightened up and yelled, 'king size and regular.' "

* "During an informal conversation period, the children talked about their friends who would be coming into kindergarten next

29

year. One of the youngsters asked if Mikie Skinner would be coming. I said I didn't know. Then he quickly replied, Missy, when he comes to kindergarten you won't boss *him* around, because his daddy's the mayor of the city.' "

* "One dark, restless day, we had a discussion on watching TV too late at night. I suggested that the children go to bed earlier and maybe they would be better little boys and girls tomorrow. One youngster popped up and said, 'Missy, why don't you get to bed earlier and maybe you'll be a better teacher tomorrow.' "

Could be. But Helen Adams was already an excellent teacher. I asked her about her attitude toward the profession. "The basis of all good teaching is a genuine love for children. All teachers should have that. With many, many persons, teaching is just another job. With some it is a profession. With me it is more than just another job, more than a profession—it is a way of life. It is the kind of life I want to live. It takes a lot of vitality."

Missy had that vitality. She went summers and got her B.S. from Wisconsin State College in 1951. She started courses in Teachers College, Columbia University, in 1955, and took her M.A. degree in Early Childhood Education there in 1958. She hoped to take a Ph.D. eventually.

"Do you need a Ph.D. degree to teach kindergarten in a small town where you are already Number One and an institution?" I asked. Helen Adams's reply told me much about her:

"The children of Cumberland deserve the best I can give them."

*   *

Part of each term, Mrs. Isabelle Mattson sat down on the job. She kept a rocking chair in her classroom and rocked contentedly in it when things went well.

During my trip to see her, I landed in Battle Creek, Michigan, on Thanksgiving Day. I ate my turkey alone. A cocktail would have helped, but Battle Creek is a dry town. I had long thoughts that day about the Kellogg Dynasty, especially Mrs. Ella E. Kellogg, the reformer, who wrote books with titles like *A Talk With Girls*. I debated giving up Corn Flakes.

The next day, Cleveland Fry, a local taxi driver, drove me to Union City, Michigan. At the elementary school, Mrs. Mattson

30

had a steaming pot of coffee ready for me. Yesterday's bleakness faded quickly.

Union City, where the St. Joseph River joins the Coldwater River, is a town of history, filled with old houses of architectural features best described as neo-American gothic. The "Plantation," now an antique shop, once served as a way station on a stagecoach route. The town was chartered in 1837, and it built a little red school house the same year. The new high school was the most modern structure I saw on my whole trip. The elementary school, four years old, was also modern and functional.

Isabelle Mattson's father came here from New York, her mother from Pennsylvania. Her maternal grandfather was a Dunkard preacher. "I still say 'boughten' bread, along with other Pennsylvania German locutions," she admitted. She was born Feb. 1, 1901, in Branch County, Michigan. This teacher, I found, was a tough-minded, independent woman, with a pioneering instinct. Her hands were strong, her skin tanned, her eyes honest. She was remodeling an old farm house, built in 1828, when I met her, doing most of the hard work with her own hands. Her husband, formerly a gold prospector, was ailing and unable to work. Mrs. Mattson's 81-year-old mother lived with her, as did an adopted son and three other homeless children she and her husband took in. It was a menage permeated with love.

Mrs. Mattson had unique teaching methods. "We set no goals in my fifth grade classes," she confided. "We make no arbitrary beginning and ending points. We just work together and advance together and we pull along the stragglers. You find the student where he is—not where he is supposed to be. I have to make allowances for each student. Some don't know how to read. Some can't spell. Age means nothing in my classroom. I give reading instruction according to each student's need and ability. The usual textbooks are not geared to my group. No one has written a textbook for my needs, and I have examined them all. I keep a lot of books exposed in my classroom, and I let the children discover them in just the way you discover something that appeals to you in a second-hand bookstore. You may think my classroom looks like a mess. I keep in it things I think a person of any age might find an interest in. In my classes I never know what is going to happen next. My students start arguments on controversial sub-

31

jects, sometimes on subjects over their heads, but I don't try to stop them. I just close the door so our loud discussion doesn't disturb other classes down the hall."

Who took part in Mrs. Mattson's discussions? It might be a boy who had a poor opinion of his abilities because his speech was impeded. The results? This boy discovers how to hatch eggs in the class's incubator, orders movies on "Egg Layers," and begins to speak before 70 children about the movies. Or two girls with an interest in music work up a talk on their own, for younger children, with pictures, and set out to teach them the history and stories of instruments and their development. They write to other rooms for permission to do the teaching. All this fits in with Isabelle Mattson's philosophy:

"The main concern I have with education is that we do not release creative ideas and attitudes. We use the pouring-in process and hope that by merely raising the level in the bottle we improve the product. Just the contrary is true."

I asked her what she thought of other teachers who taught by the book. "Victims of rigid thinking," she argued. "They don't know what is going on in educational circles. They don't read, don't attend workshops and seminars, don't attend conferences. They don't join civic clubs. They think all students are alike, give or take a few points of I.Q. The key to my system is the acknowledgment of the fact that no two children are alike in their needs and abilities. I blame principals for a lot of this. They don't go out and hire the best teachers. They let schools run themselves on a sort of inherited momentum."

She is particularly disturbed by Intelligence Quotient Tests, the questionable yardstick of a child's abilities. "As I ponder over each child's test," she said, "I am reminded of a remark that a very wise administrator made to me one time, who remembered when tests of this kind hadn't been invented. He said, 'Our teachers used to look at the children and think they could all be President. Now they look at the test results and too often think there is no use and quit trying.' I am convinced that the child whose test shows he cannot achieve satisfactorily too often has so many problems to face that he has never had a chance to do his best. Larry, who came to my room three years ago with a long record from the clinics of problems in social, emotional and academic development,

32

has gone from first grade level to fifth. And then there's the little boy who can't get arithmetic from the book, but he gets up at five every morning to milk twenty cows, earns half the milk check, which he uses to buy his own clothes and banks the balance regularly. If this isn't arithmetic, what is? Terry, who is as pretty as can be, but can't master reading, looks up from his drawing and says, with shining eyes, 'My, but I'm learning a lot this year.' "

And they did learn a lot. Much of it was due to Mrs. Mattson's constant re-charging of education's beacon. She said, "It seems to me a lot depends on how we look at education. Should we place more and more emphasis on the three R's, or should we first take a closer look at how the child feels about himself and what his concern is for others? Or how well can he understand people or convey his thought to them, or how he uses his abilities to create? Is this not a function of education? Do we help him to understand deep within himself, 'That a man's reach must exceed his grasp, or what's a heaven for?' "

To keep her students out of education's rut, Mrs. Mattson would push and pull hard during the first few weeks of school, which she considered the hardest. She would start group activities, spot students with talents or weaknesses, pull loose ends together. Then would come the rocking chair. "I tell my pupils, 'When you see me remove the rope from the old rocking chair you know you are moving ahead on your own power.' " Symbolically, the rocking chair—and the rope that prevents anyone from sitting in it—represented the class's academic progress. The more they worked, the more Mrs. Mattson felt she could rock. I saw the rocker in her class. She brought it to school when the term started, and she removed the rope and sat in it, rocking smoothly, when the class had progressed to her satisfaction.

But Mrs. Mattson didn't sit back and rock when it came to criticizing education. She was vigilant. "The school laws say you have to go to school," she argued. "The children feel this 'have to' influence. Books are handed to them and the teacher says, 'This is it.' Education is more than reading and writing and arithmetic. Education is an opportunity for us to realize our dreams, and the bigger the dreams the better.

"You must educate the total child, not the partial child or what is left over when parents and teachers have passed him on to other hands to get rid of him. He must feel wanted. He must feel he is worth something, that he has something to give. It is time we got close to the educational heart of things. Education's first function is to destroy the caste system, the stigma of being born on the wrong side of the tracks, or having the wrong color to your skin. Little teachers are little teachers because they resign themselves to being just that. They do not see the philosophy of teaching, only the practice, and the practice never varies from one year to the next. They do things by rote, never stopping to ask why."

After finishing Michigan State Normal School at Ypsilanti, Isabelle Mattson taught at Ferndale, a Detroit suburb. It was there she met a creative educator, Edgar Down. He encouraged her to try out new methods. During the Depression she established a rural workshop, the Girard Township Community Center, which enhanced her reputation as a pioneer teacher.

Now she could reflect over those years. "After 30 years of teaching, I look at some of those students and wonder why our schools failed them. Is it that we have been making the wrong approach? Have we defeated our purpose by placing the emphasis on failure? If the child can't pass the subject that the school insists he take, then he is a failure and no longer worth consideration. If I have ten-year-old students who range in ability from first grade to tenth grade, should I assume that all are capable of doing the same required work? Are these early school failures the cause of our many dropouts and delinquency cases? Does the child picture himself as no longer worth consideration because we gave him this untrue judgment of himself by our lack of perception of his true qualities? What about the child who is exceptional in some area, who comes from an environment that doesn't help him realize his gift? Is this education's problem? Should the school fill in where home and community cannot, by offering him opportunities to develop in other ways as well as in the required and standardized ones? How is it that the child may grow to feel that he can meet life as it comes and reach out, not only to help himself but also to want to help others? I feel it is because he knows his own worth and what he is capable of contributing without pride or shame. Instilling this confidence is the teacher's repsonsibility."

Mrs. Mattson's students got that desire to reach out. They

34

did help others, and their community. Her fifth graders, a few years before my visit, wanted to beautify the new school grounds. They campaigned, appealing to civic groups, and raised enough money to plant two acres and 6,000 trees and shrubs.

That must have set the old rocking chair in motion!

* *

Dr. Helen P. Maney was a talented woman for all seasons.

She was active in high school and college teaching, the city council, political campaigns, youth organizations, and her state teachers' association.

Dr. Maney was born in Geneva, New York, in 1915, went to school there and later taught history in the city's large high school. Geneva, tree-lined and domestic, nestles at the edge of Seneca Lake, the largest of the Finger Lakes. Hobart College and William Smith College give the city a pleasing academic atmosphere. Helen Maney graduated from William Smith College, and earned a Master of Arts degree and an honorary LL.D. from Syracuse University's School of Education.

Her father was a basket maker and dealer in farm produce. Her older brother was a lawyer, and under his influence she decided to become a lawyer also. But her father passed away and there was little money. So Helen became a teacher instead. She had always loved history; instead of being a fine lawyer she became an excellent history teacher. She also lectured on education at Hobart and Syracuse.

In the later 1940's, Helen Maney started a political career, filling out her mother's unexpired term on the Geneva City Common Council. Dr. Maney won her first election in 1947, and was re-elected every two years after that. She was a Democrat in a heavily Republican city, yet there was seldom a candidate eager to oppose her in her district. She more than held her own with the male members of the council as part of her work. She acted as liaison with the planning board, the city housing authority and the Senior Citizens Council. She was, when I visited her, chairman of the Civic Affairs Committee.

Dr. Maney had a quick, keenly logical mind, greatly admired on the council. As Mayor Harold Simpson said to me: "She is the stabilizer in the city council. She brings things to a logical conclusion. She does not try to dominate the discussions. She sits and listens. We wrangle, get things fouled up. Helen then takes charge. Speaking quietly, but with words that make sense, she brings us back on an even keel. She is so convincing we just have to accept her judgment. No entreaties, no misuse of womanly charm, just plain common sense. And that fine voice of hers! Have you ever heard a more beautiful one?"

I hadn't. Her voice had an oratorical quality to it, but with no bombast. It was the kind of voice you could hear from the back row of a large auditorium, not because it was loud, but because it had a bell-like ring to it.

I learned that Dr. Maney had also served three terms as vice president of the New York State Teachers Association. She was a well-known figure at all NEA conventions. She had been elected a trustee of Hobart College. Her party's bigwigs knew her. Dr. Maney showed me letters from Gov. W. Averell Harriman, James A. Farley and other leaders of the state's Democratic Party, thanking her for all she had done for New York in the classroom and in politics. In 1955, Helen Maney received from Gov. Harriman a citation for outstanding teaching.

Among the hundreds of committees she has served on was the important special committee under New York State Commissioner of Education, James E. Allen, Jr. In 1958, that commission formulated a far-reaching report, "Improving the Quality of Education in New York State Schools." It had been a special personal project of Helen Maney's for many years.

Despite all the awards and attention, Helen Maney remained a modest and humble person, willing to give credit to co-workers for accomplishments. E. B. Wertenbaker, principal of Geneva High School, called her an administrator's dream: "I never have to concern myself with what we call nuisance details when I delegate a task to Dr. Maney. She comes up with a full report, with all the kinks ironed out. She is such a good leader, she has a stabilizing effect on the other teachers. She never brings me a problem that a teachers' conference can discuss and solve. She is so fair with her students. She does not favor the prize students over the slower ones. She is a great teacher because she is a great human being. If you take the wrong side, she will oppose you. You know where she stands on every vital issue. You can trust her."

Who are today's great teachers?

Mrs. Lucille Wright, the city clerk, put it this way: "I have known Helen to stay up until three o'clock in the morning if she had school work to finish. She has never neglected one school obligation because of her work on the city council. She never looks tired. Don't ask me where she gets all her energy." Other people agreed.

I sat through two of her American history classes. Her method of teaching was the traditional one. She wrote down salient facts on the blackboard, questioned various members of the class, got clearer definitions when fuzzy ones were offered, never introduced a new topic until the old one was disposed of, and generally carried on—very well—the usual student-teacher dialectic. What impressed me was her presence, her poise, her commanding appearance, her rich, resonant voice. That remarkable voice is the first thing you notice. When she spoke, you listened, and what you heard was a well-thought-out point couched in cool, dispassionate, convincing logic.

Dr. Maney was firm, never caustic or cynical or angry. Her sympathies were broad and deep, never sentimental or on the surface. Hers was a friendship that would be lasting and inspirational, but not easily won. It would grow as the need for it grew.

Helen Maney had a patrician, classically haunting beauty. She was tall and stately. Her gray hair was tinted a lovely shade darker. Her brown, deep set eyes darted about under dark eyebrows. Her face, expressive in many moods, was handsome with honesty and character. She stood straight. Only in the privacy of her home did she bend a little, smoking an occasional cigarette, sipping 7-Up, revealing the innermost and various moods of heart and mind.

Her home was filled with books, magazines and music albums. She played the piano for relaxation. "If I come home with a problem," she confided, "I sit down and play classical music until it goes away. I'm not a good pianist. I can't draw or paint. I'm a good cook, and I have a passion for collecting recipes. But I have no artistic skills." I disagreed. Teaching was an artistic skill in the hands of a master.

Helen Maney was also a doer, a person who refused to make speeches and wait for others to act. When the city had traffic problem, she went down to the street corners and watched the lights and traffic and then made her report. On the first morning of Geneva's clean-up week, she was out sweeping with a broom. And so was every pupil in her class.

A woman of her beauty and accomplishments had to decide between marriage and teaching. Some women try to combine two careers. Few succeed. I am convinced that Helen Maney decided early in life to sacrifice all to education. With fierce pride in her mission she would mother a generation of adopted sons and daughters. "I weep over every class of mine that goes, and I welcome with open arms the class that replaces it. That's why I stay in Geneva. I know all these children and I know their parents. I don't want to leave them."

* *

Jim DeRose teaches science at Marple-Newton Senior High School, Newton Square, Pennsylvania.

In the summer of 1959, a group of 18 young chemistry teachers attended a conference at Reed College for the purpose of revising chemistry textbooks, bringing them up to date with advances of the Atomic Age. DeRose was one of these teachers. This group at Reed developed the Chemical Bond Approach to teaching chemistry, a method now incorporated into a textbook published through a grant from the National Science Foundation. James DeRose helped write this textbook and was one of the first teachers to use it in high school chemistry classes.

DeRose's Chemical Bond Approach used a central theme— the concept of chemical bonds—as an introduction to high school chemistry. The preface to the textbook pointed out that substances "can be roughly classified by their properties into three major classes. Each class of substance can be thought of as representing a particular way by which atoms are linked or joined by chemical bonds." As I listened to his classes, I knew that all of DeRose's students understood the theory thoroughly and eagerly pursued its implications and applications. Some day these young wizards would be doing research in our leading universities and industries. DeRose felt confidence in them and expected much from them. Why not? As he explained:

"I believe each individual has the right and the obligation to develop his capabilities to the fullest. Boys and girls vary mentally,

38

physically and emotionally. It is impossible for a school to provide for the needs of each specific child but it should make the attempt to achieve this ideal. The minds and bodies of our children constitute society's most important natural resource. It is the function of our educational systems not only to inform our young people but to develop an attitude of critical and creative thought."

This DeRose tried to do. He visited many high schools as guest instructor in the Chemical Bond Approach, and corresponded with several co-authors of the new textbook in an effort to work the flaws out of it. His leadership in this field brought him national recognition. In April, 1966, more than 6,000 science teachers met in New York City in their annual convention, led by James DeRose, president.

James Vincent DeRose was born in the little town of Jessup, Pa., March 14, 1917. His parents, of Italian descent, loved the soil and moved from Jessup to Bloomsburg, living on farms. Jim roamed the anthracite hills with the freedom and joy only an imaginative boy fully knows. Much of his elementary and secondary schooling was in small towns and country schools, as his family moved. He went to Bloomsburg State College, getting his B.S. in 1939. He attended classes at Temple University, the University of Pennsylvania and St. Joseph's College and in 1947 got his M.S. in education at Penn, and his Ed.D. there in 1962.

He started work on his doctorate at Penn in 1958, studying during his time-off from school. In 1960, he taught the Chemical Bond Method at Brown University's summer school.

I visited Jim and Anna DeRose and their three children, Jeanne Ellen, James Martin and William Robert at their modest home in Springfield, a few miles from Newtown Square. Jim had much to say about education. He wanted more men to go into teaching at salaries equalling other professional fields. He thought women had dominated teaching to the extent that education has developed a "she" psychology. He was lured from the head of the Chester High School science department by Dr. Kermit Stover. The reason: higher salary.

DeRose liked to push himself, his fellow teachers and his students. When Dr. Stover hired Jim DeRose, he knew he was getting a progressive man who would better things at Newtown Square. He was right. He wanted DeRose to step up the pace in the science department and bring new techniques into the classroom. The first thing Jim DeRose did was put in a request for $10,000 worth of new lab equipment. He got it. Dr. Stover appeared to be scholarly, urbane, soft-spoken, and he was. But he also had a get-it-done attitude and was not afraid to tangle with school board members and local politicians for his program. He and DeRose pushed a lot.

Jim also believed in student teachers. Several from nearby Swarthmore College would pinch hit for him when he was away on speaking engagements. On his return, he would ask the class what it had learned from the visiting teacher. "I want my students to know that there are many approaches to learning and many points of view. I don't know all the answers."

In turn, he asked much of his students. "Youngsters should be led to the realization that our great inheritance of culture is the product of man's mind and that their generation has the obligation to build a better life upon it. Our present civilization should be viewed with an attitude which aims to improve and which criticizes constructively. Education should aim to stimulate our youngsters to think independently and honestly; to be curious and probing; to question eagerly and sympathetically; to use their minds creatively; and to develop insights into problems which plague mankind."

To help other teachers stimulate their pupils, DeRose wrote two pamphlets, "A Class Exercise in Developing a Periodic Table," and "Principles of Measurements." He also co-authored "Teacher's Guide for Chemical Systems."

DeRose was slight, of medium height, with dark, wavy hair. He wore glasses, which accentuated his scholarly bearing, and inexpensive tweed suits. He seemed somewhat shy, but with a friendly classroom manner. He spoke the idiom of his students, never belittling them, but patiently getting beside them, drawing out of them the right answers while allowing the students to do most of the talking.

I heard DeRose say many times: "Let's start at the beginning again. If you do not understand each step, please say so now. It has to be clear."

He put across the idea that all, including the teacher, are engaged in a joint exploration, and that truth is the object of their search. He conveyed the impression that he had scouted the land ahead and knew the trails. He was the guide.

* *

The White House ceremony was scheduled for 12:45, May 2. The winner that spring of 1961, Helen "Missy" Adams, signed in with the guards at the gate, waited 45 minutes, then marched with LOOK's William B. Arthur into the White House, where they waited another half an hour. Missy tried to catch a glimpse of the President's office and the famous rocking chair. "I wanted to remember the color of the walls," she said later, "but I couldn't see a thing but this tall friendly figure—what a warm, accepting handshake!"

President Kennedy was in fine, Irish form, bubbling, humorous and obviously glad to be there. So was Missy. In the garden, the President, with that well-known impish twinkle, asked Missy, "What have you done to win this award?" She hesitated for a second, caught off guard. "I don't really know. I guess because I have been teaching kindergarten kids for the past 17 years in the best way I know how."

The Rose Garden filled with newsmen and cameras. Among the guests were Abraham Ribicoff, Secretary of Health, Education and Welfare; Vernon Myers, publisher of LOOK Magazine; Sterling McMurrin, U.S. Commissioner of Education; and George Watson, Wisconsin State Superintendent of Schools. The President handed Missy a microphone and told her, "Say a few words." She did. Then she was presented with a framed award certificate and a gold lapel pin by Cartier's that carried her name and the date of the award.

President Kennedy closed the ceremony with these words: "Today, the fate of individuals and nations rests upon education. In a real and immediate sense, the teachers of America hold our future in her hands. Miss Helen 'Missy' Adams is one of those to whom we owe gratitude and support. Her dedication and warmth, her struggle against high odds to become a teacher should stand as an example to future teachers and an inspiration to all Americans. I want to offer my personal congratulations to Miss Adams, National Teacher of the Year."

It was a thrilling moment.

On her way out of the Rose Garden, Missy was stopped by photographers and newsmen wanting pictures and interviews. It started a hectic week of receptions, more interviews, radio and TV shows, lunches with senators and representatives (one, thankfully, highlighted by her favorite bean soup)—and a special side trip to Columbia University to check on some courses she wanted to take.

When she arrived home in Cumberland, Wis. Missy was met at the airport by the high school band and townspeople, the mayor and state education officials. May 9, 1961, became "Missy Day." Local businesses closed for several hours. There was a parade from the Cumberland Methodist Church to Hines' Corner and west to the high school gymnasium for a program. The parade included cars carrying school and town officials, Missy and her family, a Shell Lake delegation, the high school band, a grade school band, and several busloads of children.

Missy rode through cheering crowds. Flowers and gifts were pressed upon her. It was more than a personal triumph. It was a symbolic accolade for teachers everywhere and for education itself. I never knew a town so loyal to one of its teachers. She had become an institution, much like Ruth Lee in Teague, Texas, and Ken Easter in Dos Palos, California.

The rush and pressure bore in on Missy. The strain of public appearances exhausted her. Polio-weakened, she had to give up her classroom work for a short period and rest. She soon returned. You can't keep a teacher like Missy out of the classroom.

CHAPTER TWO

*"... A good teacher is a friend to whom students are
welcome and encouraged to come for help with a problem,
be it one in geometry or one in human relations ..."*

MARJORIE FRENCH

1962 NATIONAL TEACHER OF THE YEAR

MRS. MARJORIE FRENCH
Mathematics
Topeka High School
Topeka, Kansas

RUNNERS-UP

FLOYD BASS
Science
Hot Springs County
   High School
Thermopolis, Wyo.

MRS. FLOSSIE
   BECKETT
Fourth Grade
Elementary School
Lindsay, Oklahoma

MRS. ZILPHA
   BILLINGS
Sixth Grade
John J. Flynn
   Elementary School
Burlington, Vermont

EDWARD
   BRATTRUD
Chemistry
Polo High School
Polo, Illinois

JEAN MARANI
Social Studies
Riverview High
   School
Sarasota, Florida

MRS. MARY
   PARKER
English
Sandpoint Senior
   High School
Sandpoint, Idaho

CHRISTINE
   POINDEXTER
Mathematics
Central High School
Little Rock, Arkansas

MRS. LORRAINE
   SABO
Art
Meriwether Lewis
   Elementary School
Portland, Oregon

MRS. ANNE KELL
   TINSLEY
Kindergarten
Emerson School
Flagstaff, Arizona

44

Dr. Jean Victoria Marani was five feet of educational dynamite. Her personality and pluck as teacher and curriculum director had held together an unusual school in Sarasota, Fla.

It was January, 1962.

I was on my second swing around the country in search of the National Teacher of the Year. This time I found myself in Riverview Senior High School in Sarasota.

It was a jaunty modern building, as functional as the intercom system, and as personal.

This modern atmosphere fit the teaching of Dr. Jean Marani. Dr. Marani, a dark-haired daughter of an Italian father and Pennsylvania Dutch mother, was born in Evanston, Ill., on July 28, 1924. She had spent the major part of her life in Sarasota. She loved golf and swimming. If she had a weakness, it was her fondness for fancy earrings—she owned 150 pairs of them.

It was the only weakness I found.

She was well informed in all the traditional and experimental aspects of education, and much in demand as a speaker, panelist and consultant. For every ounce of question she gave a full pound of answer. She had turned down many job offers that would have obliged her and her mother to move from a community they loved. I had a chance to meet her mother. It was apparent that Jean, an only child, was given every opportunity to advance her career. Each success fed a mother's pride. Mrs. Marani, showing me through Jean's study lined with books and manuscripts, said, "I added this room to the house to give Jean a quiet place to work in when she was writing her doctor's thesis."

Dr. Harold Alberty, of Ohio State University, noted for the

45

teachers he had trained, said of Jean Marani: "She is one of the most brilliant Ph.D. candidates I have ever taught." The two top men at Riverview, Russell Wiley, superintendent, and Freeman Vaughn, principal, echoed this judgment. Wiley said: "I made sure my own daughter took high school courses under Jean. I pay her a higher salary than most school administrators receive. Educators from all over the country come her to observe her teaching methods." And Vaughn told me: "She makes teaching seem exciting. She convinces many of her students that teaching is a profession they should enter. She is as good a teacher as I have ever worked with."

Dr. Marani was a believer in problem-centered learning. As the architect of curriculum at Riverview, she had given her students the choice of many elective courses. She strongly pushed individual research on special projects chosen by the students. They had special freedom to work, which put a premium on time and scholarship. The Riverview students seemed self-disciplined. They matured rapidly under the pressure of responsibilities given them by Dr. Marani.

Dr. Marani conducted seminars geared around small and cohesive groups of students. There was a relaxed atmosphere in the classroom. The day I visited we heard reports on communism, the life and philosophy of Gandhi, a comparison of dictators throughout history, the origin of religious holidays. Source books were evaluated. One student was preparing a questionnaire to be filled out by students in another school in Sarasota. The object was to discover if the students of one school were different from the students of Riverview in their approach to problems, or if the problems were different in kind and degree. In another seminar I listened to discussions on right wing groups, the Cold War, the Peace Corps, and racial integration. Dr. Marani made the seminars click. I knew why when I talked to her. "A good teacher," she confided, "must have warmth and friendliness, must accept every student in the room, must have enthusiasm for learning which is never dulled, must establish a 'oneness' with the class. A good teacher must be fair, sincere, look at all points of view, weight conflicting opinions, reduce the margin of error in student thinking and behavior. A teacher must have a spiritual anchor in times of storm and stress. I believe in God. Having made that state-

46

ment I do not push it upon others, and yet I teach from an inner religious conviction. A good teacher shuns self-glorification. A good teacher has fun in class. Humor relaxes tension. Once a month I ask my students to criticize me openly and to pull no punches. When one student said, 'You talk too much,' I felt properly chastened."

Dr. Marani had a staggering choice of 41 electives for her classes, including psychology, creative writing, marine biology, modern ballet and boys' home living. One of the features of "individual studies" program, Dr. Marani told me, was the counseling. Each grade had a permanent counselor who follows the class until graduation and who knows each student's needs.

"Education is no good unless it increases the student's capacity to do original thinking," she believed. "John Dewey said, 'Thinking takes time.' My students appreciate being taught up to, not down to, and what teacher can ever forget the glow that comes on the face of a boy or girl who has seen something never seen before. This glow is to the teacher what the hole in one is to the golfer. You have to make your teaching relevant to the student's own world of reality."

Dr. Jean Marani brought that reality to her seminars. We talked a lot about education, youth and the world. We became friends. Before I left, I spent an hour or so alone on the beach of pure white sand on the Gulf of Mexico. It was strewn with lovely shells at low tide. I picked up dozens, threw most of them away. Some were chipped. I began to look for the perfect shell, but like the perfect teacher, it is not always there. The sea, like education, is a mystery.

* *

The howling faces, the shouted hate, those bitter words you thought no man or woman could ever say. I heard them all, as much of the nation did, on television news programs when brave Negro children tried to integrate Center High School in Little Rock, Arkansas. That was in September, 1957. More than five years had passed since then.

Now I made my first visit to that city to interview Miss Christine Poindexter, a mathematics teacher at Central High. I was curious. Had the scars and bitterness healed and faded? You

47

cannot unmake history in a few years. You live with it, regret it, mold it, talk about it, adjust to it. Little Rock, I found, was doing all of these.

I instantly recognized the front of Central High School, caught for history's decision by newspaper front pages and television cameras. It must have been a mistake. The peace and quiet of the tree-lined streets could never have sheltered that mob. Perhaps Little Rock, when the riots broke out, was no different from dozens of other cities in the South. The civil rights issue was ready for a showdown. Time and place may have simply come together at Central High School. Teachers and students may have been caught up in one of those ugly historic moments. Perhaps.

Inside the school, I found Miss Poindexter in her office. She looked and talked like one of my older sisters in Missouri, her accent making me feel comfortable immediately as though I were hearing hometown talk again after a long absence. Miss Poindexter had great dignity and gracious manners. She first began teaching at 17 in Black Rock, Arkansas. Then came teaching jobs at places called Marked Tree, Hamburg and Osceolo. For the past 19 years she had taught at Central High. Graduate work at the University of Texas, Indiana University, the University of Missouri and the University of Arkansas kept her up to date.

"Why did you specialize in math?" I asked. Her reply told me something of the charm only a rural teacher knows. "I had a wonderful high school teacher," she answered. "His name was J. C. Eaton. He taught me to look for the true meaning behind figures. I still feel his spirit permeating my classroom. He was never satisfied until he mastered a subject. He took a college course in math when he was 77 years old. I gave that college course myself. It was a custom in rural schools years ago to give each pupil a stick of candy when he finished his course. I gave Mr. Eaton a stick of candy and he was very touched by it."

I attended two of Miss Poindexter's math classes. She taught with the traditional thoroughness we associate with good math teaching and patiently brought the slowest students up to grade level.

What is education? At Little Rock you are entitled to raise that question. And you are entitled to raise other questions, too. What happened to Christine Poindexter during those September

48

days? "I was 'purged' you know," she told me. "I was one of the teachers who took a stand in favor of integration. It was a moral principle with me. I told the authorities that I believed in education for all, regardless of race or creed. I was purged for saying this. Even members of my own church congregation snubbed me and said harsh things which cut me to the quick. Some of them complained about me to my mother. She told them, bless her heart, 'I support my daughter's views. We have no regrets.' She was 85 at the time."

"What about your present students, do they feel any stigma?"

"Of course they feel it, but they are working harder than any students I have ever taught. They are trying to make up for things by achieving high honors. There never has been a time in our history when young people were better than they are today. I say this with deep conviction. They are studious, they are generous with their time when it comes to helping worthy causes. They are tolerant. Today at Central High School there is not the slightest discrimination against the Negro students. It was not the students who caused the trouble in Little Rock. It was the parents. Parents who teach lies to their children are always a problem.

"During the crisis here, even when troops stood guard, when the press and radio folk were crowding around the school looking for something sensational to report, not one class was missed, not one teacher was absent. Inside the building work went on as usual. Most of the students deplored what was going on outside the building. I know. I was there."

J. W. Matthews, principal, praised Miss Poindexter's stand against the local bigots. "She was a tower of strength to me in the crisis." On his desk was an ashtray with the words, "Cheer Up!" I pointed to it. He smiled. "I had some grim moments," he said.

Some teachers I talked to tried to make excuses for what happened. Others, like Christine Poindexter, quietly practiced what they taught. A redemptive force was at work in Central High. Miss Poindexter thought it was creating a new climate of freedom and justice. If so, she must take some of the credit for creating it.

One young man who transferred from the all-Negro Horace Mann High School in Little Rock to Central High was Ernest Green. He had wit and poise and got along well with the white students even during the worst days of the crisis. He went on to do graduate work at Michigan State University. One summer between terms he came to New York to work for LOOK Magazine. He was assigned to the research department under me. We never discussed Little Rock all the time he was on my staff. At summer's end, when it was time to return to college, Ernie Green and I talked about Christine Poindexter. He was delighted to know I had interviewed his teacher. Then he paid her a student's compliment—hardly modest under the circumstances. It told me much about Christine Poindexter's role in 1957. "When you write to her," Ernie told me, "send her my best regards."

* *

Lindsay, Oklahoma, a town of 4,500 in the Washita River Valley, is a region of great fertility, contentment and good schools. Mrs. Flossie Beckett, a fourth grade teacher in the Lindsay Elementary School, was one solid reason the schools were so good.

Lindsay is known as the "Broom Corn Capital of the World." That, with oil and gas, makes it prosperous. This has helped education. On one side of a pleasant Lindsay street is a huge new high school; another new elementary school gleams on the other side. This was where Mrs. Beckett taught.

I first chatted with Guy Robberson, superintendent of schools, in his posh office—complete with electronic devices—in the high school. He was excited about Mrs. Beckett's winning a Teacher of the Year nomination. In Oklahoma you have to be very well known to get this nomination, for it is a statewide competition with each county thrusting forward its own favorite son or daughter. I was anxious to meet this Flossie Beckett who had triumphed over so many formidable rivals.

Robberson walked with me across the street to the elementary school and Mrs. Beckett's neatly decorated classroom. She was well-dressed, in her middle fifties, composed and pleasant. She had beautiful auburn hair, almost reddish, that made her look younger. She was a grandmother when I met her. She had married and raised her family—two girls and a boy—until 1943 when teachers were needed so badly. The boy, the youngest child, was in the fifth grade, so she decided it wouldn't hurt the children if she went into teaching. She finished a nine-week school term for a teacher

50

who had resigned and began going to college summers to get her degree. The experience didn't hurt the family at all; both daughters have become teachers, too.

Flossie Beckett moved gracefully among her pupils. She had lots of motherly love to pass around and each child got his share. She loved the corner of the world she was in and the Oklahoma children who passed through her door. Parents of young children have a right to know what kind of teacher they turn their child over to—very few exercise this right. The enrollment of a child in school is an act of faith—unless there's a teacher like Flossie Beckett. No parent in Lindsay worried about his child in her class.

Flossie Beckett won the hearts and minds of fourth graders. Hers were fiercely competitive. Mrs. Beckett would ask a question and all hands would go up, so quickly and so vigorously I was afraid arms would be wrenched from sockets. There was an eagerness to be praised, to excel. Like all good teachers, Mrs. Beckett made sure each child had a taste of success before the bell rang. This was a joyful class. Learning was such fun when everyone got into the spirit of it. Being dull is a teacher's cardinal sin. Flossie enlivened her classes with 35mm and stereo slides she and her husband, Si, who worked in the nearby oil fields, took during trips through the national parks to visit their children and grandchildren. The fourth graders loved it.

The Becketts also took up gardening as a hobby, and won more than 100 ribbons and prizes for their flowers, mostly roses, at the county and district fairs. Mrs. Beckett outlined her gardening role: "Si does the work and I pick the flowers."

Flossie Beckett's fourth graders saw more than a teacher behind a desk. They responded to her because she responded to them, thinking of their education even while on long-distance trips and taking photographs for their classes, or bringing in flowers to brighten the classroom. She was like the person Plato had in mind when he wrote, "Those having torches will pass them on to others."

* *

You sit in the Greyhound Bus Station in Albuquerque, New Mexico. You must stay there for three hours waiting for the bus to Flagstaff, Arizona. Your plane flight has been wiped out because of bad weather. You have missed the Santa Fe train. The bus is last choice. With limited success, tired mothers pacify tired babies while men in cowboy boots and sombreros sit silently and roll cigarettes. It is 7:30 early in a lonely evening, and dark. You climb on the crowded bus, pass through miles of beautiful country, but see none of it. Your companions are mostly Mexicans and Indians. The girls wear slacks and sneakers. No one talks. It is chilly. The towns stretch 50 miles apart and there are 300 miles of desert to cross. Nothing—no light from trailside houses or clinging villages—disturbs the hallowed hush and void of darkness.

And yet from time to time an Indian arises from his seat, walks to the front of the bus, the driver stops and the Indian steps off into the black nothingness. The first few times you squint and peer out to see what he sees and you do not. There is nothing out there. How do these Indians instinctively know when to get off the bus when there are no lights or markers? You sense you are in a land of mystery, a land set apart for those who can live with its secrets.

The weary night wears on. Through the glass top of the upper tier of the bus you mark a single star, and it becomes your traveling companion, compass and comforter. Your mind dully recites part of the childhood rhyme, and catches itself. Your other companions sleep, twitch, snore. One woman's feet are badly swollen from being on the bus too many days and nights. At 2:40 a.m. you pull into Flagstaff between banks of snow. There are no taxis. The only noise is the bus fading off, and then the crunch of your shoes in snow as you pick up your bags and walk down deserted streets in search of a hotel—any hotel. The air is sharp, clean and cold. It almost hurts city lungs. You realize you are in high altitudes. Ah. You spot a hotel sign. The night clerk sleepily tells you that you are in luck, there is just one room left, the hotel is filled with weekend ski enthusiasts. You are too tired to unpack your bag.

Church bells awaken you and you remember it is Sunday. You had forgotten. The sound in juke boxes and loudspeakers from endless stations and terminals still echoes in your ears.

Later, you take a taxi to 914 North Leroux. A name plaque showing above a snowbank identifies "The Tinsleys." The bell rings, a nurse in uniform answers the door and calls Mrs. Tinsley.

52

Who are today's great teachers?

(You learn shortly that Anne Kell Tinsley's husband, William, a dean at Arizona State College, is now in the terminal stage of brain cancer, and that Mrs. Tinsley gave up her kindergarten classes six weeks ago to be with him.)

You are not prepared for the warm welcome you get, but, in looking back later, it should have been what you expected. Anne Tinsley is a tall, stately, gray-haired woman with a charming Mississippi accent and all the graciousness of ante-bellum South. The living room is a neat assemblage of antique furniture, books and pictures, and you sense that two cultured people have put into this room every object that reflects their love for one another and their philosophy. Mrs. Tinsley pulls back the drapes of a window and shows off her terraced garden, snow-covered now, but which would be alive with flowers when spring crept back to keep its promise. "Flowers are my hobby," she admits.

The conversation moves smoothly into her girlhood in the South. "My sister and I often went boating with an eccentric youth by the name of William Faulkner. He wrote my sister a sonnet. She said, 'He may be a poet, but he doesn't know much about handling a boat.' When his book *Sanctuary* came out my mother said, 'Anne, you don't dare read it,' and to this day I haven't. I don't care much about the things he writes about, even though I recognize his place in American literature."

She plans to take over her old classes for one day for your benefit. "You can't travel this far and have all your plans upset. You ask about the Indians. They are difficult to teach. They want our brand of education, but they do not accept its responsibilities. They break appointments. An Indian mother may bring her child to school one day in the morning and bring it to school in the late afternoon the following day. I once thought that the little Hopi girls were backward because they would never step forward to recite. I then learned that Hopi custom and religion demands that the girl child always remain in the background and must never be so bold as to step forward. My little Indian girls were simply obeying tribal injunctions. All my Indian children have an aptitude for art. They have an instinct for design. You should see some of their paintings, their pottery, handicrafts. Some come to our churches, but they take the hymns literally. When the hymn says, 'make joyous sounds,' the Indians beat on drums or shake their rattles.

My husband wonders if we ever really convert the Indians, whether there is an inner mysticism not wholly convertible. He thinks we take away from them something beautiful without replacing it with something quite as beautiful. We know that the Indian has an inner spirituality he never confides to us and which we can never fathom. He shows it in many ways. He will stand silently every day watching the setting sun—reverently. We don't always do that, but sometimes I think we would be better off if we did."

She shows a book written by her Indian friend, Mrs. Elizabeth White. It is called *The Sun Girl* by Po-Lin-Gay-Si (Hopi for "Butterfly"). It is a charming book for children, which Mrs. Tinsley read to her kindergarten pupils. She also offered Piki bread made by the Indians from blue corn and pinon nuts, an Indian delicacy.

You ask her views on education. She quotes Ruskin: "The purpose of all education is to acquire power to bless and redeem humanity." She then adds quoting from memory, "Mary Beard says that 'action without thought is perilous, and thought without action is futile.' Spirit means more than academic background. Only weeds unfold naturally, other plants need cultivation. A child is like a plant. You have to study it, must know what makes it grow. We can love children without truly knowing them. Knowledge comes from long study and experience and maturity. We should evaluate ourselves more often. We must learn from other teachers. I left college teaching to go into kindergarten. Don't ask me why. It would take too long to answer. I just enjoy getting down on the floor with children and looking at the world through their eyes. This is education on the ground floor."

Anne Morrow Kell was born December 5, 1910, in Pascagoula, Miss. She went to Mississippi State College for Women in Columbus, took her masters degree at Teachers College, Columbia University, then taught at Bemidji State Teachers College, Bemidji, Minn. In 1943–44 she was a first grade teacher in the McGuffey School of Miami University at Oxford, Ohio, where William Holmes McGuffey compiled his famous "Readers." She went to Arizona State Teachers College in Flagstaff in 1946, where she met and married the dean, William W. Tinsley in 1946. In 1947, Mrs. Tinsley joined the staff of the Flagstaff Public Schools.

She had given much. Mrs. Tinsley helped found the kindergarten system in the state of Arizona. Parents scrambled to get their children into her classes. Without her skills, many Indian children might have become simple "blanket" Indians. The Flagstaff school district is the second largest in the United States. It covers 7,000 square miles, bigger than Rhode Island and Delaware combined. Some students live 45 miles away and bus in every day. There were about 300 Indian children in the school when I visited.

Monday morning classes with Mrs. Tinsley were a tearful reunion. Her pupils had not seen her for weeks. They hugged and clung to her. Dr. Tinsley sent the class a basket of fruit. Mrs. Tinsley gave a lesson on citrus fruits and how to distinguish one from the other. Then they ate them. A lime was held up. "What's this?" A little girl called out, "A baby citrus." When Mrs. Tinsley had trouble with the squeezer another girl said, "You are a callous kangaroo," and everyone laughed. Later there were naps to soft music and classes in the gym with dancing to a record that described the movement of the wind. It was a lovely day.

Flying back to Phoenix that night in bad weather you are the only passenger on the plane. The stewardess politely tries to make conversation, but your thoughts are back in Flagstaff. You have passed into this mysterious land, something happened, touched you, now you are leaving. It will take time for its beauty and harshness, its kindness and cruelty to make its mark.

Dr. William W. Tinsley passed away April 6, 1962, nine weeks after my visit.

* *

W. A. Oliver, assistant superintendent of schools, picked me up at the hotel in Portland, Oregon, and drove me to Dr. Lorraine Sabo's school. Dr. Sabo taught art, and found special meaning in the work of her students.

The first thing I noticed about the Meriwether Lewis Elementary School was the excellent paintings and drawings hanging in all the offices, classrooms and corridors. It was almost a museum.

Dr. Lucile Field, the principal, gave Dr. Sabo complete freedom to supervise the school's art program. She confided: "I don't envy the teacher who has to fill Lorraine's shoes." After meeting her, neither did I. We started the day with a coffee break in the faculty lounge. Dr. Sabo was a tall, handsome, well-dressed woman with hazel eyes and dark hair salted with flecks of gray. She had been married two years. Her husband had just accepted a job with Bell Telephone Laboratory in New York, and they were leaving the next day. Dr. Sabo was giving up her teaching. This unexpected development meant that we would have to consider disqualifying her as a candidate. She had already resigned and I could not observe her teaching methods. But we did talk about teaching.

She told me her teaching philosophy. "You have to understand the feelings of children—know how to deal with their changing personalities. You must give them something of yourself. You should never let your home problems warp your teaching personality. Children like to have things well organized in the classroom, for they often come from unorganized homes. Children must feel security in the classroom. Teaching is like acting. Each day you put on a performance. If you click, your audience is with you."

Lorraine Sabo was born in Chicago in 1921. She took her master's at Columbia University in 1955 and an Ed.D. there in 1959. When her parents moved to Portland, Oregon, earlier, she joined them after teaching in a tough Chicago school "behind the yards," in the stockyard district.

Lorraine Sabo was concerned with the gradual stifling of a child's imagination that occurs in most schools. She saw this first in their art.

"Most children love art," she told me. "But some did not have a three-dimensional sense. All children's art is good up to a certain age. It has a primitive simplicity and it is spontaneous. Children draw familiar things, home, dog, cat, tree, parents. From the fourth grade on they start to become self-conscious and self-critical. They lose the simple touch. The adolescent boy shys away from art. He thinks it is sissy, or that people will laugh at him. His personality is beginning to change and his art with it. 'Who am I?' he asks. He is no longer a child, not yet an adult. He lacks self-confidence."

I asked her if she found it difficult to head a school art department and work out a school program. "With art there is no ready answer to things. It is individualistic. We know what the answers are in mathematics. In history we have definite facts and dates. In art there is nothing quite as definite as all this. Your program for teachers has to be flexible. Your hope is that children

56

will find art a good counterpoise to the more material aspects of civilization. Art is simply an effort to communicate something. As teachers we are obliged to furnish the techniques for this communication."

She talked to me in this easy fashion for two hours. "When my pupils grow up they will not have the feeling of being afraid and inhibited and lack creative satisfaction," she said. "All I ask of them is that they see things through their own eyes, that they put something of themselves into their creative work and discover something about themselves in the process.

"I have tried to awaken the art instinct in children who may not have a chance to go to great art galleries and see the masterpieces during their creative years."

Her success opened new worlds to these children.

* *

There was some snow on the mountains and Mt. Baldy had the whitest peak. Baldy sets the seasons. As teacher Mary Parker said to me: "We tell our children they can't go swimming until the snow is gone from Baldy."

Sandpoint, Idaho, my destination, is built on one of the deepest and most picturesque lakes in North America, Pend Oreille (pronounced Pon-du-ray). The drinking water in Sandpoint is soft and icy cold, even in the heat of summer. Richard L. Sodorff, the high school principal, mixed it with bourbon, his home remedy for an infected tooth I had. That may have had something to do with my praise of it. On the way to a roadside steak house to meet Mrs. Mary Parker, Dick warned me: "Mary will no doubt turn down an invitation to have a cocktail, but if you wish to be a gentleman and ask her that will be perfectly all right." As soon as we were seated "Miss Mary" ordered a dry martini.

Mrs. O. B. Parker—"Miss Mary" to everyone in Donner County—was nearing sixty when I met her. She was an attractive woman, honest and open, and her guilelessness appealed to me. She opened her house to her students. She organized a high school group called "The Bibliophiles." Three times a month they met in her home and discussed books, danced, listened to records, polished their manners. There were no social or academic barriers

57

to membership, and boys and girls from the more under-privileged families mingled with those of the rich. This club was democracy in its Greek sense, and Mary Parker was imbued with the Socratic spirit. She was the presiding genius.

When I visited her high school classroom, her English literature class was studying Barrie's *The Old Lady Shows Her Medals.* Students read it aloud. When a strange word was encountered in the reading, Miss Mary would stop the class and have the word checked in the dictionary. She also gave pointers on diction. She combined literature with the theater, reading with acting. She prepared the class for the day's play by giving a lecture on J. M. Barrie, the author. Her room was filled with books, most of them paperback editions of classical literature. Mrs. Parker bought these books herself, from her own paycheck. The students borrowed them freely.

There was a permissive atmosphere in her classroom, but the resulting informality never got out of hand. Teenagers can be a trial. Miss Mary took the wise view that the fun of learning must be retained. Her sense of humor never left her. If you are not prepared to share the teenager's upside down life, you must at least be able to laugh with them. Mary Parker could.

Mary Parker was born in Curlew, Washington, in 1902. Her father ran a general store on the Colville Indian Reservation, and she remembered him driving a team of eight horses a hundred miles to pick up supplies. There were no roads or bridges, just poorly defined trails. Rivers had to be forded at some risk. In 1913 the family moved to northern Idaho. Mary's father became a dairy farmer and built a creamery. Mary loved this rural life, but she wished to become a teacher. She went to the University of Idaho.

After college, Mary began teaching. She married in 1926 and moved to Sandpoint. But a regulation barring women from teaching in the Sandpoint schools kept her from there until 1947. Then, with a serious teacher shortage, her husband on the school board, and Sandpoint High School in desperate need of an English teacher, Mrs. Parker got the job—on a temporary basis. Twenty years later, she was still in it. She took a year's leave when her son was a senior at the school. He thought it might be embarrassing to him to be in her classroom. She understood.

Who are today's great teachers?

Mary Parker was a well-known, understanding teacher. She looked out for her students. "Miss Mary" often wrote college professors at universities her students attended, telling them that a certain boy or girl shouldn't be overloaded with tough courses the first year. "Nurse them along," she pleaded. Her advice was often heeded, and it saved several students from becoming college dropouts. Her interest in them was lifelong. She kept in touch, and when they got into difficult times they came back to her. "She's a whiz," wrote a University of Idaho professor to principal Dick Sodorff. "Her students are doing the best work of any we have on our rolls."

Four years after I met her, on July 26, 1965, Miss Mary passed away. Her loss was a loss not only to Sandpoint, but to the ideals of education everywhere.

* *

Spokane, Washington, to Thermopolis, Wyoming, is a short distance as the crow flies. But it was dead of winter, and I was not a crow. I spent one day trying and flying, but got no farther than Casper, Wyoming.

The three-hour bus ride from Casper to Thermopolis was a lonesome Sunday safari into an uninhabited area blanketed with snow, an area where mountains were always in sight but never reached—until the very end. I saw herds of antelopes pawing through the snow to the frozen grass below. Occasionally, the bus stopped at barren hamlets with their lone filling station and a cluster of frame houses. I drank a cup of good coffee at the bus stop in Shoshoni. Pretty soon we would be in Wind River Canyon, and as the bus lurched along the winding road of the magnificent gorge you could feel it sway and shake from the impact of the wind. We descended toward Thermopolis along a trout-filled river with "white water." In the Owl Creek Mountains we could see cave openings high up and half-hidden.

In Thermopolis, I got a room at the Emery Hotel. Since it was Sunday I didn't want to call Floyd Bass, knowing that teachers have few enough days to themselves. Instead, I buzzed N. O. Mikkelson, superintendent, and from that moment on I was inundated with the town's overflowing hospitality. Some of the friendliest people in the world live in the loneliest places. Isolation brings out the best or worst in man. Here was the best.

Floyd Bass headed the science department of Hot Springs County High School. He taught biology. He made class work a joint adventure. He stimulated scientific inquiry, but the results of research in the laboratory frequently went beyond his original expectations. He showed me his new lab equipment, including an incubator. He was proud of the fact that this was the best high school lab in Wyoming. The day I was in his class, frogs were being dissected. Floyd showed me the importance of studying the frog in terms of understanding anatomy. Students named each muscle to me.

Bass stressed original research. He had one advantage over other teachers: Thermopolis is a living laboratory. Big Springs, the world's largest mineral hot springs, gushes water at a temperature of 135° Fahrenheit. Twenty-two lesser springs are also in the area. People come from all over the world to drink the waters and take the mineral baths.

Floyd Bass assigned several students to analyze these waters. Many forms of life exist in them. Two of his students also studied the algae from Big Springs and discovered what may be a new antibiotic. Bass kept all the research reports of former students. They are neatly filed and cataloged by subject, and form a valuable research archive.

"We begin our year with the study of the cell," Bass explained, "study the frog for comparative anatomy, then go on to the detailed study of the invertebrates. We also study the microscopic life of this part of Wyoming, and we make hundreds of slides. I keep about 25 permanent slides from each student's collection, and we are building up a sizable microscopic library, well indexed. There is a great deal of gold here, plus uranium, and beneath Thermopolis are mysterious catacombs. These catacombs cause some of our houses to settle at crazy angles. There is so much to explore. In Wind River Canyon alone one can see every geological era. It is a perfect lab for a geologist. Two of my girls are working on nutritional problems. They are making cookies from algae. Other students are working with rats, driving these animals insane and then bringing them back to sanity through special diets. We are trying to discover new fertilizers. One man

60

just outside town has a garden irrigated by waters from the mineral springs. The vegetables he grows are larger, more tender, more nutritious, tastier than any found in the commercial markets. After we sample these vegetables we no longer want to eat the ones we get in the stores."

Floyd Bass was born in Geddes, South Dakota, Feb. 1, 1923. He married in 1951. His wife, Glenyce, worked in a beauty shop and she used the family car. Floyd drove a comfortable old beat-up pickup truck to school. They had a son, Steven, and a daughter, Sally Jo. In the summer, Floyd worked in the oil fields to supplement his teacher's salary.

He sent top students to regional science fairs, got scholarships for the needy, and spent much time advising elementary school teachers in his field.

Before I left, one person offered to fly me back to Casper in his private plane. Another wanted me to stay over and go moose hunting in Jackson Hole. This is the kind of friendliness you find in Thermopolis. Mrs. Bass pot-roasted my first moose meat for me and it was delicious. Floyd had shot the moose on his last hunting trip and had put it in the deep freezer. The tragedy of the American bison is well known. I was glad to learn that Wyoming was trying to protect its moose population. Some hunters have to wait years for a permit to shoot them.

The state protects other natural resources, too, like excellent teachers. Floyd Bass was one of them. He had the common touch. He wasn't stuffy. He avoided the role of intellectual. Few in the town would have called him "egghead"; most would agree that he was a regular guy. And, yet, perceptive John Magnetti, the principal, could say of Floyd, "He's a college professor, really, but don't tell him I said so. We might lose him."

They wouldn't. The folks in Thermopolis thought too much of Floyd Bass to let him go easily. And, in return, he thought much of them.

* *

Marjorie French sat in her office and I walked in unannounced. She was tall, slim, chic. Her gray hair enhanced her angular face. She had bright eyes, a quick smile, a puckish humor.

She looked lovely the morning I met her. It fit her mood.

61

Her students had wanted her to wear a red dress the day I came. They liked her in red. I arrived a day early, so I will never know what impact the red dress would have made on me. Sewing was her hobby and she made many of her own dresses. "I had just kicked off my high heels when you entered my office," she told me later. "Did you notice that I had one shoe on?" I hadn't.

Marjorie and I had fun that day in Topeka, Kansas. She supervised mathematics teachers in 14 Topeka schools, and taught a few classes, too. As a rule, Kansans and Missourians don't get along together. Old border feuds have left many scars. When William Allen White wrote his famous editorial in the Emporia *Gazette*, "What's the Matter with Kansas?", most of us Missourians had a lot of answers, none complimentary. The nicest epithet Kansans have for us is "Pukes," which indicates the depth of friendliness. The rivalry reaches its apex each fall when the University of Kansas and the University of Missouri meet in football. Marjorie and I were graduates of those two rival schools. But I was so taken with her, I quite forgot the ancient prejudices. Later had she suddenly yelled, "Rock Chalk, Jayhawk, K.U.!" I might have joined her in this spine tingling call to arms.

We drove around the city visiting all 14 schools whose mathematics courses she supervised. Most of the buildings were modern, some so new the debris left by the builders was still being carted away. Freeman French, her husband, was director of music in one of them, and when we arrived unannounced he was directing the school band. It was the first time Marjorie had ever dropped in to watch Freeman work. He was surprised almost to the point of embarrassment. After the rehearsal, we stepped into the corridor and Marjorie and Freeman held hands. I recalled my short conversation with Miss Grace Helms, a veteran teacher in Topeka, who said: "I had a lot to do with Marjorie going into the teaching profession. I sized up her potentialities. I also helped her choose the right husband. I introduced Freeman to her. I made sure they danced together and got acquainted."

Freeman and Marjorie had so many things in common. They both loved music and the theater. They loved to go dancing together. Both were avid sports fans and never missed Topeka High School's football and basketball games and track meets, and they yelled as loudly as anyone at the rallies.

62

Who are today's great teachers?

Medford Street in Topeka, on which the Frenches lived in a modest home, is not unlike a thousand other streets in the heartland of America. Frame houses sit on ample lawns and newsboys on bikes hurl rolled-up newspapers with flagging accuracy, hitting the front porch or an occasional dog or rose bush. On the French house lawn was a set of croquet wickets, for Marjorie and Freeman and his brother Vernon, who taught at Washburn University in Topeka, waged many a croquet war across that ground. Vernon lived with the Frenches as did Marjorie's mother. She had seen Marjorie through Kansas State University (BA) and the University of Kansas (MS) after her father had died when she was eight.

Now Marjorie French had become an outstanding teacher. It was a joy to watch her work in the classroom. It wasn't showmanship. It was simply teaching at its best. Her lightning-fast mind flashed and sparkled and lighted up mathematical problems for her students. Her students, responding to her questions as a symphony orchestra responds to the baton of its conductor, came up with the right answers. The smile of approval on Marjorie's face told me—and them—when they were right. Toward the end of the class, Marjorie threw out some quick questions calling for quick answers, arrived at without pencil and paper. Watching for upraised hands like an auctioneer at a fast sale, Marjorie would point a finger and the correct answer would spring forth in a short time, faster than I could write down the question. It was a virtuoso performance. That teacher was mighty proud of her students.

After class, Mrs. French stepped quickly into the hall, and as the students filed out she greeted each one with a friendly word, a pat on the back, or wink—and always a smile. Why? "The psychology behind all this is that I establish personal contact with my students in a relaxed mood," she told me. "We have just finished a serious discussion of a serious subject, straining our mental powers to the utmost. In there I am a teacher. Out here I am a pal."

One of the texts used by Marjorie French was *School Mathematics Study Group*. SMSG, as it was called, was a serious attempt at curricula revision in the field put together by math teachers of all levels. Marjorie was going to Stanford University

63

the summer after my visit to work with Dr. E. G. Begle, the prime architect of SMSG. She was playing a leading role in the revision of this material.

Marjorie French was well known. When a delegation of educators from New Zealand came to the United States to study the methods used by math teachers, they visited Topeka. When they saw Marjorie French they wanted her to come back to New Zealand with them to revitalize the teaching of mathematics there. But she loved Kansas and its kids, and stayed.

Dr. Giles Theilmann, director of instruction in the Topeka Public Schools, told me about a boy with a psychological problem who needed expert guidance. He was sent to see a psychiatrist. The visit was a disappointment, so the boy went to talk things over with his teacher, Marjorie French. He later said, "I got more help from Mrs. French in five minutes than I got in half an hour at the clinic." All the boy needed was a bit of mothering.

That was the way Marjorie French preferred to teach— close to her students.

* *

When you were with Edward Brattrud for a few days you drew strength from him. He made you ashamed of your petty little fears and misgivings. You find yourself measuring your cynicism against his faith. He made you think nostalgically of the old-fashioned goodness of your parents and grandparents who went to bed at night and got up in the morning with the fear and love of God in their hearts. He was not a Sunday school teacher in a lab apron. He confined his remarks to chemistry and related subjects. His spiritual influence was not verbal at all. It was more like a strong oak tree or sunset. Wilbar Craig, principal of Polo High School, put it less poetically: "Ed has guts."

Polo, Illinois, was more difficult to reach than Thermopolis, Wyoming. I negotiated with a taxi driver to take me the last 50 miles. We drove along the Rock River, from Rockford, on a Sunday afternoon. I profess to be an expert on America's winter landscape, having seen most of it in the months of December, January and February. I have seen our magnificent country in black and white, and remember it as an etching. What I wouldn't give to see it in summer, as a painting.

Who are today's great teachers?

The taxi driver and I covered all of Polo in a few minutes, and learned that there were no motels in the area. I was obliged to stay in the Marco Polo Hotel, then in its 92nd year. The mattress rattled as though it were filled with corn shucks, and a few senior citizens, who were the hotel's permanent guests, shared a hall bathroom with me. I developed an affectionate regard for the place, however, thanks to the hospitality of Naomi Coats, the proprietress, who washed my dirty shirts without charge and secured some brochures on the history of Ogle County. I took her picture, had it enlarged, and I'm sure it still hangs over her desk. There was no telephone in my room, but a man who had lived at the Marco Polo for 40 years told me I should be thankful for this blessing. To tell the truth, I was.

In 1856, Polo had a population of 2,500. Today, it has the same number. The town was called Buffalo Grove at first because herds of buffalo rested in its shady groves during the hot summers long ago. Old Zenas Aplington, the founder of Polo, agitated for a high school as early as 1859, but it wasn't built until 1868. The townspeople had to think about it and sleep on it. The new high school, built in 1956, was modern and functional. The wealthy dairy farmers and the tradesmen who cater to them were not stingy with funds. The teachers were excellent and well paid.

Ed Brattrud, the high school chemistry teacher, met me at the Marco Polo. I noticed that he walked with a slight limp and carried a cane. Three years earlier he had fallen down a flight of stairs and injured his leg. The June before my visit to Polo he had to have his leg amputated. By Thanksgiving he was back in the classroom. In his chemistry lab, he was constantly walking around, and he lectured standing up. None of his students took much notice of the limp. He was just as active when he was at home helping his wife Virginia and their sons Gale and Mark with household chores. I saw much of the Brattruds. It was Lincoln's Birthday, the schools were closed and I spent a good part of the day in their pleasant little home not far from the high school.

Ed was articulate on education. "I was once asked what I taught. I said that I teach students, not science. I am more concerned with attitudes, attitudes which will motivate students to do their best and work up to the limits of their capacities. I teach that each experiment in chemistry is a way of seeking the truth.

I feel that a good experiment raises more questions than it answers. Learning is tentative. The spirit of the search is everything. The slow student challenges me. My responsibility to him is greater. I can help him find his place in society. There is a lot of dignity in self-determination."

Ed was so interested in the personal touch that he went through the school yearbook each fall before opening day and memorized the names and faces of all the students enrolled in his classes. He found out as much as he could about the parents and home background of each student. Then, on the first day of school he addressed each student by his or her first name, inquired about an ill parent or a lost pet or a change of residence. The school term began on a friendly, personal basis. "When I studied the school annual to fix names and places in my mind I made no attempt to find out about the grades these students made. That might prejudice me. I do not care about grades. Grades mean practically nothing to me. I am more interested in aptitudes and attitudes. There is far too much talk about I.Q. ratings. I am more interested in the Intestinal Quotient than in the Intelligence Quotient. I do not go along with the hackneyed classification of redbirds and bluebirds—the slow ones and the fast ones. In my classes the strong are morally and spiritually bound to help the weak. The world at large is just an extension of the schoolroom in this respect—strong countries have to help the weak ones."

In Brattrud's class that help was never absent. I found him the most conscientious teacher I had encountered. He was a perfectionist without losing the human touch. He came to school early, ahead of everyone else. He set up the laboratory equipment for the day's project. He had the students do their lab work in pairs, but he changed these pairings constantly so that the slow learners got a chance to work with the brighter ones, girls with boys, extroverts with introverts. "Social adjustments should start early in life," he believed.

Brattrud was an ardent conservationist. He deplored the pollution of our streams and rivers and air, and he wrote his master's thesis on the subject of water pollution. He took his master of science degree from Illinois State Normal University, and also did graduate work at Kansas State Teachers College and Colorado College, some of it helped along with a National Science Foundation grant.

Ed felt that the key to success in teaching was thorough and careful preparation. "My students are entitled to the best teaching I can give them," he said. He was a fastidious person, paying close attention to detail. He could have been very sober, but his sense of humor carried over this burden. We laughed about many things. His passion for self-improvement could not be written off as a fault.

Willis E. Pittenger, the superintendent, saw him this way: "Ed has a knack of teaching I find hard to explain. He is not a spectacular teacher. I suppose it is a sort of spiritual quality. He has zeal. He sees the statue in the marble, the oak in the acorn. He sees the adult in the child. He is caught up in the vision of a more glorious America than our fathers ever dreamed of, and all great teachers have that vision. If they have this, you do not have to worry about what textbooks are used, or what tests are given."

Few people worried about Ed Brattrud. He was self-sufficient. Brattrud could go into the research departments of big industry any day he chose. He resisted this temptation. He was an expert on precision instruments and served as a consultant to companies in this field. But primarily, he saw himself as a transmitter of knowledge to young minds. To him, personal gain seemed a selfish goal when put up against the possible benefits to mankind.

* *

My 30-day trek ended in snow-covered Burlington, Vermont. Because of the snow, I took the train from New York. It was a long train with many coaches. Some of the coaches were removed when we reached Springfield, Mass. We lost a few more at White River Junction, where all the Dartmouth College boys got off. By the time we reached Essex Junction, which serves the Burlington area, we had one coach left. I was on it. The trip had taken nine hours.

Mrs. Zilpha Watson Billings taught the sixth grade at the new John J. Flynn Elementary School in Burlington. The classroom was filled with familiar objects. The chairs were too small for me, as usual, the walls were cluttered with "art," and the smiling children, some with a missing tooth or two and the proper quota of freckles, gave me the feeling I had been there before. Zilpha was blue-eyed, sandy-haired, neatly dressed. The first thing you noticed about her was her poise. She was relaxed and friendly and had a proper amount of New England reserve and character, just short of appearing stiff and stand-offish. Her friends called her "Peg." The whole school had a happy atmosphere, thanks to Mrs. Doris Somaini, the principal.

Zilpha Billings won her bachelor of science degree from the University of Vermont in 1935. She had been teaching ever since. Her husband, Richard, was an executive with the New England Telephone Company. Their son, Robert, was a freshman at Boston University when I met him, and their daughter, Barbara, was a freshman at the University of Vermont.

Mrs. Billings was a remarkable classroom teacher. During my first hour in her sixth grade I listened to what she called "Expert Reports." Each pupil had a chosen subject to investigate and report on: nursing, the FBI, Robert Frost, newspapers, bird skins and the like. Each report contained a bibliography and was neatly bound. Mrs. Billings was trying to teach her students to do research on subjects of their own choosing.

Her teaching philosophy was sound and inspiring—and strict. "One of the first things a child must learn is self-discipline. If he cannot control himself, he is not prepared to contribute to society. My classroom is informal, but purposeful. The children help plan the work. Each child learns that he will get a fair hearing. I expect the best from each child and will not compromise with half-hearted efforts or evasion of responsibility.

"In these rushing, troubled times a child needs, more than ever before, to have his island of happiness, peace and security. Often this security can be nowhere except within himself. I teach my pupils that much of their peace and security comes from within, and that they must help create it. Everyone has bad moods, but bad moods are not something a child has to keep. Even eleven-year-olds can learn to do this. They need to think less of what they are not getting and more about what they are not giving. I teach my pupils to understand the innate worth of each person's contribution to the world. I open up to them the vast regions of the universe where they, as future scientists, writers, explorers, doctors, housewives or teachers may help change the course of man's destiny. In whatever niche we find ourselves we can make a contribution. Facing my pupils at the beginning of a term, I feel like a diamond cutter. In front of me is a veritable fortune in the rough, which, with the proper cutting and polishing may become an art treasure for the world. I would hate to be a teacher and not have that outlook.

"The secret is to get at the heart of each child's problem. To do this for a whole classroom is a big job, but it can be done if the teacher has the will to do it. The rewards are worth the effort. A good teacher is a growing teacher, ever adaptable to new ideas, material and media; ever mindful of the need for objective criticism from supervisors and other faculty members; ever alert to the need for new goals for continued growth."

The day I was there, Mrs. Billings's pupils surprised her with a charm bracelet bearing the inscription "Teacher of the Year." She was touched by this, and could not repress tears. Things were getting sentimental. I waved my hand over the heads of the kids and pronounced, "I now dub you boys and girls the Class of the Year." They fell for it, all laughing, and the tension was snapped.

* *

The year seemed to pass quickly, and here we were again in the Rose Garden of the White House to honor another National Teacher of the Year. I like to think of Marjorie French as she was that day, May 14, 1962, at the White House. After the award ceremony, President Kennedy called the chief usher of the White House and asked him to show all of us through the mansion on a privately conducted tour. Marjorie was as excited as a little girl as she hefted the gold dinner service and peeked into the kitchen and the President's private dining room.

After she won the National Teacher of the Year Award she was besieged with invitations to compile textbooks, write professional articles for teaching journals, make speeches, head up committees and research groups, appear on television and radio. She was featured on the cover of *This Week* magazine. She took her high honors and increased responsibility in stride.

She and Anne Kell Tinsley, of Flagstaff, Arizona, and Mary

Parker of Sandpoint, Idaho, got together after writing letters for a time, and visited the Grand Canyon.

Marjorie's mother collected all the congratulatory letters, plaques, medals, photographs and telegrams that flooded the house after she won the award. There were whole scrapbooks of clippings. A special room was filled with the record of her achievement, and was promptly dubbed, "The Hall of Fame." It was funny at the time and brought many laughs and jokes. It doesn't any more.

Marjorie French died of cancer in Topeka, Kansas, on July 5, 1965.

Topeka names its schools after famous persons. In 1967, Topeka's newest school was named the Marjorie L. French Junior High School.

CHAPTER THREE

"... It is my hope that I may be able ... to inspire further study on the part of my students, to instill a sense of right and wrong, to awaken an interest in independent study, which will lead to the development of the kind of person who derives satisfaction from the human values ..."

ELMON OUSLEY

1963 NATIONAL TEACHER OF THE YEAR

ELMON OUSLEY
Speech and World Problems
Bellevue High School
Bellevue, Washington

RUNNERS-UP

MRS. MARJORIE
BEHRINGER
Biology
Alamo Heights High
School
San Antonio, Texas

MRS. GLADYS
BELDEN
Home Economics
Albany Union High
School
Albany, Oregon

MRS. ALMA
BLUNCK
First Grade
Swanson School
Palmer, Alaska

HELEN ESTES
English
Manchester Senior
High School
Manchester,
Connecticut

MRS. BONA
GORDEY
Mathematics
Orville Wright Junior
High School
Tulsa, Oklahoma

SIMMS
MC CLINTOCK
Social Studies
Crossett High School
Crossett, Arkansas

DANIEL
RADAKOVICH
Problems of
Democracy
Glasgow High School
Glasgow, Montana

NAOMA
SORENSON
First Grade
Franklin School
Salt Lake City, Utah

MRS. MABEL
STAATS
English and
Journalism
Southwest Miami
High School
Miami, Florida

72

1963

In Manchester, Connecticut, on my way to visit the first teacher for 1963, I stopped to ask a mailman for directions to the school. "Do you know Miss Helen Estes?" I inquired. "Sure do," he replied, "I went to school to Miss Helen."

Most people in Manchester have been taught by Helen Estes. Miss Helen, as they call her, was head of the English Department in the town's high school. For a long time, she had had a strong influence on Manchester's education. She had taken her BA degree at Wheaton College in 1924. She taught at Norwood High School, Norwood, Mass., for three years and came to Manchester in 1927. She has been there ever since, establishing a record and tradition not likely to be surpassed. She has had a profound creative impact on successive classes of seniors over her 35 years in Manchester. Principal Edson M. Bailey, since retired, wrote to me: "When an administrator is privileged to work with teachers like Helen Estes, it is easy to organize and administer a good school program."

The postman knew his town, and I soon arrived at the high school. I was impressed by the building, which, I found out later, cost $5 million and held 2,500 students.

I spotted Helen Estes in that teenage flood that flows through high school corridors when the bell sounds. I recognized her from a photograph. Before we broke our handshake, she whispered, "Please Mr. Burke, don't let anyone know why you are here." I think she was truly embarrassed by the whole turn of events.

As I stood beside her, she seemed very small. But she gained stature and authority in the classroom. On the way to class we were nearly bowled over by two boys. "Boys, no running!" Miss Helen yelled. They stopped dead in their tracks, grinned sheepishly and apologized. This little lady had the voice of a Marine Drill Instructor. "My, I didn't know my voice was that loud," she said with a laugh. "This reminds me of my girlhood in Maine. I was walking down the street in winter and a pack of dogs ran out and snapped at the heels of two ponies being ridden by children. I had never seen the dogs before, didn't even know their names, but I shouted, 'Go home!' and every dog in that pack turned and ran with its tail between its legs. That was when I discovered I had a tone of authority in my voice..."

"Were you born in Maine?" I asked.

"No. I was born in China. My parents were missionaries. Later my father became a teacher in China. I was sent home when I was a few weeks old and was reared by an uncle and aunt in northern Maine. I was too young to have any memories of China."

Her face was a palimpsest upon which was written faith, affirmation, self-discipline. She expected the same from her students. How did she view her role as a teacher?

"Education is discovery: discovery of the marvelous world of color and sound, of movement and hidden forces; discovery of the enduring rewards of warm, mutually generous human relationships. The educated classroom teacher will be prepared to point out the many paths worth exploring and to stimulate the development of skills which can make possible 'fortunate journeys.' It is the teacher's privilege to have a part in the learner's delight over many primary discoveries."

Miss Helen supervised 17 teachers in her English Department. They pulled together for an ideal. "Whether for appreciation of the concepts of Aristotle or of the fantasy of *Alice in Wonderland*, the potential discoverer needs intellectual tools: training in vocabulary, in recognizing implications, in interpreting metaphor, in response to verbal textures. Again the teachers, in successive years, have the conviction that, in supplying the tools, they are equipping explorers for the future."

I attended a staff meeting. Miss Helen had brewed coffee for all, and served cake. Then the war started. Some of the teachers opposed a system Miss Helen had initiated. Others defended it.

74

Her system was this: In what she termed the "Individual Program," Miss Helen required each student to take on a special category of assignments over and above the regular classroom work. Extra points were given for the added effort. Helen Estes started the program because she believed that most high school students were capable of doing more work than the minimum required, especially if the extra work dealt with special interest subjects and provided better preparation for college.

One teacher arose and fired at the others: "I keep my students busy enough without adding Miss Helen's individual assignments. I think it places too heavy a burden on students, and it places a lot of extra work on me. When a student in my class makes an 'A' he has earned it. I hate to see it jeopardized by extra-curricular involvement."

"Some of my pupils gripe about it," added another teacher, "but after they have graduated they come back and tell me how grateful they are. They have had to work that hard in college, so why not develop this habit while still in high school."

There was more argument. Miss Helen sipped her coffee and listened. I sensed that those who opposed her most vehemently were really quite fond of her and had high respect for her. They reflected her own policy of encouraging honest difference of opinion. There were no "yes men" in her department.

Miss Estes carefully designed and modified her program to fit the economic and cultural patterns of the community. Manchester, in the old days, had a paternalistic society built around the powerful Cheney family, who owned silk mills in town. Workmen imported by the Cheneys made Manchester a melting pot. The Cheneys ran the schools, as everything else, and put up money for them. But the silk mills eventually shut down, the family fortune dwindled, and the schools had to be taken over by the town. It's done a good job since.

Helen Estes and two other teachers lived in the old Cheney mansion. They bought and refurbished it after it had fallen into disrepair. It was a comfortable old house, filled with antiques, with high ceilings and tall windows down to the floor. Bookcases lined the walls, giving it the atmosphere of a president's house on the campus of a small New England college.

Miss Helen had been reading William Golding's *Lord of the*

Flies the day I was in her home. I'm sure she read *Catcher in the Rye* when her students were going through the "Salinger phase." She kept up, with beneficial results for her pupils.

Helen Estes was a writer at heart. In 1934, she started "The High School World," a full page of school news written by her students and published weekly in the Manchester *Evening Herald*. It has come out every week since then under her able editorship. She also wrote articles for professional journals.

She knew what a student needed to become a writer: "To the youngster who has learned to distinguish gneiss from schist, a rock ledge is no longer a mere mass. 'Crimson' and 'scarlet' come to have separate identities in capturing experience for the beginning artist and for the young poet. Few boys and girls would explore their musical listening beyond temporary tunes were they not guided to find pleasure in more complex and permanent music. Elementary experiments in physics and chemistry can excite the will to penetrate further the cause and effect of natural laws. The teacher can rejoice that, from the immediate experience, a boy or girl may develop a lifetime of discoveries in the material environment."

Miss Helen Estes helped make that discovery possible for a town-full of children.

* *

I crossed North Dakota and eastern Montana, riding the *Empire Builder* of the Great Northern Railroad, one of the last of this country's excellent trains. The countryside was a panorama of loneliness. Few trees grew except along the banks of shallow rivers. Very few towns, or scattered ranches, sprouted along our route. To me, this was beauty.

When the great empire builder, James J. Hill, strung a railroad across this empty country there were no towns to speak of along the right-of-way. The stops were called "sidings." Some railroad clerk in St. Paul called Siding #45 "Glasgow, Montana," and the name stuck, even though there were no Scotsmen there in 1887. A town sprang up, filled with frontier saloons, but little happened except devastating floods from the Milk River. Then came 1933 and Franklin D. Roosevelt announced that work on Fort Peck Dam would soon start. It did and thousands of workmen came to the Glasgow area. Now, 16 miles from Glasgow, is an Air Force Base, part of SAC, and there are 7,500 people there, more than the town of Glasgow itself. The children from the base come by bus to Glasgow High School.

In this part of the country, the school bus links all children. Education reaches out to every corner of our land, offering opportunity to each dreaming boy and girl. They ride great distances for their dreams.

Daniel D. "Bunny" Radakovich, the teacher I was to interview, came to Glasgow High School after a long journey.

Here's how Arnold Campbell, owner of the Campbell Lodge, where I stayed, described Bunny's background: "Bunny Radakovich was a product of the seamier side of Chicago. When the Civilian Conservation Corps was established in 1937, boys like Bunny were plucked from the city slums and brought to remote rural areas like Montana. Bunny came to Glasgow and he liked it. His parents had been killed—I never found out how—and he was just a poor orphaned kid determined to make something of himself. After awhile, his CCC outfit was sent to Utah. Bunny wrote to me from there and told me he would like to come back to Glasgow and go to school. I told him to come ahead and that I would look after him. He worked at odd jobs, and I loaned him some money. Later, when he was fighting with the Marines in the South Pacific, he would send me a Government bond every time he could afford one. He continued to pay back all I had staked him to, and I never knew a boy who worked harder for an education."

Bunny Radakovich looked like a professional football fullback. As he lectured in class, leaning on the flimsy rostrum, I expected it to crumble under him. He never wore a coat in the classroom and kept his sleeves rolled up. He grew up with them rolled, always ready for more work.

Bunny told his own story this way: "My father was Yugoslavian, my mother, Irish. I came from Chicago, but I don't like cities. I like a place where everyone knows you by your first name. After I was mustered out of the Marine Corps, I worked my way through the University of Montana, played football, baseball and golf. I did four years' work in three by going to summer school. I got married in 1947. I began teaching at Glasgow

High School in 1951, and also coached the football, wrestling and track teams, and was assistant coach of the basketball team."

He gave up coaching after a few years. "Teaching is more important to me than coaching. Many ex-football players like me never grow up, and they think that sport is everything. If you are a good teacher you have to concentrate on more serious things."

To Bunny Radakovich, one of the most serious things is Communism. Glasgow High was the first school in Montana to offer a course on the Soviet Union's political and economical program, and it was Radakovich's idea. "We cannot compete with the enemy unless we know what he is up to," he explained. His classroom was filled with books and pamphlets on Communism. In his lectures he pointed out the structure of capitalism as it exists in America, showing his students how this differed from the economic and ideological system behind the Iron Curtain. His classes debated and argued from all points. It was a lively hour.

The people of Glasgow raised money to send Radakovich to San Francisco to attend a conference on the study of Communism, proof enough that they approved of his program. This came at a time when many Right Wing extremists were denouncing similar programs in our schools as subversive. Alarmists didn't scare a tough Marine like Radakovich.

I went to the Radakovich home for lunch. The house sat on the top of a high hill, and was large enough for Bunny, his wife, three children, Linda, Michael and Janice, a cat and a dog. "Snob Hill," said Bunny, jokingly. "Up here we look down on almost everything." He showed me parts of the house he had built himself, including a rumpus room in the basement. Here, too, were his books. He kept physically fit by playing golf and officiating at basketball games.

The high school in Glasgow looked small, shabby, and poor compared to the luxury plant I had just visited in Manchester, Connecticut. But the glory of the American school system lies in the fact that the coming together of the right students and the teachers can happen anywhere. Glasgow, in Valley County, Montana, is remote from any large city. It lacks theater, opera, and art. But good books and good teachers, the age of air travel, the growth of the communications media bring culture to it.

78

Who are today's great teachers?

Students there, like those in most places I visited, knew what was happening in the world. Part of this is due to Bunny, and his courses. He encouraged debate and argument. Almost anything went as long as a student demonstrated his reasoning powers and his eagerness to speak for himself. "To me," Bunny Radakovich confided, "and to most teachers, that is the real aim of education. I do not want my students to parrot back to me quotes from my lectures. I want them to do their own thinking. I'm like the man who fires a gun at a track meet. I get the runners started, but they have to run the race themselves."

* *

It was 18 degrees below zero. I landed in Anchorage, Alaska, with thermal underwear, parka, overshoes. Anchorage was refreshing. It has hotels with international food and lobbies where Japanese and Swedish airline stewardesses mingle with sourdoughs.

If I were planning to become a teacher, I think I would choose Alaska as the place to start my career. The opportunities and challenges there are greater, the rewards seem more satisfying, the people are friendlier and more sympathetic. Drawn together through the isolation of the long winter, the people of Alaska place extra value on humanity and on their mutual lifelong adventure.

Now the problem: How to get to Palmer, Alaska. Bush pilot? Train? I had the feeling of impending Great Adventure. I called Mrs. Alma Blunck, the teacher I wanted to see, in Palmer, to let her know I was on my way. The moment I reached her by telephone she said, with friendliness and eagerness, "Henning and I are driving into Anchorage today to do some shopping, and we'll be happy to pick you up at your hotel." My luck was still holding!

The main Alaskan roads are kept open all year round. The only danger is breakdown and a night in the sub-zero temperature. Cars parked overnight are plugged into an electrical heater from the house. I rode 40 miles through icy, snowy country unlike any other I had seen before. The Chugach Mountains plunged sharply into the valley and the bay, and motionless rivers waited out the long winter. The sun set around 2:30 that afternoon.

I saw my first moose on the outskirts of Anchorage.

Henning Blunck was of Danish descent. He met Alma in Illinois. They married and, with true pioneering instinct, moved to Alaska after hearing a lecture by Father Hubbard, the "Glacier Priest." They drove up in a farm truck and took two cows with them. Alma played nursemaid to them on the bouncy trip over almost impassable roads through long stretches of uninhabited country. The Bluncks chose the Matanuska Valley as their home. In New Deal days, this part of the Alaskan wilderness was advertised as a paradise for hardy settlers, a place where, with luck and hard work, you could make a quick fortune in agriculture. Matanuska turned out to be the graveyard of dreams. Many families couldn't stand the long Alaskan winters or cope with the tragically short growing season. Midwestern farmers, used to long and hot summers, had trouble adapting to these conditions. Many who came grew homesick, discouraged, broke—and returned. But a few stayed on, and conquered the weather and the soil and slowly fell in love with Alaska. They succeeded in the Matanuska Valley.

Henning and Alma Blunck were among them. They owned a large ranch and a herd of dairy cattle, offspring of the cows brought with them from Illinois. They were part of that band of Matanuska "first comers"—oldtimers who had made it.

I arrived in Palmer with the Bluncks on a weekend. Father Nugent, the parish priest, called to say hello. With time to spare, I sampled the little known but widespread and sincere Alaskan hospitality. Here are people with cold hands, but warm hearts.

Alma and Henning drove me out to have dinner with the Sam Boyds, also Alaskan "first comers." Mrs. Ada Boyd served delicious moose steak, much like roast beef. The Boyds told me that dozens of moose cross their farm nearly every day at certain seasons of the year. There are more moose in the Matanuska Valley than in any other part of Alaska, but severe winters and hunters have decimated their ranks. One teacher in Palmer told me that she often had to run out into the playground and grab small children and bring them inside to prevent them from being trampled accidentally by moose that wandered by. Mrs. Boyd, a pioneer teacher in Alaska, died a year or two after my Alaskan visit, as did Father Nugent.

80

Who are today's great teachers?

I also visited the home of another teacher, Mrs. Margaret Cope, who'd come to the valley in 1939. Her husband, a bush pilot, had lost his life in a plane crash at Juneau. "When we came here," she said, "school classes were held in private homes and in boxcars. Look what teachers like Alma Blunck have accomplished. Look at our fine school buildings today." William T. Zahradnicek, superintendent of schools at Palmer, became Alaska's Commissioner of Education the year after I met him. Everyone called him "Mr. Z."

Alma Blunck taught first progressive—a transitional group of pupils in the first grade who weren't quite ready for promotion into the second grade. Most of her students at the Swanson School in Palmer were slow learners. A few were mentally retarded.

Alma kept a progress report on each pupil, measuring mental development, social adjustments, and specific problems and observations. These reports were almost as thorough as the case reports of a psychiatrist.

To handle a class like this required special training, patience, compassion. Alma had all three. In her class were 17 boys and girls. With skill, she might be able to move a few into the second grade immediately; others stayed in the first for a year or so. The theory behind first progressive was that children should not be pushed too quickly into another grade if they haven't the preparation, or the mentality, for it.

Alma was doubly needed. Ed Smith, president of the board of education, told me that parents liked to put their children under her direction in first progressive; they trusted her. Moreover, Alaska in 1963 had no schools for retarded children. There were only two psychiatrists in the entire state. Alma's classes were an experiment. The project was originally the idea of Mrs. Barbara Smart, whom I met, and other Palmer teachers began testing it.

Daily, Alma faced a wide range of problems. She had to be mother, teacher, best pal, psychologist, ethnologist, linguist, stage designer, and artist at the same time. She had some Indian and Eskimo children to teach, and their backgrounds set them apart from the newcomer to Alaska. I tried to make friends with one little shy Eskimo boy. Alma said he had been attacked by a sled dog, and his face still bore the scars of the struggle. If you laid a hand on him, he went to pieces. He relived again the horror of being bitten by a savage Malamute.

Alma talked about her pupils. "These kids are rebels. They do not take to society at first. They are timid, aloof, moody. In about a year and a half, they begin to adjust, slowly at first, but with increasing speed. I do not like stereotyped children. I encourage individuality. We have no problem with the mentally retarded ones."

I realized what a pioneer Alma was. Great things are waiting to be done in Alaska. There will be a growing demand for more schools and more teachers. Alma was in the vanguard. She was the leader. She devoted all her time to promoting the welfare of her fellow teachers, and had helped raise standards and salaries. It would be difficult to name an important convention of teachers in Alaska, vast as it is, that Alma had not attended and influenced. She was known to more people than any other teacher in Alaska. Alma received her Master of Education degree from the University of Alaska and did graduate work at the University of Arizona.

The Bluncks had two married daughters, Mary Cullison and Elizabeth Stapleton, and eight grandchildren. One of the daughters lived in Palmer.

It must be pleasant to have moose and Indians for neighbors, and to walk knee-deep in lush wildflowers and grasses among delphinium nine feet high, and pick strawberries the size of your fist and cabbages that weigh up to 50 pounds. I left Alaska with the happy feeling of meeting the true settlers.

I received a letter from Alma Blunck in June, 1966. She and Henning had moved to Tucson, Arizona, but they had kept their Alaskan ranch as a summer home. "I teach a class of retarded in Tucson's largest district. They are brought by bus from the poverty pocket in the district. They are tough in action and and language. They are Catholic, Spanish-speaking, and of Mexican descent."

Arizona was kinder to Alma's arthritis than the blustery Alaskan weather. In Tucson, her work continued: "I am going to go to the University of Arizona this summer and begin specializing in brain-injury and its effects upon children."

82

Who are today's great teachers?

Now, two states will benefit from Alma Blunck's teaching. Schoolchildren in both can be grateful for that.

* *

I had not slept during the all-night flight from Anchorage to Seattle. On the way to Fairbanks I stayed awake so as not to miss the massive bulk of Mount McKinley, America's highest peak. I needed a shave, and I was bone tired. The taxi ride from the airport to Bellevue, a wealthy suburb of Seattle, was delayed by the traffic snarl caused by 75,000 employees of the big Boeing plant trying to get to work. Fog hung over the city.

When I got to the huge high school building and met Harold Heidenreich, the principal, I begged permission to go to a motel and sleep off my fatigue. I was not mentally alert, and I thought an interview at that time with teacher Elmon Ousley would be unfair to us both. Meeting strangers day after day, and being fully aware of my mission and the heavy responsibility that accompany it, consumes a lot of energy. I never lost sight of the fact that I was the ambassador for LOOK Magazine, the U.S. Office of Education, and the Council of Chief State School Officers.

By early afternoon, I was ready to return to the high school and begin. I met Elmon Ousley, and he invited me to one of his advanced classes in world problems. It resembled a New England town meeting. A young man stood at the rostrum and acted as moderator. Debate from the floor was intelligent and spirited. Ousley stood near the moderator to advise him; he was an expert in parliamentary practices. He had good political savvy and could have made an outstanding Congressman had he gone into politics instead of teaching. He was as good a politician as he was a teacher.

Ousley was an adroit debater, a responsible citizen who took part in civic affairs, a tireless worker for the NEA and other educational groups. He was the author, along with Dr. Orville Nelson of the University of Washington, of a guide for the teaching of speech in high schools.

He seemed shy when I first met him. He was humble and self-effacing. He was not a showman. I followed him around for a day or two and began to admire his quiet efficiency, his gift of understanding, his capacity to take charge when a situation called for leadership and direction. He had a way of making a planned action seem impromptu. He was the completely organized and disciplined man, but it did not come easy, and there was just a whisper of sadness about him at times, born of the knowledge that all dreams do not come true.

Ousley was born in Spokane, Washington, December 22, 1911. His pre-school years were spent in the mining country of northern Idaho. The family later moved to Bend, Oregon, where he had to travel seven miles to get to school. Later the family moved to Colfax, Washington, and Elmon entered Washington State University. He had been a teacher at Bellevue High School since 1939.

Everyone called Ousley "BZ." It was a nickname he picked up in childhood. "BZ" was a character in the Harold Teen comic strip. Just before I met them, BZ and his wife, Dee, had taken a trip around the world on a sabbatical leave. The poverty, ignorance, and suffering they saw in countries like India gave a new purpose to their lives. To BZ it was an unforgettable example of human degradation caused by illiteracy. The best cure for poverty and disease is education. "When Dee saw hungry masses of children in India, she wept openly," he told me. "She could not touch food for several days—it seemed sinful to eat well when thousands were starving." The Ousleys used hundreds of feet of colored film on their trip, and gave illustrated lectures after they returned. All the proceeds from these lectures were sent to the needy people they had met on their travels. The lovely home of the Ousleys on Lake Sammamish is always filled with the sound of music, BZ's hobby.

Bellevue had a model school system, the result of good planning. Elementary schools were built on 10-acre sites to house 400 to 600 students; junior high schools on 25-acre sites to house 600 to 800; and high schools on 45-acre sites to house 800 to 1,000 students. Salaries of teachers were well above the state average.

Much of this was the result of the leadership provided by two men who had gone to school together in Colfax, Wash., as boys—Harold Heidenreich, the principal, and Elmon Ousley. I had dinner with these two men, and we talked about education for three hours. I asked BZ to define the term "educated man." He paused and said: "He should have the necessary mastery of the intellectual tools of his era, and should understand and appreciate the values of his country, and should use his knowledge for the betterment of people everywhere."

Ousley was known throughout the Northwest as a winning debate coach. I could see how this came about. In his classes, every student was encouraged to stand up and speak his mind. But the remarks had to be addressed to a specific subject and the argument advanced had to be logical. It was never difficult to pick a team of good debaters from a classroom of students who thought for themselves, and who exchanged opinions according to set rules of fair play and parliamentary procedures. These boys and girls were astonishingly well-informed and articulate. I was told that 85 percent of the Bellevue seniors went on to college. Ousley could take much credit for this.

Elmon Ousley did not use textbooks in speech classes. Students learned by doing. He stressed the art of listening. Ousley himself was the textbook. His goal in teaching was to prepare young people for their duties as citizens—world citizens, if you shared his vision.

He said: "It is my hope that I may be able, through a wider field of knowledge, to inspire further study on the part of my students, to instill a sense of right and wrong, to awaken an interest in independent study, which will lead to the development of the kind of person who derives satisfaction from the human values—what are common and which may be shared by all men."

* *

Albany, Oregon, a town of about 14,000, huddles on U.S. Highway 5 which starts deep in Mexico and winds northward to Alaska. It was founded in 1848 and opened its first school in 1851. Albany is in the lush Willamette Valley, and the Willamette River flows by the town. Albany was a labyrinth of school districts. When I was there, there were 22 separate school boards and 22 separate school budgets. I soon found out that a complex situation like this produced a split faculty, one group being for reform and overhaul, and the other content with the town's status quo. Mrs. Gladys Belden, the head of the home economics department of Albany Union High School, joined the more liberal bloc. There were problems. "Tax" was a dirty word in Oregon. Pay-as-you-go Oregonians resisted the imposition of taxes, and this affected their education system.

I felt like an intruder in the home economics department. I was surrounded by girls, most of them short and brunette. Gladys Belden, tall and stately, seemed to tower over her students. Her blue eyes and dignified bearing matched her temperament. She could be mother confessor in private moments with these girls, but in the classroom she was all business. Every moment of her school day was planned in advance by Mrs. Belden. She was reluctant to kill time, even with me, important as my visit was. I talked with her walking from room to room, dogged her steps with notebook in hand, and finally persuaded her to pose for some pictures. Posing for anything was not an easy thing for her to do.

I sampled cakes and cookies the girls baked in the large and well-organized kitchen. Unlike math problems, this was something I could understand and appreciate. I hustled from cooking class to sewing class, and from there to the stage of the auditorium where a fashion show was being set up.

Later, Mrs. Belden took me to a pep rally in the auditorium, about the size of an armory with the acoustics of a tile shower. The school band was out in thundering force. The noise deafened. Students sat in class groups, and the juniors tried to out-cheer the seniors in competitive bouts of noisemaking. Mrs. Belden was a sort of den mother to the whole school, and she was roundly applauded at the pep rally.

Gladys was a native of Washington, but her parents had moved to Stillwater, Oklahoma, when she was small, and she went to high school and college there, specializing in home economics and education at Oklahoma State University. Her husband was a lawyer, but poor health forced him to discontinue his practice, and with five children, the Belden financial situation became acute. Mrs. Belden looked for a teaching position. "I have been asked if my teaching has been approved by my family. Actually, it has enhanced our home life. My family enjoys the idea of my being a teacher. I bring home new books and new ideas, and there is stimulating family discussion. My husband has a strong interest in my work." Once involved in the profession, she was determined to go as far as she could. She has attended summer schools and conferences, maintained active membership in local and state educational associations, written a column on homemaking for a local newspaper, taken part in political campaigns, made speeches, and revised the State Department of Education's manual, *Homemaking Education in Oregon's Schools.* Principal Stanley Czech said he always went to Gladys Belden when he needed advice or wanted a job well done.

"Homemaking education has given me an opportunity to know and work closely with girls at a formative and challenging age," Gladys said. "Tremendous changes in homes and communities have followed closely upon technological advances. Emphasis in home economics has changed from the simple teaching of skills, such as cooking and sewing, to include serious consideration of problem solving, creative thinking and management of all kinds of resources. Our civilization is not as home-centered as it was in our grandparents' day, and the teacher today must have a broader knowledge of social problems, of psychology, and of the electronics revolution."

The Beldens had five children. David was a sophomore in high school, when I met them, Margaret a junior; Sharon was a freshman in college. There were two married daughters, Mrs. Beverly Boyd and Mrs. Joyce Cary, and three grandchildren.

Why did Mrs. Belden want to teach?

"Attitudes are as important as anything else. You have to like young people enough to want to help them with their individual problems. You must have a real interest in learning. Classes should be small. My work is complicated by the fact that home economics is a catch-all for girls who are not going to college and who plan to marry early. They are not too interested in scholarly subjects. If I cannot persuade them to go to college, I can, at least, prepare them for the responsibilities of a modern housewife. I show them how to prepare nutritious meals at minimum costs, how to make their own clothing, how to manage a family budget. I also teach them how to participate in community affairs, and point out the responsibilities of good citizenship. I interest them in the P.T.A. I encourage them to keep informed of what is going on in the world. There are many undeveloped areas of usefulness and creativity for the emancipated American woman. Ignorant women, lazy women, are a drag on this nation."

"I ask them to keep track of every penny they spend on themselves, and every penny their parents spend on them for one full year. Then they begin to realize how much money is involved in their education."

Mrs. Belden also mentioned Federal aid to education. "We need it," she argued. "We owe it to our country to keep our schools as good as we can and need to make them. Schools should be out in front, not lagging behind. We need more democracy in our schools, less paternalism. We should have freedom to make experiments, for educational methods and objectives are not fixed, but fluid. We face new problems. We have greater and greater responsibilities. We need more and better teachers, better pay. Further, we need new or revised textbooks."

Mrs. Belden, and other teachers like her, help push against these barriers toward a better educational system in this country. The more they succeed, the more we benefit.

* *

Naoma Sorenson had taught first grade in the Franklin School in Salt Lake City, Utah, since September 19, 1918. She still lived in the same neighborhood she knew as a child, not far from her classroom. In that classroom, I watched Naoma Sorenson build sturdy little characters block by block on an unshakable foundation. From her rich experience she knew every inch of the road each child would take. It was a happy journey for all.

When I got off the plane at Salt Lake City, I thought for a moment I was back in Alaska. It was 18 degrees below zero with a sharp wind sweeping around the mountains. I was glad to get to my warm hotel room. I thought I would call up Naoma Sorenson and invite her to dinner. But there were 316 Sorensons and Sorensens in the city telephone book. I was told later that Naoma's father, a railroad man, was Danish, but that he spelled his name the Swedish way. "Naoma" was a modification of the Biblical "Naomi."

Miss Sorenson was born in Pocatello, Idaho. The family moved to Salt Lake City, and lived in a section of town on the wrong side of the tracks marked by rows of houses occupied by the families of the railroad men. They still stood and Naoma pointed them out to me. She graduated from the University of Utah in 1918, and took her BS degree there in 1937. Naoma told me she received a salary of $600 a year during her first year of teaching.

Boyd Pexton, the youthful principal of Franklin School, told me that Naoma was the first one in school in the morning and the last one to leave in the evening. She was a strong woman. "I was injured at the time my appointment as principal came through, and Naoma acted in my place until I could throw away my crutches. Things were running so smoothly when I got back, I had no difficulty at all. She is about the most wonderful person I've ever known. She spends a lot of money on her first grade pupils, her own money. If she needs new books or equipment and our budget is tight, she buys what she needs out of her own pocket. If a poor child comes to school without a lunch basket, Naoma feeds him. She keeps a supply of milk and cereals on hand. I've known her to buy a child a new pair of shoes because his old shoes had holes in them. She's been doing this for years and she never tells anyone about it."

When I finally found Naoma Sorenson, she drove me around Salt Lake City, showing me Brigham Young's homes, "The Beehive" and the "Lion House" where he lived with his many wives. Naoma was an active member of the Church of Jesus Christ of Latter-day Saints (Mormon).

Naoma Sorenson was the pivotal teacher at Franklin School. She was the soul of the place. A luncheon was held in her honor the day I was there, and several top administrators in the city school system were present. The state legislature was holding its sessions, and the newspapers were filled with stories about the lawmakers wanting good roads and good schools, but kept saying that the state was spending too much money. The people wanted no new taxes. They spurned Federal aid. Later, there was a teacher revolt in Utah. They got fed up with bad pay, crumbling schools, and the fact that they had no bargaining power.

Miss Sorenson was a "mother hen" teacher, constantly looking after each member of the flock and scratching up intellectual food for young and hungry first grade minds. They seldom balked at her. She stayed with fundamentals and the true and tried prac-

89

tices. She pecked away at ignorance with phonetics and the good old English alphabet. She gave each pupil a sense of sharing in the day's adventures. Her classroom was a social microcosm, a nest of straw democracy. Responsibilities were shared equally, and selfishness gave way to the common interest. In Naoma's world of little people, good manners prevailed and the firm Mormon ethic glowed like a candle.

Self reliance is not an exclusive Mormon virtue, but all Mormons teach and preach it. Miss Sorenson believed in rewards and punishments, and each pupil had the joy that came from having one's efforts appreciated and praised. She left her mark on every child she taught. Memories of her will last a lifetime.

Naoma Sorenson worked hard to get single sessions in first grade, even though this meant hiring extra teachers. Thanks to her efforts, only one school in Salt Lake City had double sessions when I was there.

Much can be said of Naoma. Maurine Jones, a teacher at Franklin School, offered this insight: "Naoma is the epitome of all we hope to become as teachers. She is flexible, but she has rigid standards. She has a tremendous sense of fairness. She is not easing off as retirement approaches. She is working harder than ever. She is still studying ways to improve her teaching." This same Maurine Jones was Utah's Teacher of the Year nominee in 1966.

Someone else said of this warm teacher: "Every day of her life is an outstanding achievement because of the help she has given a child, a fellow teacher or a friend, during that day."

Naoma Sorenson's own credo: "No child is unimportant."

* *

When her daughter died of polio, Marjorie Behringer could have turned all her attention on her two sons and husband. Instead, she turned it on a classroom, and became a teacher.

Mrs. Behringer always had the "touch" of a teacher. As a young girl, Marjorie taught a blind child to read.

Marjorie Behringer kept me busy. Her school, Alamo Heights High School, was some distance from downtown San Antonio. I got out there in an over-heated taxi. Normally the climate is warm, but when I was there the weather was chilly, thanks to

90

one of those blue winds that sometimes blow down from Kansas. The taxi driver was complaining about the cold weather. After Salt Lake City, I felt comfortable in San Antonio.

Alamo Heights High School was big and impressive looking, somewhat on the swanky side. One might call this school "Ivy League" in comparison with other schools in town, if such a term applies in mesquite country; 95 percent of A.H.H.S.'s seniors go on to college.

Marjorie Behringer, a true Texan, stood straight and tall, looked you squarely in the eye, and was warm and friendly and hospitable. This biology teacher was an articulate humanist with a sharply-honed mind.

Marjorie was born in Boerne, Texas, northwest of San Antonio, on May 21, 1912. Her parents died when she was a child, and an older brother, one of a family of nine children, acted as guardian. Later, a Methodist minister and his wife moved to the ranch and looked after these children. Marjorie worked harder. She showed me her hands: "See these slightly crooked fingers. They got that way from teaching calves to suck milk. We took them from their mothers when they were born and taught them how to drink milk. This saved us from having to wean them later on."

She recalled a happy childhood in a lovely setting of foothills, lime trees, and open spaces. "I once caught an armadillo by the tail," she said, "just as it was escaping into its hole. I held it for dear life while my sister ran for a crowbar. In prying the armadillo out of the hole, the crowbar pierced the animal's shell and it died. We were horrified at what we had done, and cheated of spending money as well, for an unblemished armadillo shell sold for 50 cents."

Marjorie's modest home had that lived-in look you recognize as carefree and sensible. It was almost old-fashioned in its cherished objects of furniture, family portraits, and keepsakes. Her youngest son was still in high school, her oldest son in college. When I visited their home, a teenage Cuban exile, Juan de Miguel, had just arrived, and had been made an immediate member of the family. Ed Behringer, Marjorie's husband, an ex-Army officer and teacher, spoke fluent Spanish (as did Marjorie), so Juan felt quite at home. The Behringer home is headquarters for teenage boys.

I missed Marjorie's lectures in her classroom, but she showed me her well-equipped biology laboratory. It was filled with "specimens," such as a pickled baby armadillo, a monkey's skeletal remains, test tubes of carefully nursed viruses that one girl had extracted from a San Antonio sewer, an aquarium filled with "crawdads." There was also a pickled rattlesnake, looking mean even in death. One teacher said to me: "When I visit Marjorie's kitchen I never throw out any odd-looking dishes of stuff lying around. These are probably rare specimens Marjorie has picked up somewhere and is experimenting with."

Marjorie Behringer's students regularly won top honors at science fairs. Like Floyd Bass of Thermopolis, Wyoming, she encouraged her students to do original research. She showed me the work being done by the girl who had isolated viruses. To help with the experiment the student had rigged up an old phonograph turn-table which kept in motion the test tubes of sewage bacteriophage. This girl had just missed winning a prize at the science fair at San Antonio College on two occasions, and she was making her third bid. Behringer-trained biology students carried away so many first prizes she withheld her entries some years to give other teachers a chance.

"I also promote field trips, and the terrain around San Antonio is interesting," she told me. "We also have one of the best zoos in the country because of the favorable climate. My students make constant trips to the zoo."

Marjorie had reached the top salary at Alamo Heights. She had given college teaching a thought, but felt the need for her was greater at Alamo Heights. She wanted to write a novel when she found time, had a few chapters of it on paper. I suspect it would be good.

She had this to say about teaching: "Young people are influenced by a teacher's every word and gesture. Students can be given a desire to love and to share, to tolerate, to sympathize and to understand. Or, woefully, they can be influenced to grab, to hide, to hate, to lie, and to cheat. The teacher must remember that the self-importance of each child is all-important. Never betray a child's trust and confidence. If you teach grade school pupils, remember how you felt when you were in grade school. If

Who are today's great teachers?

you teach high school students, remember how you felt when you were a teenager."

Marjorie Behringer practiced what she taught.

* *

Few teachers give much time to their pupils before the bell rings. Not so with Mrs. Bona Gordey. She got to Orville Wright High School in Tulsa, Okla., at 7:15 a.m. Then, students with math problems—or those absent for a few days—came to her before classes for help and catching up. This had been her habit for years. Without these early morning sessions, many pupils would have dropped behind. Only once was she late, when her car stalled in a heavy snow and she walked the remaining two miles to school.

It wasn't surprising that the late Sen. Robert S. Kerr sent a telegram to Mrs. Gordey in October, 1962: "We in Oklahoma are all very proud of you and your outstanding achievements." This was not a perfunctory message. Sen. Kerr knew her personally, and had a genuine interest in her various educational activities.

An editor from Prentice-Hall publishing firm went out to talk to Mrs. Gordey about the textbook, *Mathematics—First Course*, which she co-authored with Brown and Sward. After attending a few classes, she said: "I've been all over the country talking to math teachers, but I've never seen anyone like Mrs. Gordey. She is the best."

Mrs. Gordey had the practice of reading a sketch of some famous person every morning before getting into the math problems. Her classes loved it. The day I was there, she told them about George Washington Carver, born a slave. "Each of his days was filled with learning," she said. "Labor is a thing to enjoy." She repeated it slowly. She told us that Carver, as an old man, came to Tulsa for the ceremonies when a school was named after him.

Bona Gordey felt that junior high schools were coming to an end. "We're gradually going to get rid of them," she told me. "It was a noble experiment, but it doesn't work, as some of us are beginning to realize. The job of integrating two separate school plants and curricula imposes an extra cost and burden upon us. The old idea of a four-year high school is finding favor with a few of us who are old enough to remember how things were prior to the junior high craze that swept the country. The basic premise was wrong: the idea of putting our unwanted in-between students off in a building to themselves. Young people need the experience of growing up together in a democractic way; the younger learning from the older ones, the more sophisticated ones. Imitation of someone you look up to is a powerful force when you are young and awkward and seeking your way."

The Orville Wright School is built in the round. It has three tiers. A long corridor takes you full circuit on each floor, and you might find yourself going around and around except for the color schemes. A teacher might say, "My room is in the blue section, third floor." Or another, "I'm in the yellow section of the first floor." You soon orient yourself by colors. When I visited the Gordeys in their home, Mr. Gordey asked me, "What do you think of the color scheme in Bona's school?"

"It's new and different," I replied. "How do you like it?"

He laughed: "I'm color blind."

The Gordeys had no children of their own, but they spent time with the neighborhood kids, watching three generations grow up and move away, and the classroom children were never neglected. Bona had a Cuban refugee boy, Jose Nunez, in her class the day I was there. She made him feel wanted.

Bona Gordey's classroom manner was jaunty and assured. Her voice was that of experience. She pointed her finger and got a quick response. She managed her questions in such a way as to quiz, correct, and stimulate at one time. She had the salesmanship and showmanship of a medicine man, she bantered, chided, and challenged her audience to sell the product—math. She laughed a lot, too. Tension and math, she believed, don't mix. And she pushed, always saying: "Don't guess. Think!"

"I learned early that success in directing educational growth has a direct relation with the pupil's desire to learn. As a teacher, I have spent much time trying to excite the curiosity of the pupils so they have this desire to learn. When this desire is strong enough, nothing can stop the learning process. I just get out of their way and watch them grow in skills, understanding and knowledge."

94

Who are today's great teachers?

Bona Gordey was just as excited about teaching today as she was when she first joined the Tulsa public school system in the 1920's. She still had the same energetic drive and competence. She was still active in Methodist church work, and still supported Tulsa's museums, symphony orchestra, and little theater. Many prominent Oklahomans studied under her. They still kept in touch.

* *

Simms McClintock was a Horatio Alger hero. He was a great success as a social studies teacher at Crossett High School in Arkansas.

I had expected to find a sort of backwoodsy type of town, provincial and coon-doggy. To my surprise, Crossett was planned right down to the last brick, reeked with modernity, and was set as neat as the tidiest New England village. It was owned, lock, stock and barrel, by the Crossett Lumber Company and the Crossett Paper Mills up until 1948, and is in the middle of a massive forest of Southern pines, some 120 feet tall. Simms McClintock drove me miles and miles into the heart of these beautiful dark-green, deer-filled forests. In this land, the mills do a $50 million a year business, and employ 2,300 local people. The mills have been taken over by the giant Georgia Pacific Company.

In the paternalistic days, the big mills made their workers live in company houses. There were two types—the homes built for the executives, and the cheaper houses for the workers. All were painted gray, and all looked alike. A paint manufacturer, cashing in on the blandness, put out a paint called "Crossett Gray."

The mills decided who was to be mayor, sheriff, and town treasurer. They supplied most of the money for schools.

Then, after 1948, the company relinquished its control, free elections were held, and the town planner started putting up handsome school buildings, a town library, a new auditorium, widened streets, new parks, swimming pools, trees. Crossett became a beautiful small town in Arkansas instead of an eyesore.

You have to know all this about Crossett in order to understand McClintock as a teacher. In such an environment it was

95

easy for him to be a liberal and have modern views in pedagogy and civil rights. Mill executives, many from the North, wanted their children to grow up in the liberal tradition. A progressive atmosphere permeates the city.

McClintock was proud of his students, and bragged about the members of his all-male "Key Club," made up of honor students. "I make the 'Key Club' boys wash dishes now and then in the school cafeteria to rid them of snobbery," he said. The club was trying to bring a YMCA to Crossett, agitated for a place where elderly folks could go for relaxation and for a children's room at the local hospital.

"Simms is wrapped up in his teaching job," Hugh Willis, the principal, told me. "It is his whole life. He teaches students rather than subjects. He is the most cooperative man on my staff. He is always asking me, 'Is there something else I can do?' That is an old-fashioned virtue which is dying out. Few teachers ask for the extra load.

"Simms also wrote the text for our courses, World Culture I and II. He visits our guidance staff constantly to get background material on our students and their home life. This is the mark of a good teacher."

Willis continued: "We have 6,000 people living here, and we have 3,050 Negroes in our school system. The town itself is small, but the school district embraces 212 square miles, and many Negro students are transported to Crossett by bus."

Simms McClintock was born in Lake Village, Arkansas, on July 1, 1927. He served in the Army during World War II, served again during the Korean War, had been all over the world, studied at Hendrix College (planning for the ministry), Columbia University, the University of Lausanne, and the University of Colorado.

As a boy he delivered newspapers and saved his money for school expenses. Although brought up in the Deep South, he learned from his father, "The War Between the States is over, and we must build a new nation." Simms was strong for civil rights. "I deplore the situation at 'Ole Miss,'" he told me, referring to the violence and murder surrounding the admission of James Meredith to the University of Mississippi.

Simms worked hard for the good of all teachers. He had

a sense of mission, and willingly served as president of the Ashley County Education Association, the Crossett Education Association, and the Arkansas Council for Social Studies.

He made a fetish of good citizenship, using the "laboratory practice method" which emphasizes problem solving in teaching young people about responsibility, decision making, and living in society. In addition to his regular classroom work in high school, Simms coordinated the social studies program in all the grades from one through 12. He had gone to Nebraska and Oklahoma teaching clinics to demonstrate the master teacher's techniques in the area of social studies. He was somewhat of an authority on economic theories and practices. He was interested in local and regional history and held memberships in various historical societies.

Simms McClintock was a bachelor and he lived in a trailer at the edge of the forest. The trailer was book-lined and comfortable, allowing concentration. I asked him why he lived alone, and he said he wanted to save money for graduate study toward a Ph.D. at the University of Texas. He already had a Masters from Columbia University.

Sims was also a lay preacher in the local Episcopal church, and he took me to visit the rector, Charles B. Hoglan, Jr., a young intellectual with modern viewpoints. The two men obviously found in each other's company the mental stimulation needed to overcome provincial dry rot. They seemed sophisticated and urbane.

McClintock pushed his students. He had them studying economics by pretending to buy stock, then recording the buying and selling transactions, and keeping track of the total.

The sign over his classroom read: "Through This Door Pass the Leaders of Tomorrow's World." He and his students took it seriously, though, and never lost sight of that responsibility and challenge.

* *

Mabel Staats was known for her energy and stamina. She was also noted for her beautiful speaking voice.

When I arrived in Coral Gables, Florida, I went to Southwest Miami High School. I had spent a night in a small hotel managed by Cuban refugees and filled with exiles. All night they argued in Spanish. I was determined to find another place to stay, so I checked out before breakfast and went straight to the school, carrying all my baggage. My gear was not what you would expect to see in Florida. I had a parka thrown over my arm, the one I had worn in Alaska, and I carried a pair of heavy overshoes. I was told that Mrs. Staats was home with a virus and a bad case of laryngitis, that it would be days before she could return to the classroom.

This was my last stop, and if I could not see Mabel Staats I would have to go back to New York with nine teachers in the bag instead of ten. I called her to whine a bit. To my surprise, she answered the phone. Her voice sounded weak all right, but I began to think there might be an outside chance of seeing her at work. She listened to my woeful story. "Come to see me tomorrow morning at my home at nine. You'll be surprised how resonant my whispers can be. If my voice fails, we'll write notes to each other."

Mabel Staats was a poet as well as a teacher. Her new book, *Bright Quarry*, had some excellent poems in it. The lines she wrote about her late husband, J. Riley Staats, chairman of the geography department at the University of Miami, applied to her, too.

"The words will dim upon the fading page,
But in the lives he touched there will reflect
Those attributes we cannot fully gauge,
And we shall sketch him best in restrospect.
The deeds recorded are but half the truth;
All else lies written in the hearts of youth."

I drove up to her home in Coral Gables, just across the street from the University of Miami campus. She lived in a charming house, which she designed, and the front of it displayed lacy grill work in the New Orleans fashion. A bougain-villaea vine, in flower, grew over the door, and around the house were flaming hibiscus, the pentis, the ficu, the mango, sea grape, bauhinia, thunbergia and other exotic plants.

It was the same inside the house: old furniture, pieces that belonged to her father, a braided rug her mother had made, and cases filled with rare glass and china. We talked in her living

98

room for three hours. "I teach American literature by choice," she whispered. "Teaching is hard work. I have been tired, worn out, angry at times, but never bored. Each day is different. I taught in junior high school for many years. Many teachers think junior high students are immature. I love these unwanted ones. I taught them to read well and to write well. I have made some anthologies of the exquisite poetry they wrote. I helped them find themselves. I made them write their poetry in the classroom, with no help from their parents. I never assigned a topic for a poem or an essay. That is fatal. I set the mood for the creative act, but my students had to select topics of deep significance to themselves. I have never found the student who couldn't write something worthwhile, given the opportunity and encouragement."

Mrs. Staats' classes were overcrowded; some had 40 to 50 students. She read and criticized more than 500 papers a week, and taught a journalism class that prepared the school newspaper, *The Southwest Lancer*, which won national recognition.

Mabel Staats was not just a teacher, she was a force in the community. She had sold war bonds, made speeches, run a traffic campaign, and organized town meetings. Her students had prepared 82 one-minute scripts for radio station WVCG for use on holidays and special occasions. The theme of these scripts was, "America is words of freedom, deeds of courage."

Mabel was in *Who's Who of American Women*, was named Outstanding Woman of Dade County (Florida) and received the Classroom Teacher's Award from the Freedoms Foundation at Valley Forge. She had headed at least 15 civic, cultural and church organizations.

She was born in Vermilion, Illinois on June 26, 1905. She married J. Riley Staats in 1935, and they moved to California, Pa., where Dr. Staats taught geography at California State Teachers College. Mabel earned her BS there in 1937. She took her Master's degree at the University of Miami in 1955. She began teaching during World War II in California, Pa., while Dr. Staats was with the Office of Strategic Services.

Mabel Staats employed useful little ideas and devices to stimulate the poets in her class. She emphasized to them the use of their dreams and emotions. She pushed writing on subjects

99

outside the classroom. This avoided tones of a "lesson." She urged young people, who seemed afraid of solitude, to embrace it for the inspiration it generates.

Mrs. Staats started her poetry classes with exercises in cinquains, which forced the students to an economy of words and a concentration of image. A cinquain's largest and most rewarding segment is submerged, suggesting far more than is said in the five tight little lines. The class then moved to working on a common theme—death, rain, spring, the sea, the joys and sorrows of young love, a subject dear to the teenage heart. By using the theme, the students could keep notebooks in which they jotted down descriptive words or cognate ideas. Hopefully, from these notebooks would come the poetry Mrs. Staats sought in her students.

Mrs. Staats pointed out that the lives of each student made good subjects for poems. She often quoted from her own work and used it to illustrate how her own joys and tragedies have affected her. She would ask: "What am I trying to say? What mood do I want to create? What words or phrases do I use that will contribute to the effect I am striving for? What form seems best suited to my mood and thoughts? What symbolism can I develop? Have I used the modern idiom, current speech which seems natural?"

Mabel Staats worried about helping her students express their ideas effectively without destroying their original thoughts. It is a delicate balance.

For about a year after I met her, we exchanged letters and poems. They were postludes to our brief encounter. Thumbing through our letters I find I ended one with a little Japanese poem I had just run across:

"leaf
   brush
      our cheeks
         again."

* *

It is always an exciting moment to find yourself at the gate of the White House grounds. You have to be properly identified on a typewritten list held by one of the guards.

100

Who are today's great teachers?

I met Mrs. Elmon Ousley in a Washington hotel lobby the morning of the award ceremonies, but Elmon hadn't returned from a Congressional hearing on an education bill. The limousines that would take us to the White House had already arrived. Elmon Ousley, although a good and fast talker, would never get by that White House guard with the list. "Dee" Ousley wasn't perturbed. "BZ will be here," she assured me. She was right. He came in at the final minute.

It was a gray morning. There was a nip in the air and the threat of rain hung low over the capital. Plans to have the ceremony in the Rose Garden were changed at the last moment. The television and newsreel cameras were set up in the "Fish Room" of the White House executive offices. The room was packed with photographers. President Kennedy was late in making his appearance, we found out later, because of a meeting on the crisis in Laos. But he soon came out smiling, freshly groomed, and in a relaxed mood. He quickly mentioned that giving an award to a teacher was a delightful change of pace from the affairs of state. "Dee" Ousley handed the President a small cardboard box tied with a ribbon. She announced that it was a gift for "Macaroni," Caroline Kennedy's pony, and that it had been sent by the governor of Washington. The President insisted on opening the package, and fumbled with the ribbon. It was an apple. The President laughed, and said: "That pony gets too much to eat as it is. I'm going to keep this apple for myself."

President Kennedy invited all of us out to the Rose Garden to see how lovely it was. A group of college students were on the White House lawn, getting the stage set for a concert they were going to present that evening. The President went up to the edge of the terrace and waved to the students and shouted, "C'mon up here." They did, in a leap and a bound, and the President announced, "I want you to meet the Teacher of the Year," and introduced Elmon Ousley. It was a delightful and charming gesture, much like the man himself.

After the ceremony, the Ousleys and I piled into the limousine to return to the hotel for the press conference. "Dee" handed me an album and a pen and asked me to sign my name. I did. "Whose signature is this one just above mine?" I asked. "President Kennedy's," she replied. It was undecipherable.

"How do you like your tie clasp?" I asked BZ. The men who win the National Teacher of the Year Award get tie clasps, the women get lapel pins.

"My God," exclaimed Ousley, "the President didn't give it to me."

None of us had noticed that this part of the ceremony hadn't taken place. The apple had distracted all of us. The President, we learned later, had put the tie clasp in his pocket while he was unwrapping the package.

Someone was sent running back to the White House to see if a press secretary could obtain the tie clasp from the President. We waited a few moments on the White House grounds, and the runner soon was back with the President's own tie clasp. Later, a reporter for one of the Washington newspapers, getting wind of the mistake, got the original, too. President Kennedy had it in his coat pocket all the time.

Another unexpected incident had taken place after the stroll around the garden. A member of our official party had discovered that her handbag was missing. She suddenly remembered that she had left it on the table in the "Fish Room." She tried to find her way back, but got lost in the White House. She opened a door and stepped through it, only to discover that she had walked into the President's private dressing room where he often went to freshen up. And there stood the President. He bowed politely and escorted his unexpected guest to the door. Nothing was said between them.

Following his award, BZ Ousley took several months off from teaching and went around the country making recruitment speeches for the National Education Association. He was about the best emissary education ever had, and he worked hard to get his message across. I still find teachers who tell me they remember his visit, and the impression he made.

CHAPTER FOUR

*"...I touch the face of humanity each day in my classroom,
for I teach the ambitious and the indolent, the brilliant
and the slow, the mature and the immature. I listen to a
16-year-old lay his soul bare before me in a few minutes..."*

LAWANA TROUT

1964 NATIONAL TEACHER OF THE YEAR

MRS. LAWANA TROUT
English
Charles Page High School
Sand Springs, Oklahoma

RUNNERS-UP

MRS. LETHA
  DICKINSON
Fifth Grade
Lincoln School
Riverton, Wyoming

WILLIAM
  DUNWIDDIE
Social Problems
Neenah High School
Neenah, Wisconsin

HAROLD FRAZIER
Mathematics
William Hall High
  School
West Hartford,
  Connecticut

FOSTER GREEN
Mathematics
Prescott Senior High
  School
Prescott, Arizona

MRS. ROY
  GUTHRIE
English
Memphis High School
Memphis, Texas

MRS. MARY
  ARROWSMITH
  MACE
Third Grade
Brennen Elementary
  School
Columbia, South
  Carolina

THOMAS MANLEY
Biology
Selinsgrove High
  School
Selinsgrove,
  Pennsylvania

JOHN RAGLE
English
Springfield High
  School
Springfield, Vermont

MADALEN
  SAUBER
Special Education
W. K. Dwyer
  Elementary School
Anaconda, Montana

1964

Every school needs a Dunwiddie.

William E. Dunwiddie taught social problems at Neenah High School in Neenah, Wisconsin, using a textbook he helped develop and write. Then he coached the debate team, spearheaded a council of teachers that met with the school principal to discuss current problems, organized the school's musical programs and "hootenannies," and directed the committees of the student council. He spent his whole life helping others.

Dunwiddie was born at Fox Lake, Wisconsin, in 1920. He knew America at the grass roots level. He gravitated toward teaching quite naturally—his father was a school superintendent.

Bill was good-natured and smiled easily. He was so direct and honest you dispensed with flattery and "front" and met him on his own terms. He was a family man. His wife, Mary Jane, shared his outlook on life and his educational ideals. The Dunwiddies married in 1942 and had four children, Alice, Jane, Peter and Tom. Bill played the recorder, his wife the piano, one girl played the cello, and the other three children played violins. Two of the children were in the high school orchestra, one of the finest in Wisconsin. The family operated as a unit. Material things were unimportant. Alice took care of the budget. One of the boys had baked bread the day I was there. "The family took a vote," Bill said, "and we voted unanimously not to buy a television set. We thought it would take too much time away from our music and our reading."

Good classroom teachers should not be wasted in administrative jobs. Dunwiddie had administrative skills, but his milieu was in the classroom, and he was happier there. His whole philosophy was based on the daily teacher-student confrontation. "Today's students are more responsive than ever," he asserted. "They respond to quality, reject the shoddy in education. Their questions are serious, and you have to answer them honestly. You must share the anxieties of your students as well as their moments of intellectual exhilaration."

Miss June Tenckhoff, dean of women at Neenah High, said: "Bill is the most cheerful person I have ever worked with. I have never seen him lose his temper, and certain adolescent antics can be pretty exasperating. I can work myself up into a real feather and foam about something that gripes me, but Bill always remains calm. We look at educational issues and problems in the same way. Bill is always sending me a newspaper clipping about some subject we have been talking about and will write on it, 'What do you think of this?' All teachers should have the desire and willingness to swap ideas. Bill is quite a singer. He also acts for the Riverside Community Theatre. He has courage. He is willing to experiment. The ultra-conservative type of teacher is wedded to the status quo. Not Bill. Even those who disagree with him respect him, for no one ever doubts his sincerity."

A good illustration of Dunwiddie's own philosophy and his classroom fulfillment of it was found in his work with a high school teacher in neighboring Appleton. These two educators took the intellectual elite from both high schools and formed them into a seminar. Leading artists, writers, industrialists and government officials visited this seminar and lectured to the students. It gave the students better depth and perspective. It also brought rival high schools into scholastic cooperation, a distinct contrast to their bitter Neenah-Appleton football rivalry.

The day I was there, Dunwiddie had written these words by Thomas Jefferson on the blackboard: "Error of opinion may be tolerated where reason is left free to combat it." It formed the core of his lesson for the day.

Dunwiddie did not lecture. He did not foist his own view on his students. He asked questions. He loved to start a panel discussion with no holds barred. Bill arranged his students in a horseshoe so that they faced each other. He acted as moderator in the open end of the horseshoe. "I enjoy classroom teaching," he said, "because it approaches the old Greek concept of happiness—

106

Who are today's great teachers?

'the exercise of vital powers along lines of excellence, in a life affording them scope.' I have found, as have so many teachers, that no one learns so much as the person who tries to help others learn. I have been in Neenah High School since 1949, teaching the modern problems courses, and coaching debate. I like to coach debate teams. Debate attracts students who are intellectually gifted, who are articulate, and who are well informed. Good debate calls for intensive research in the subject to be argued, and nothing is more important to the college-bound student than the organized research for facts and the familiarity with basic reference tools. The benefits students gain from participation in debate are of lasting value in a wide variety of situations and vocations."

Bill took his bachelor of science degree at the University of Wisconsin in 1942. Then he did a 17-month hitch in the Navy. He took his MA in education at Ohio State University in 1947, and was a John Hay Fellow in graduate studies at Harvard University in 1961–62.

In his spare time, Dunwiddie wrote. He found out the hard way that it is much more difficult to write a textbook for teenagers than to write a novel, biography or travel book. It has to be up-to-date, free of prejudice, well-illustrated, made to fit a certain grade level, written with conviction. Dunwiddie did it. His excellent textbook, *The Problems of Democracy* (written with Horace Kidger) is objective and thorough and written in an easy style.

It formed the central reading for his seminars. The students were free to attack it, branch out from it. For Dunwiddie, the intellectual probe was the important thing.

He wanted his pupils to think for themselves but to respect the other person's point of view. The rapport between Dunwiddie and his students was excellent. He was obviously their friend and leader, and no one thought of getting out of line.

* *

The trip to Anaconda, Montana, was depressing. It involved middle-of-the-night plane flights, fitful periods of sleep in cold hotel rooms, and long waits in dreary bus terminals. By the time I reached Anaconda and the Marcus Daly Hotel, I wondered why I'd come.

Anaconda was in one of its periodic slumps. The ore processing had been shifted to Butte. You looked up a hill at the smokestack of the Anaconda Copper Co., and it belched smoke down on you. It was still working, but local workmen grumbled about layoffs and slowdowns. I got the feeling that the Anaconda Copper people owned everything in sight; that stirring industrial history had been written here.

On the morning of January 8, 1964, I went out to the W. K. Dwyer Elementary School to interview Miss Madalen Sauber, teacher of special education, a euphemism for "mentally retarded." She was the best paid teacher in town, and by all odds, the happiest. She was a vital person.

Her pupils ranged from 8 to 12 years old. Her effect on their lives was astonishing. None of them will get beyond the mental age of 13, unless special operations can correct organic defects.

A lovely girl sat all day doing crayon work. She could not read or write or spell her name. But she had been accepted by other children and she was cheerful, now. At first she had been frightened, morose and withdrawn.

Another girl, 13 years old, who looked no more than eight, was a typical mongoloid when Madalen Sauber took charge of her education. She was sent to the Mayo Clinic for corrective treatment. Miss Sauber knew exactly what the follow-up program should be. The child's IQ crawled ahead eight points. She progressed.

Miss Sauber had special shoes made for a boy with club feet, and he was no longer self-conscious about his appearance. He was learning to use the typewriter, and seemed so happy with it Miss Sauber thought he might have some mechanical ability.

"Our biggest goal is to keep these children out of institutions," Madalen told me. "They come to me shy, defeated, unloved misfits. Many are antisocial, aloof, bewildered. I have to conquer their shyness, teach them to enjoy one another's company, make them happy to come to the classroom and to perform the many little tasks I set for them. Already they can count the milk cartons each morning and deliver the proper quota to each class. You have no idea how much they enjoy this responsibility.

"All I can do is teach these children to read and write, build up their confidence. I can teach the boys enough skills to enable them to do odd jobs, and I can teach the girls enough to enable them to obtain domestic employment."

The state of Montana provides $3.00 for these retarded children for every $1.00 provided for normal children. Still the need is overwhelming. Madalen Sauber was paid more than other teachers but there are not enough Madalen Saubers. She had to go to more schools to keep abreast of new methods in teaching educables and trainables—harsh, sociological terms for these kids. She had attended five colleges for training, getting her Master's in 1957 from the University of Montana.

Madalen began to teach special education in the W. K. Dwyer School in 1957 under a remarkable principal, Miss Mary Dolan. Special classes for retarded children were in their infancy in Montana in those days, and Miss Dolan gave Madalen Sauber a free hand. A few parents were critical of the program; they didn't understand it. Wouldn't these children somehow be shunned by the normal kids? Madalen Sauber brought the parents around not by argument but by classroom results.

Miss Sauber said: "Today's world stresses adequacy of performance for approval and society sets much importance upon the ability to function normally. While wanting to be loved, appreciated, and valued, the retarded child cannot compete without experiencing failure and rejection if judged by standards applied to normal children. This, in part, explains why placement in a special education program is considered necessary. I believe education, training, and research hold the keys to a better future for the retarded child. It is my goal to be part of that future."

Madalen was born in Gold Creek, Montana, and her parents still lived there when I met her. Her father ran a grocery store, but he spent a lot of time hunting and fishing in the virgin lakes and forests of the Continental Divide. He took Madalen with him as often as possible, and she became a crack shot. The mounted head of a moose she had killed was brought to the school the day I was there.

When I said goodbye to my little friends at the W. K. Dwyer school, they hugged me and held my hand. It was a touching farewell. Madalen insisted on driving me to Butte. It is not one of those lovely places you see written up in travel magazines, but a drab, cheerless town in need of a coat of paint. I saw it in the dead of winter, with a cold. Mining towns need spring flowers to camouflage their grime.

Shortly after my visit I received an invitation to a wedding. Madalen Sauber was to marry Clayton Burt. She wrote to assure me that she would continue her career. I was glad to know that. After seeing her work and the problems in her classroom, I knew she was a vital person to these lonely Montana children.

*   *

In the summertime, Riverton, Wyoming, is a good jumping-off place westward toward the Jackson Hole country and the Tetons. But in January, it is raw, cold, brown landscape.

A few years ago, Riverton was a provincial cowboy town of 6,000 people and countless grazing antelopes. Then, in Gas Hills just outside of town, uranium was discovered. Goodbye rawhide. People found out that Fremont County had more than 20 million tons of uranium ore deposits.

By the time I reached Riverton, there was just enough educational ferment going on to make things interesting. The teaching machine was bound to follow the Geiger counter and the isotope. I heard the "tick, tick" of progress. But you can't make liberals from conservatives by mixing them with teams of hot-shot physicists and engineers. Just before my visit, an attempt to raise the school budget and hire more teachers was defeated. When I was there, Riverton's public schools didn't have a single kindergarten class! But the town had an airport.

Brain waste is appalling. Of the 1,000 children entering the fifth grade in Riverton, only 604 will graduate from high school. Forty percent will be dropouts. Letha Dickinson worried about this.

Mrs. Dickinson was a motherly type of fifth grade teacher in Riverton's Lincoln Elementary School. She had gray hair and an engaging frankness and simplicity. She reminded me of my boyhood Missouri teachers.

Letha Leola Farley was born on April 1, 1904, on a farm in Phillips County, Kansas. The family moved to Akron, Colorado, when she was four. She walked nearly two miles to school, which was held in the spare room of a neighbor's home. Later, towns-

110

people cut a church in two and hauled off one-half for a new school building. That's the way things got done in those days. Letha's father owned a Reeves threshing machine, and drove it from ranch to ranch during the busy harvest season. She helped her mother cook for the harvest hands.

"I can remember," Letha said, "when I accepted a summer teaching job in Route County, Colorado. I lived at Jack Terhune's and walked a half mile to a one-room log structure nestled among the wild columbines and shimmering aspens we called 'quakers,' at an elevation of 8,250 feet overlooking Yampa Valley. I had 14 pupils."

To pay her way, she had to drop out of college for a term to teach school. She went to Colorado State Teachers College and also attended Western State College, the University of Wyoming, and the University of Colorado, broadening her usefulness as a teacher.

While attending a meeting in the courthouse in Fort Collins, Colo., she met the principal of the local high school, Norman R. Dickinson, and they were married on May 31, 1931. The birth of a daughter almost cost her life, and she spent two years under a doctor's care. She and her husband, during the lean years, made only $75 a month teaching school. But they never gave up teaching.

I went to Mrs. Dickinson's fifth grade class as pupil number 32. The other 31 were around age ten, and at least two had mental ages less than that. There was no provision for special courses for the retarded, so these slow learners were distributed throughout the school. I sat next to one of these children, an attractive boy, full of good-natured fun. When Mrs. Dickinson asked him to write down words, he filled his paper with meaningless doodles. He put his hands over them for fear I would discover the fact that he couldn't spell a single word. Later, Mrs. Dickinson gave some special attention to my friend. He tried hard, but progressed little. In this crowded public school, the boy was already a lost cause. Letha Dickinson had to keep the rest of the class going at top learning speed, but she also patiently watched over the retarded lad as a shepherd watches over straying lambs.

"In our surge to upgrade education, we should review our

111

child psychology and allow children to be children while they are children," Mrs. Dickinson argued. "Streamline—challenge—yes, but not push them into adulthood. We must provide the 'climate' for learning. Each segment of education is important in its own right. One step along the way in education is just as important as the next step."

* *

Prescott, Arizona, on a Sunday afternoon, dozes. Especially its airport.

There was no transportation into town. A friendly man wearing a cowboy hat and levis, who had just said goodbye to a Hindu student, was the only person there, and seeing me standing forlornly with my luggage, he came over, introduced himself, and offered me a ride back into town. I thanked him, and said I'd probably call a taxi. "You may have a long wait," he said, and renewed his invitation to ride with him. When people out in Wyoming and Montana, Utah and Arizona offer you hospitality, they mean it. To reject hurts their feelings. They are just naturally friendly, and they like to give a stranger a hand. I had a pleasant ride to my hotel. Mr. Bucholtz, it turned out, was an engineer, the student from India a friend of his sister's.

The next morning at 6:30 my telephone rang. Mrs. Sarah Folsom, county superintendent of schools, wanted to know if there was anything I needed, anywhere I wanted to go. "Yes," I replied, "I need a doctor and I want to go to the hospital." I felt terrible. I had a bad cold. Mrs. Folsom rescued me, took me to the hospital, pulled rank and got me a shot and a prescription. By nine we were at the high school, and I met the man I had come many hundreds of miles to see, Foster Green, the math teacher.

He was a mild man, and I soon found that I could learn more about him by talking with others. Sarah Folsom had much praise for this lovable man. "I nominated him for the Teacher of the Year award because he's about the only teacher in Yavapai County I've never received a complaint about. He is an ideal community leader. His daughter was ill two years before she died. She had a rare disease that required expensive treatments. The Greens gave every cent they had, which wasn't

112

enough. The good people in this town raised enough money to meet the hospital bills. Foster never missed a class, never missed a Sunday at church, never complained, never asked for help during this tragedy. That's the kind of man he is."

When a fellow needs a friend, Providence often sets him down in the right spot at the right time. Prescott is such a place. Foster Green was a deeply religious man, and every Sunday at the Baptist church he made a point of greeting strangers and making them feel at home. When I had dinner with the Greens, in giving thanks at the table, Foster made a pointed reference to my cold and asked that I be made the object of a special blessing. I felt better.

Willard M. Fetterhoff, the principal, was one of those men you love to talk to. Lacking an ashtray, he unscrewed the lid from a jar and put that in front of me the moment he discovered I was a heavy smoker. Fetterhoff was very fond of Foster Green. "He was here when I came to Prescott. I was a Latin teacher in those days. We became fast friends. We even correlated Latin and algebra."

Fetterhoff continued: "The number one objective in education has to be citizenship. Teaching pupils to think is not the number one objective. We have as our duty the maintenance of the American Way of Life. That's where Foster Green comes in. He is an exemplary citizen. He sets a good example for the students. I've been his principal for 17 years and I have never had one student lodge a complaint against him. I can't say that about the other teachers. He comes to school ahead of the students, stays late. He will come over here on Saturday to help students catch up on their work. Each summer he studies the list of his prospective students, and finds out who their parents are. He has spiritual strength for emergencies. The kids love him. He never treads on any student's personal dignity."

I went to Foster Green's classes in algebra. He always opened class with a funny story involving mathematics, to relax the tension.

He was very much like "Mr. Chips." He was humble and kind. He never chided his students. They never embarrassed him. They did their best for him at all times. To do less would be a betrayal of trust. He kept reminding them that college lies ahead.

He started with simple problems and turned them into complex ones. This was mental calisthenics. He made sure everyone in class understood the problems before going on. There were never any laggards taking refuge in half-solutions. He stopped, took time out, and helped the perplexed student to a complete understanding of the mysteries on the blackboard. He never sprang a quiz on his classes. He told them weeks in advance when the quizzes would arrive.

There were no surprises in Foster Green's classes, just mutual respect.

* *

Amarillo has memories for me. Right after the turn of the century my parents were among the trainload of Missourians who went to the Texas Panhandle to buy thousands of acres of unfenced, uninhabited land. I was taken along. I remember visiting my uncle who owned a huge livery stable and feed barn. That and a scant dozen houses constituted the whole of Amarillo. But Mother and Dad took one look around and decided that the spot was too far from civilization, too uninhabited. They could have bought land for pennies an acre.

The lonely wasteland they rejected is now dotted with oil wells and gas wells. The buffalo trails I remember are now superhighways. I took a bus from Amarillo to a little town called Memphis, population 3,260. We went straight as a die across Route 287, right into the center of a cotton growing region. Everywhere you walk in Memphis you see tufts of cotton blown from trucks on their way to the gins. You find yourself flicking bits of cotton from your trouser legs. At night, the smell of burning refuse from the cotton gins chokes the air.

Mrs. Roy Guthrie, the teacher I had come to see, apologized for the odor and hoped that I didn't have asthma. She picked me up at the town's best hotel, a 75-year-old venerable edifice that lacked room telephones, porter service and baths. A bowl and pitcher stood on the commode. Roy Guthrie had climbed the stairs earlier to invite me out to dinner. He showed me his postman's badge on his shirt as his credentials, and we went downstairs and joined Mrs Guthrie, who was a sweet, gray-haired, friendly lady. I sensed that she was a good school teacher.

114

Who are today's great teachers?

My hosts insisted that I see the town, so we went back on Route 287 again. I saw acres of baled cotton awaiting shipment. We got out of the car and inspected a new community hospital about to open. "How far does Route 287 go?" I asked. "To Denver Collo-ray-do," answered Roy. This was the charming pronunciation in this corner of Texas. When I visited Mrs. Guthrie's English class, the girls read with what sounded like an Australian accent.

Mrs. Guthrie told me that she wanted to be a teacher even as a child. "I rigged up an empty classroom and placed apple boxes in it as desks and I taught an imaginary class. I astounded my sister by asking her, "How do you spell chrysanthemum?"

"I'm now 66 years old. I began teaching when I was 16, and except for a short term as County Superintendent of Schools, I have been a classroom teacher ever since. I live and die a thousand deaths in the classroom, for I want to pass the vision along to young people who need it. By vision I mean the panoramic view of new life seen through a door just opened."

My school day was a busy one. One of Mrs. Guthrie's students, Exie Hugh, became my chauffeur. He drove me from place to place, and always got me back to school by the time my teacher's class started. I asked Exie, who was a bright student, what college he was preparing for. "I'm not going to college," he said. "I'm going to work on my father's farm." In a prosperous agricultural area this decision is not an unusual one. I could imagine Exie's ten-gallon Texas hats getting more and more expensive as his status as a cotton grower increased over the years.

There were 23 seniors in Memphis High School (built in 1923) when I was there. Mrs. Guthrie's senior class in English had only 11 students in it, barely enough to furnish the cast for one of the Shakespearean plays she had under rehearsal. She stressed fundamentals, laboring over etymologies and asking her students to break down words into their Latin roots. They did this with ease. She borrowed a corrected theme on an opaque screen so that every student could see what the errors were. Up there, they seemed even more inexcusable. The girls read poetry like John Donne's "Death Be Not Proud" to the accompaniment of a class organ.

Mrs. Guthrie used the "fused program" in her Memphis classes. She explained. "In most schools you have 4½ months of grammar, and 4½ months of literature. I feel you have to fuse grammar and literature day by day. I do not like the term 'subject approach.' I do not like to choose a term subject like 'love' or 'family' or 'patriotism.' Students get tired of such a contrived subject emphasis. I prefer to settle on types of literature for a good part of a term, such as the short story, the essay, poetry. I teach the importance of the verb in communication."

Mrs. Guthrie's philosophy was this:

"I believe in youth. I feel that young people receive too much criticism, and not enough confidence and counseling. I believe that most high school students want to improve their lives, want to study to learn rather than to receive grades.

"I strive daily to instill in my students principles of personal worth, self-discipline, triumphant living, and ultimate development. I want them to know that I am their friend, and that I will help them with 'all I have' at any time—day or night, summer or winter—when they call me, and that their confidence in me will be absolutely guarded."

W. C. Davis, the superintendent, called Mrs. Guthrie "a natural." She imparted qualities of learning you don't get from books alone. I got the feeling that her retirement would be an almost tragic loss to school and community. She was the cultural conduit for a town that needed something better than an oil-pipe connection with the outside world.

Mrs. Roy Guthrie had spent all her life in and around Memphis. She was born in Wise County, Texas, Feb. 26, 1898. Her parents brought her there in a covered wagon. It wasn't until 1950 that she earned her MA degree from West Texas State College. She had graduated from Memphis High School herself, way back in 1914. Two World Wars took place between those important graduation ceremonies. She watched her students go off to fight in them. Later, she taught the children and the children's children of those who returned. Mrs. Guthrie would have been a good English teacher in any school in America. Memphis was the lucky town that got her.

* *

Lawana Trout was a composite of all the good teachers I had ever met. I came to use her as a standard when I walked into a classroom.

116

Who are today's great teachers?

Her stamina amazed me. She thought nothing of taking her high school English students 110 miles into Oklahoma City to see a performance of "Antigone." No distance was too far to go for education.

But her tenderness touched me deeply.

I arrived in Sand Springs, Oklahoma, late in the afternoon, and Lawana's classes were over. I called on her anyway, and we had a pleasant chat. Her school day never ends. She often went out to see students who couldn't attend classes. This was such a day.

We got in her car and drove to the poorer section of town. "I'm going to read to a sweet little girl who has cataracts in her eyes and who hasn't been coming to school. She needs an expensive operation, but her parents can't afford it. She need not know who you are or why you're here. I'll just tell her you are a friend of mine."

We stopped in front of an unpainted, sagging house, with boards on some of the windows. The front yard overflowed with huge broken slabs of concrete that had been dumped there. We had to pick our way through it. We knocked. A woman with a friendly face, but in shabby clothes and straggling hair, asked us to come in. On a bed, half-dressed, lay her husband, recuperating from a heart attack and too feeble to shake our hands. "He's been this way for more'n a year," the woman said sadly. A small boy rested on the foot of the bed. In the next room sat little Mary. She got up and shook hands and smiled when Lawana spoke to her.

"I've brought you a reading of 'The Raven' on a record, Mary. Today we are going to study Edgar Allen Poe."

I have never seen such a beautiful child. She was small, soft-spoken, quick-minded. Lawana and I took turns reading. Mary retained every word. Her memory was exciting. She sat enraptured, oblivious to the tragic poverty around her.

"These people are proud," Lawana said when we left. "They are not defeated. They have just had a run of hard luck." But I had the sinking feeling that the run wasn't getting better.

Educators in Oklahoma knew about the excellence of her methods, and they asked Lawana to train other teachers at Central State College. She also revised the state course for the study of English. And she was an expert in speech therapy.

"Most people have one of two views regarding my attempts

to heal ravaged adolescent lives. With a gush of sickening prattle about my undying devotion to saving 'the poor and neglected misfits,' some people stereotype me as a 'do-gooder.' At the other extreme, my friends and associates preach against my sacrifice of time, labor and peace of mind for a cause that one lone individual cannot perform.

"I teach as I do because I must. There is no alternative. You saw one Mary, but there have been many 'Marys' to me, with different names and problems, but with the same pathetic and exquisite sensitivity that begged to be accepted, understood and loved. I have not given my life to teaching; it has given life to me."

Lawana Hooper grew up a farm girl, helping her father drive tractors and harvest the hay crop. She had been born in Hastings, Okla., April 26, 1932, when the Depression and Dust Bowl blew across this land. She later took her BA from the University of Oklahoma and a Master of Teaching Arts from the University of Tulsa.

In 1952, Lawana—which is an Indian name—married Verdine Trout, and their son Robert Edwin was born in 1959. When I met the Trouts in 1964, their Sand Springs home was filled with books. Verdine, a teacher, was a Civil War buff and had many books on this subject, and Lawana was an ardent collector and reader of books about the Renaissance. After Irving Stone had done his book on Michelangelo, Lawana invited him to lecture in Sand Springs. Stone was so impressed with Lawana's knowledge of Renaissance literature, he waived his usual lecturer's fee. "I don't charge teachers like you anything. How could I?"

Lawana was teaching English in the Charles Page High School in Sand Springs, a suburb of Tulsa, when I first met her. She was just 34, pretty, wholesome, dynamic. In the classroom, she was poised, dignified and serious—firm rather than shy, delicately attuned to the shifting moods of the teenage psyche and ready for any intellectual contingency. "I touch the face of humanity each day in my classroom, for I teach the ambitious and the indolent, the brilliant and the slow, the mature and the immature. I listen to a 16-year-old lay his soul bare before me in a few minutes.

"As a teacher, I have an important image to paint for the public as well as for my students. An ugly act or thoughtless word from me means a disfiguration of the image of my profession. I

118

accept the fact that to the public I am 'the school,' that I am 'education.' In accepting the responsibility to teach, I am aware that I need to grow constantly in knowledge and experience. I know that learning will not occur for my students unless I am able to transform my wisdom into a challenging stimulus for their imagination."

The Trout home was a cultural center for high school students. They came to play records, to read, to make dates, to have parties, to find the counsel they needed. Often one of them would be in trouble. Once, Lawana risked her life to help straighten out a member of a teenage gang, even facing threats from the boy's father.

I asked Lawana how she got her work done with the house full of noisy high school students almost every night. "I just go in my den and close the door. The kids pop corn, make fudge and listen to records. They wash all the dishes, and when bedtime comes they straighten up the living room and kitchen and go home. Many children lead lonely lives. They know they can come to my home and enjoy a social evening. No one is ever invited. The door is always open."

The evening I was there, a teenage girl joined us for dinner. "She's been living with us for weeks," Lawana said later. "Her stepfather is an alcoholic and he mistreats her and her mother. The girl called me one night around 2:30. 'Come and get me!' she cried. I hurriedly dressed, jumped in the car and drove over and rescued her from her stepfather. She's been staying with us ever since. I want her to finish the term at high school, and I want to keep her from harm."

Not long after I visited her, Lawana Trout accepted a teaching job at Central State College in Edmond, Okla., and she and Verdine sold their house in Sand Springs. "This morning I turned in my keys and said farewell to my principal and superintendent," she wrote me. "We all had a good cry and I feel miserable. I know that I am closing a vital chapter in my life, perhaps the most important one. There is so much of me here in Sand Springs. I feel incomplete now that I've left. Students were enrolling and they begged me to stay, which didn't help matters."

She hated to leave the students. Lawana kept in touch with her former charges in Sand Springs, even her problem children.

119

But life continues, and life sometimes continues downward for some of us, like Mary and the young man Lawana had plucked from gangdom. There just wasn't another Lawana Trout to look after them.

* *

What does a South Carolina Teacher of the Year do after a tough day in the classroom?

One of Mrs. Mary Arrowsmith Mace's daughters confided: "She comes home at night, removes her shoes, puts her feet on the table and says, 'God, what a day I've had!' "

Not all of Mrs. Mace's days got that bad. But the third grade in Columbia's Brennan Elementary School could really make her feet hurt.

Columbia, S.C., must be a sea of blossoms in the spring. When I saw it in January, it had a tired look. There was a chill in the air that seemed incongruous if not inhospitable. History lent some warmth to its old streets and houses. Woodrow Wilson was born in Columbia, and it was there, in a Hampton Street basement, that the poet Henry Timrod lived and sang. Riding in from the airport I passed through neat new suburbs, and as I neared the old section of the city, I saw depressing rows of flimsy houses occupied by the Negro poor. The Negro slums, particularly the section called Powell's Pasture, contrasted violently with the lovely white homes in the Heathwood section. The Old South was there.

Mary Arrowsmith Mace was a tall, stately woman of great charm. She was at home among the magnolia trees and wisteria vines. Her educational aims were as fresh and experimental as the latest textbooks. She spearheaded the drive of the South Carolina Education Association to get the state legislature to pass a bill calling for higher pay for teachers. The legislature accepted the SCEA recommendations, the first time in its history it had acted on the association's proposals. Mary Mace made this breakthrough.

She told me that South Carolina ranked so low among states in expenditure for education that she thanked God for Mississippi. "Only Mississippi stands between us and last place," she said. "The turnover in our teaching staff is incredibly large. Many of our teachers move to Florida and other states that pay higher salaries. We are victims of the 3-M's—moving, marriage and maternity."

120

Who are today's great teachers?

Mary Mace held an MA from the University of South Carolina, located in Columbia. She kept in close touch with the university and enrolled her two daughters there. Both were studying to be teachers. She was born in Kingstree, S.C., and took her BA from Erskine College, graduating magna cum laude. Her husband, A. P. Mace, was a civil engineer, and highly educated.

I got some idea of Mrs. Mace's versatility as a teacher after a long talk with Miss Carol Hill Mundy, principal of Brennan Elementary. Mrs. Mace, Miss Mundy told me, had taught high school classes, and was best known for her work with sixth graders. "She had never taught third grade before, but since she acts as an advisor to primary teachers she decided she ought to have some actual classroom experience with third grade pupils. I gave her my blessings and she is doing a fine job, as you will see when you visit her classes this morning."

I watched Mrs. Mace in a class of 35 children, much too large for one teacher to handle. I am constantly amazed at the boundless energy of third graders. They cannot remain still for more than a few seconds. Teaching them to be tidy, respectful, group-minded, unselfish and attentive is a herculean job. Mrs. Mace held out, against the odds, and did a wonderful job.

"The class and I were overstimulated by your visit," she told me. A stranger in class with a camera slung around his neck was marked for attention. In a hundred different ways I was asked to share a morning of their little lives.

I liked the scholarly atmosphere of Brennan Elementary School. Miss Mundy had surrounded herself with talent. Eight of her teachers held Masters' degrees. One, Mrs. Helen King, is a poetess of some renown in the South. The school was matriarchal in a cosy way, even to the name—it was named after Francenia Brennan, a principal. Its all-female cast kept alive a sort of sorority pride and loyalty. The school is situated near fashionable Kilbourne Park and the Heathwood residential section and the children lived close to school. No school buses were needed. Neighborhood pride in the school kept it well above the state average scholastically.

There were no Negro families in the immediate area, and integration was an academic question. When the day finally comes, Mrs. Mace seemed to think that reason and patience would bring about a smooth transition. If she's behind it, all will be behind it.

121

Mary Mace was this kind of teacher. As the school librarian, Mrs. Louise Windham, phrased it: "Mary is the most unselfish person I know. She doesn't care a doodle bug about the limelight. 'Run and ask Mary' is the rule around here when people want things done. Superintendent of schools, Guy Varn, depends a lot on her. She is unusually brilliant, knows so much about so many things."

* *

William Hall High School was top drawer. The students were sophisticated and college-oriented. The boys sprouted "ivy" perspectives and the girls thought in terms of Mount Holyoke, Smith and Radcliffe. West Hartford, Conn., is liberal in its thinking, generous in its support of education, demanding in getting school officials and teachers of the highest quality. In return, it paid high salaries.

Harold R. Frazier, mathematics teacher, had to be exceptionally bright to win the state Teacher of the Year nomination, not only over the rest of the teachers in Connecticut, but also over his able colleagues in William Hall High. As one of his fellow teachers put it: "I was skeptical about these nominations until I heard that Hal Frazier had been chosen as Connecticut's entry. The choice was so exactly right, I just can't get over it. His being chosen has raised my opinion of the award a hundredfold."

Robert Dunn, the principal, younger looking than Frazier, turned his office over to me for my interviews. It was examination time. No classes were being held. Frazier was monitoring.

Dunn said: "The impact of personality is the greatest thing in teaching. Success in teaching is not vertical. One rapid promotion after another is not the goal. Take Hal Frazier. He was offered the top math job at the Brookline, Massachusetts, High School, at a big hike in salary. He turned it down. At Brookline, he would have been the administrative head of a large math department. Here he can devote all of his time to classroom teaching. He even teaches in college during the summer term. Our motto here is 'Delight as you instruct.' We are trying to repudiate George Bernard Shaw's jibe: 'If you can't do anything else, teach.' Shaw himself said he wished he could retract that statement."

Harold R. Frazier was born July 15, 1924, in Ohio. "Most of my memories of my early youth in Youngstown center upon the

122

effects of the Depression on our family," he told me. "I don't think my father ever recovered from the losses in money, property, and pride. My mother accepted the view, 'it was God's will.' We were almost destitute. I saw education as the one way to escape degradation and poverty. I did well in high school, scholastically and athletically. I was awarded the Amos Miller Scholarship to attend Oberlin College. At Oberlin, I became aware of the full depth and insight of knowledge. It was 1942. We were at war. I volunteered for service in the Air Force. The consequent loss of identity as an individual with emphasis on the larger group, the constant reliance on rules and regulations for all procedures and decisions, the lack of explanation for certain actions and seeming arbitrary actions of Fate all produced an awareness of myself as an individual embedded in a much larger complex of forces than I had perceived in college. My training as a meteorologist and subsequently as a navigator strengthened my feeling that I would function most effectively in a system which was not considered closed and complete. After returning to Oberlin, I was inspired by my mathematics teacher to go into the teaching profession. My first teaching job was at the Oakwood School, a Quaker co-educational boarding school in Poughkeepsie, New York. The philosophy of the Society of Friends, that there is that of God in every man and that one always works for its realization, was warmly received by me. For eight consecutive summers I attended Columbia University, where I took my Master of Arts degree in 1954."

Frazier had benefited from two National Science Foundation awards. One of these gave him the chance to work with John Kemeny and the Dartmouth College mathematics staff at Phillips Andover Academy.

In turn, he had given much to William Hall High's students.

Hal Frazier joined the faculty in 1954, right after "Sputnik." Americans were worried about their science lag in high schools and colleges.

Vernon Graham, another W.H.H.S. teacher, and Frazier decided to set up a teaching workshop for modern math. Many townspeople, including some of the school board, opposed this bold new approach. But the two brilliant men stuck together, inviting open debate. They got it. Graham tells the story: "Hal came to me one day and said, 'I think we should attend a Board of Education meeting.' He wanted to know what our bosses were thinking. We went. We were stunned when someone got up and criticized the new concepts of math. Hal and I had the feeling that something big was on the way in our thinking regarding math, and we both jumped to our feet and made an eloquent plea for the newer approach. Hal has the gift of making a complex problem seem simple, and he knows how to trim his language to the layman's mental viewpoint. When he got through explaining things, the board members gave us the green light to teach math as we thought it ought to be taught in the Atomic Age and the Space Age."

After spirited public meetings, the two teachers won. Hal Frazier and Vernon Graham had a free hand. Frazier's classes were firecrackers of learning. He was a modest man. Graham had this to say about him:

"Hal has the most refreshing approach to math of any teacher I have ever known. He is creative, he's an artist, maybe a frustrated architect for all I know, but he is constantly excited by the joy of discovery, the discovery of new facets of mathematics, by new and challenging questions asked by bright students, new applications of old mathematical theories. His classroom is a 'conversation' of minds.

"If you taped the lectures of most math teachers you would hear the droning voice of the teacher 95 percent of the time, with an occasional interruption of a student or two. This monologue is usually based on old textbooks that should be updated or thrown away. Not so in Hal's classes. A tape recording of his classes would be the exact reverse—student voices prevailing, Hal asking a question or two. He knows exactly when to add his own words. He may be the best teacher I have ever known. What a dynamic person he is. To top it off, he has a delightful sense of humor. Students love him because he never has a superior attitude."

Frazier, while driving me out to meet his wife and three children in his woodland hideaway in Simsbury, talked about young people. "The high school students today are the best we have ever had. Do not let anyone tell you anything different from that. Why are they the best? They are more serious, they are more demanding of high standards on the part of the teacher. They expect you to know your subject thoroughly. They want you to give your best. Teaching math is a humbling experience. Right now I have a boy in

124

my class who is a mathematical genius. His thinking is so advanced he is always several jumps ahead of me. I can teach him very little. He can teach me a lot. He never likes to appear cocky in front of his classmates. His mind is so fertile, so lucid, so mature you wonder how a boy his age comes by such gifts. We need to re-examine our attitudes toward youth.

"Our current crop of boys and girls hate the term 'teenager,' hate its connotation. They are not nearly as delinquent as their parents. The breakdown of communications between parents and children is due to the tendency of parents to regard their offspring as irresponsible brats long after that moment of sudden maturity and grasp of reality has turned these so-called teenagers' thoughts inward to feed upon themselves."

Graham admired Frazier's attitude toward his students. He saw his friend as an all-around person, and described him this way:

"Hal's classroom has the relaxed atmosphere of friends discussing a topic of mutual interest. Even though his knowledge of mathematics is profound, he has so many other interests you hate to type him as a math teacher. Catch him between classes and he may be reading a volume of poetry or a book on art. When he built his house, he was the architect and did a lot of work himself. He paints, he constructs Calder-like mobiles, uses old bits of native stone to make modern pieces of sculpture. He's a complete man. He sees life whole. He sees math as a path of logic a man must tread to arrive at the nature of things. He sees it, not as something fixed and static, but as something expanding and creative, a key to unlock many closed doors."

Michael Stephanian, the vice-principal, was young and personable. All the administrators in William Hall High School were young, collegiate-looking in the best sense of that term. They ran their high school like a college. These men were able and far-sighted beyond their years. Stephanian said: "Sunday morning before we go to church, Hal and I play golf together. He's the high school golf coach. He also coaches our soccer team, and it is one of the best teams in New England. I teach English. Usually English and mathematics teachers are on different wavelengths. But Hal and I try to correlate our two subjects. He even tried to use a verbal approach to a non-verbal area. He thinks of math as an art. The heart is the teacher. Hal's got plenty of heart. The outstanding

125

teacher is one who has tasted of life, who knows what life is all about. A student is always trying to find himself. Hal is always there, ready to help this seeker."

* *

John Ragle, Boston-born son of a Harvard-trained doctor, struggled to avoid the image of an elite social background.

He joined the crew of an old wooden fishing schooner in Gloucester, Mass. This rugged vessel headed for the Grand Banks. For 40 days and nights, the leathery-faced, hard-swearing fishermen manned the nets, chewed tobacco or swapped yarns in reeking quarters where each bunk had to be shared by two fishermen. They sprinkled the floor with sawdust from time to time to cover the tobacco juice, and to keep it from getting slick. The layers of spit and sawdust grew six inches thick, the accumulation of several years of neglect.

John Ragle couldn't stomach chewing tobacco. So he put flattened Tootsie Rolls in tobacco wrappers pilfered from an old salt. He went through the motions of taking a chew now and then, spitting the chocolate as expertly as his companions spat tobacco juice.

On land, Ragle began a medical course at the University of Chicago, then joined the Army Air Corps for World War II. Afterward, he studied humanities at Harvard University, interrupted by illness and exhaustion a couple of times, and a few years of hard work to earn his living. He taught English and French at Governor Dummer Academy in South Byfield, Mass., wrote a biographical piece on founder Jeremiah Dummer, and won his Master's in English at Middlebury College. Ever since the war he wanted to study English literature and learn its rich, ever-changing language. The desire to transmit this heritage to young Americans became a passion and goal. He set about to find a good public high school where the caste system of the private academies would be replaced by the more democratic exercise of individuality.

He received an appointment at Springfield High School, Springfield, Vermont. This was one of the most important things that ever happened to Springfield and John Ragle. The sons and daughters of the machine tool workers of "Precision Valley," as Springfield is nicknamed, knocked off Ragle's glossy veneer. His refinement of mind and manners had a cultural impact on students.

126

Who are today's great teachers?

Springfield, like Rome, has seven hills, and if the Black River is no Tiber, it is nonetheless a river of history—the history of the machine tool industry. The Jones and Lamson Machine Company, the Fellows Gear Shaper Company, and the Bryant Chucking Grinder Company clack-clack away, producing key machine tools. New school buildings were on the drawing boards for Springfield. But the Yankees on the school board and the local citizenry simply wanted to know just where each dollar was going. There was keen interest in education, for most of the town's machine tool executives and top workmen are college-trained men and want their children to go to college.

Springfield is an old town. The high school building seemed almost as old. But Springfield High School, small in enrollment, shabby in appearance, had already produced four John Hay Fellows —John Ragle and John Bateman, teachers; Russell Heath, principal, and Winston B. Keck, superintendent. After Ragle introduced me to Bateman, he whispered, "There's the finest teacher I have ever met." Others thought the same of Ragle.

"We didn't know how this young man who had led such a sheltered life would adapt to our industrial community," said Russell Heath, a kindly, soft-spoken man. "We soon found out, much to our delight, that he joined in all the civic activities of our town, made friends with everyone, and was accepted by the community wholeheartedly, not only as a regular fellow, but also as a leader and a cultural asset."

The first English class I attended had 15 students in it. Another seminar-type group had 11. They were busy with various stages of their paper work, improving their skills in punctuation, diction, and sentence structure. Each student was encouraged to spend more time on the phase of study he thought he was weakest in. The students were given a two-week period to polish their writing skills and to reach, stage by stage, the level of achievement set by Ragle. He did this for balance.

"I have strong faith in the fundamental worth of young people and in their potential for good," Ragle said. "At the high school age this potential lies largely untapped; as they become men and women it may be either dissipated or become the motivating factor in their lives. The force of any social order for good or for evil is the sum total of the individual worth of every person who is a part

127

of that society. It is imperative that mankind turn this vast and complex array of strengths, skills and insights to the pursuit of what is right and good."

The day I was there, a film strip on "Hamlet" was shown to the class, with running commentary and questioning by Ragle. It was a sort of Shakespeare lab session. Along with a study of the English classics, Ragle let each student choose his or her own modern novel. I do not try to force upon them the novels I may like, for taste in reading is highly individual."

Ragle encouraged all his students to give their original views. Under his leadership there was wide informal discussion of the pros and cons of topics. Ragle took off his coat, sat among the students, and seemed to become a senior member of the class. "I do not believe in a permissive atmosphere that can get out of hand and jeopardize discipline, but I am just as firmly against regimentation."

John Ragle lived in a modest little house, on one of the higher hills, with his English wife, Sheila, and their two adopted children, Allison Claire and John MacLaren. John's final adoption papers had been court-approved the day before I arrived, and the house was filled with great happiness. Mrs. Ragle's mother was visiting them the day I was there. Her husband was an engineer who was sent to Germany right after the war to inaugurate that defeated country's industrial rehabilitation.

Sheila MacLaren was a nurse specializing in midwifery in a Springfield hospital when she met John. She was an intelligent young woman of quiet manner and engaging charm, tremendously sympathetic with her husband's high ideals and willing to make financial sacrifices for their fulfillment. His younger brother, Thomas, was president of Marlboro College in Vermont, and another brother, Richard, was a glacial geologist. The whole Ragle family seemed to have been brilliantly endowed.

"I'm not the executive type," Ragle told me, "I just love to teach English. I run dry after each class, so I insist on having some time to myself. I give a lot of extra time to my students in and out of class, but I do not open my house to them at all hours. For one thing, the house is too small, and we have small children to take care of. I feel that students must learn as much as they can about themselves, learn to use their talents. What a student is doing in

128

Who are today's great teachers?

class does not stick unless the self-discovery side is achieved. We have a big responsibility in helping students discover themselves, and in discovering their community functions. Such discoveries are very exciting when they happen. We have a lot to learn from elementary teachers when it comes to handling individuals. We don't give these patient, skilled, dedicated teachers enough credit. They are the ones who shape the direction of young minds."

John Ragle knew what life was all about. He taught from a rich experience. Somewhere in Ragle's makeup was a yen to be a writer. I asked him about it.

"Oh, I've been through it all," he said, laughingly. "I took a whole year off and spent all my time writing enough short stories to fill a book. I sent them to publisher after publisher and never got any of them printed. But I learned more about writing during that year than I ever learned in school. I recommend that every English teacher try to write short stories. Novels are easier to write, require less precision and art."

Ragle was interested in teaching students who might not have the academic skills for college. He was active in a plan of teaching similar to the one given at Cincinnati University. His pupils with vocational aptitudes went to high school for a period and then worked as apprentices in the local machine shops. They earned while they learned. The local industry also furnished scholarships and other aids. It cut down the problem of school dropouts. The sturdy Vermont character rebelled at the thought of supporting shiftless people not interested in bettering their condition.

Ragle rebelled at a deeper idleness. "Through the centuries there have always been individuals striving toward knowledge— toward what is right and good. In all ages, men have made great strides toward it; yet in every age momentous discoveries have been diverted to serve little ends. The hope that the progress of some men toward good ends will someday become the progress of all mankind must find its impetus in the young, who must learn to use the best that is in them."

*   *

I rode the bus from New York City to Selinsgrove, Pa. It was Sunday. Crowds poured from churchs along the Lehigh Valley.

The ride was long and winding through the mountains of the

129

depressing anthracite region. Dingy towns clung to bleak, ruptured hillsides. Whole mountainsides had been turned inside out and the scars lay unhealed, barren, desolate and ugly.

Empty school buses stood parked in rows in puddles of water left by melting snow. The churches along the highway were crowded. Some of them were crowned with bulbous Old World onion-shaped domes. Suddenly, we left the hills behind and the Susquehanna lay ice-jammed and silent before us. Soon we reached Selinsgrove on the Susquehanna.

The school buses rolled on Monday. I met teacher Thomas R. Manley right after his biology lecture in the auditorium of Selinsgrove High School. He had introduced team teaching in biology, and it had proved so successful in Selinsgrove that there was talk of its statewide adoption. He stood on the stage, showing colored slides of sponges, coral, sea anemones, and other marine life. He explained Darwin's theory of coral reef formation. Over a hundred students, the combination of five separate classes, listened.

Manley, dressed in his lab smock, wore glasses, and looked every inch the college professor. He also lectured like one. I thought, how lucky these students were to have a teacher of that caliber to guide them through the labyrinths of modern science.

Manley had an assistant, plus two student teachers from Susquehanna College and Bucknell University, who supervised the laboratory experiments and assigned textbook readings. The class groupings were by attitudes, and instruction was geared to Manley's lectures, which were also geared to intelligence levels. The integration achieved by Manley's team teaching experiment was a revelation to the school administrators. Team teaching was relatively new, and many schools were reluctant to adopt it. Much depended on the ability and imagination of the key teacher who coordinated the program.

Tom told me about his job. "As long as I'm healthy, I want to go like a house on fire. I never tire of doing things that interest me. The old timers resented my coming to Selinsgrove High as head of the biology department. I was young and brash. I wanted to change things. They wanted the status quo. One day I called all the reactionaries into my office and I told them, 'If you can show me you can teach a biology class better than I can, I'll quit. I'm willing to let the students be the judges.' We have been good

130

friends ever since. I get all the students on my side. Then I get the parents on my side. If students and parents believe in you, you don't have to worry. Many teachers try to curry favor with the administrators. I'm not here to give lessons to the superintendent and the principal. I'm here to help students. I never snub a student when I meet him, no matter where it is. One boy who had failed in every class but biology told me, 'You're the only teacher who talks to me.' "

Manley showed me a speech he was preparing for a group of student teachers. It shows how outspoken he was: "The security of tenure made safe the positions of incompetent, lazy, and uninspired teachers who slowly rot or die in the classroom. To a large degree, this static condition of education for long periods of the past lay in the hands of administrators who, no better than their teaching staffs, were satisfied to rule over faculties as little gods from whom all wisdom and resources flowed. Within every school there are increasing numbers of teachers who realize that respectability as a teacher necessitates more than six or seven hours a day of expounding from a textbook. These breakers of the status quo are the ones who become the focal point of student interest within the school."

Manley took his BA degree from Fairmont State College in West Virginia, in 1940. He enlisted in the Air Force when the war started. Afterward, he returned to West Virginia University and earned his master of science degree in genetics in 1946. He taught school for a few years, and organized several horticultural centers, performing many unique floricultural experiments. He was invited to attend Ohio State University by the Ohio Florists Association, and he was asked to teach horticulture at Western Reserve University. He also became the horticulturist at the Garden Center of Greater Cleveland. As a boy, he had loved growing gladiolus. He became an authority on gladiolus as the years passed, and he went to Vermont to become a partner with Elmer Gore, one of America's leading gladiolus growers.

But teaching was his first love, and he moved to Pennsylvania and took a job teaching biology in the Selinsgrove Area Joint Schools. He bought a farm nearby and grew acres of gladiolus. He did a big business.

Manley showed me his gladiolus farm and his country home.

131

He had rehabilitated several boys convicted of petty crimes, who had served time. He got them out on parole and put them to work on his farm. They went straight, and moved on to better jobs.

In Manley's big barn, a foreman and two helpers were sorting gladiolus bulbs for shipment. Trays of bulbs were piled from floor to ceiling. Manley had 120 acres of rich land on the banks of the Susquehanna, near Liverpool, and about 30 acres were devoted to gladiolus. He had experimented with soils and fertilizers and had grown 150 bushels of corn per acre. He borrowed $40,000 to start his gladiolus business, and was making a fine bushel of money from it.

I was constantly amazed by his energy, his knowledge, his ambition. Manley drove toward goals with an almost cocky self-assurance. He couldn't understand why any teacher should hide behind false modesty, minimize his talents, lose out to less competent teachers. Manley wasn't likely to do that. He spent a year at Yale University as a John Hay Fellow. He spent his summers in 28 northern counties of Florida studying a vanishing species of butterfly. About all that is known of this rare butterfly was discovered by him. He held a National Science Foundation Research Fellowship at Yale when I met him.

Manley and his wife, Evelyn, were remodeling their old farm house, and Evelyn and Lance, their son, bought antiques at auctions and refinished them. A daughter, Natalie Anne, was a freshman at Penn State University when I was there. Evelyn was a teacher in special education in the Selinsgrove Elementary School. With a woman's prerogative, she took a slightly dim view of her husband's preoccupation with gladiolus farming and butterfly chases through Florida swamps, but she did it good-naturedly.

"We met while attending the same school in West Virginia," Evelyn said. "Tom had a picnic date with my roommate, but she could not go, so Tom asked me if I would go in her place. I went, and Tom climbed to the top of a tree and was swinging from branch to branch like Tarzan. The limb broke and he came crashing to the ground right at my feet. With this incongruous beginning our romance blossomed into marriage."

Evelyn Manley gave me another glimpse of Tom. "Now and then the deer come down from the hills and nip off the top of the gladiolus. One year, they were ruining our crop. We called the

132

game warden. He said, 'Tom, take your gun and go out and shoot them.' What does Tom do? He goes out looking for them in his noisy tractor, knowing they will not come within shooting range. Or he goes out and tells me he has forgotten his gun. The fact is, he just doesn't have the heart to shoot a deer."

Tom Manley also wrote and produced musical comedies for his high school. His friends insisted that he could crash Broadway if he set his mind and energy to it. Maybe so. Manley had a good public relations sense. He knew how to promote the things he was interested in. Most teachers do not; they are too timid.

Manley had several students working on projects of an advanced nature and was coaching them to win honors at science fairs. His students were consistent winners of regional championships at these fairs, and some had placed high nationally, including his son, Lance.

The day I visited his classes, two or three students were making detailed records of the habits and responses of the Oriental cockroach. Last year his students came up with a new species of moth by removing the sex glands of the female moth and transferring them to another female of a different kind. One boy, who was on the verge of dropping out of school, got a new lease when Manley got him interested in snakes. Now the boy is a recognized authority on reptiles and corresponds with college professors. Since Manley was an authority on butterflies, he had trained a few students to do advanced work in the biological functions of lepidoptera.

There was scholarly excitement in Manley's lab. The student teachers from nearby colleges felt privileged to work with him. With good reason. A teacher of his caliber is as vital as the coal in those dark hills. Or perhaps as bright a spot on the educational landscape as a gladiolus on an anthracite pile. Manley later became associate professor of biology at Bloomsburg State College.

* *

The day President Johnson gave Lawana Trout her award, Miss Blanche Crippen, assistant executive director of the Council of Chief State School Officers, set up an educational television interview between Lawana and me. It was impromptu, without benefit of script. We talked for about 15 minutes. It was my first television appearance as well as Lawana's, and we had butterflies

133

in our stomachs. We held hands like kids just before the lights and cameras were turned on. But when the taped version of our interview was shown at the NEA convention in Seattle, no one could believe that Lawana's brilliant exposition of her philosophy was a spontaneous and unrehearsed performance.

President Johnson, in giving the award at the White House on May 4, 1964, also named her to the Presidential Scholars Committee, made up of distinguished Americans. She met some of her fellow committee members at the White House on June 10th. These were great moments for the little girl who once told her secrets to her favorite tree on a farm near Hastings, Okla.

In presenting the National Teacher of the Year award to Lawana at the White House ceremony, President Johnson said: "I have started my career in the classroom, too, and sometimes I feel that I have returned to the professions now. In these times the Presidency offers a great educational challenge and responsibility. While the pay here is appreciably better, Mrs. Trout, than in the public schools, the tenure is appreciably less certain.

"We are honored to welcome Mrs. Trout to the White House this morning. In honoring her as the Teacher of the Year, we honor an outstanding woman and a most useful citizen. In a higher sense, we honor one of our society's most valuable professions, the profession of teaching.

"In this free land, the minds of our young are our most valuable resource. The classroom teacher is always the steward of that resource. For our prosperous Nation and our growing population, no challenge is greater on our horizon than preserving and raising higher the standards of public education. . . ."

After the ceremony, Lawana made many trips, gave many speeches, worked on a textbook, made television appearances, moved from the high school to the college level, took care of her small son while her husband was in another city doing graduate work at college. I worried about the strain of all these activities on her health. But Lawana was strong. During a summer clinic in Princeton, New Jersey, she demonstrated to other teachers how to cope with tough kids from slum areas. She quickly won over groups of knife-carrying, dope-trafficking boys who were normally allergic to education and hostile to teachers. I never worried about her after that.

CHAPTER FIVE

*"...I teach the pleasure of working hard. And we laugh.
Every day it is my responsibility to teach how to laugh,
as well as how to be serious. We must look at ourselves,
see our foibles, laugh at ourselves, and sometimes
go about repairing that which we laughed at..."*

RICHARD KLINCK

1965 NATIONAL TEACHER OF THE YEAR

RICHARD KLINCK
Sixth Grade
Reed Street Elementary School
Wheat Ridge, Colorado

RUNNERS-UP

JOHN MC MANUS
Music
McMinnville High
School
McMinnville, Oregon

ELEANOR
PARKER
English
Laconia High School
Laconia,
New Hampshire

MRS. KATHERINE
ROBINSON
Resource Teacher
Glenwood
Elementary School
Charleston,
West Virginia

MRS. NELL
THOMAS
English
Greenville High
School
Greenville,
Mississippi

1965

The train from Washington, D.C., to Charleston, W. Va., snakes along the banks of turbulent rivers through the Appalachian Mountains. Unpainted shacks, many abandoned, sagging listlessly, lie scattered along these banks. Well-dressed businessmen in the train's dining car glance casually out the window. They may say to themselves, "Appalachia," then forget it.

What good is education if it doesn't put an end to "Appalachias"? Jobless miners could find employment in other fields if they had a high school education. Better housing, better living conditions could result from higher levels of schooling.

What chance does a child of poverty have of getting an education and then getting out? Little chance. What, then, are the chances of a poor, blind child?

Mrs. Katherine B. Robinson knew the answers. In Charleston, where she taught, she was called a "miracle worker." She taught blind children in the Glenwood Elementary School, which—uniquely—was a part of the regular Charleston public school system, not a school for the blind. Her story was the story of a small miracle.

Some persons think of blind children as being "retarded." Mrs. Robinson bristled when she heard this. She knew it was cruelly false. "More often than not the blind child is more talented than the normal child," she would argue, "because the loss of one faculty is compensated for by the intense development of the other senses." Mrs. Robinson's sightless pupils kept up with students who had normal eyesight. This was considered impossible before her time.

She had given 18 years to the study and teaching of blind

137

students. She taught nine pupils when I was there. Some, she hoped, would eventually go on to college. They were carefully screened, and had to be bright. Katherine Robinson then took over, and made them feel that they could make it.

I entered her classroom with some misgiving. I was afraid I would feel sorry for these children, or might say something wrong. Before the day ended I heard happy laughter and felt warm waves of friendship. The most cheerful voice of all was Katherine Robinson's.

I sat down with the children and was introduced to them. They were going to read. "Mr. Burke has but two eyes," Mrs. Robinson said, "but each of you children has ten fingers. Show him how good you are." They did, reading Braille faster than I could follow in the conventional manner.

Keeping these blind children up with the regular classes was tough. Katherine Robinson converted all the subject matter, all the lessons of the other teachers in Glenwood Elementary School, into Braille with special equipment she had in her office. She used every mechanical device she could find. Once or twice she had to invent some machine badly needed in her work. She would transcribe the lessons into Braille, which she had taught herself to read, and make tape recordings of upcoming lessons. Her pupils listened to the recordings and memorized them. Their retention was phenomenal.

Mrs. Robinson stayed up late almost every night running off copies of classroom material on a Braille machine. She collected books in Braille, and her classroom had the World Book Encyclopedia, which is 145 volumes in Braille, and an unabridged standard dictionary, 36 volumes in Braille.

Ideally, there should be one teacher for every three blind children. It takes a lot of patience to teach Braille to a beginner. But once a blind child has mastered the Braille system it is possible to read rapidly enough to keep up with normal children. Mrs. Robinson's children, working in advance, learned their lessons and then joined the other pupils in the regular classes. They raised their hands and answered questions as well as anyone.

The rewards of attention seem greater for the blind child. I met a little blind girl, about ten years old, in these classes, and gave her a book of poetry I had selected from the shelves. She

138

read it with her fingers more rapidly than I could with my eyes. She didn't make a single mistake.

Then we talked. She told how she could ride a bicycle, ice-skate, bowl and play games. She went to basketball games, was a Girl Scout, sang in the school choir, and did all the things that appealed to her.

I visited the Robinsons. Katherine's husband, William Beverly Robinson, also an excellent teacher, had just given her a Hammond organ. She loved to play classical music. She also was the musical director of the Glenwood Elementary School, and put some of her blind children in the school choir.

Katherine Robinson was born in Charleston, and went to school there. In 1934, she graduated from West Virginia State College. She had majored in music, but when the chance to help blind children came along she knew the "call." She did graduate work at Hunter College in New York City, and served on the President's committee on Unemployment of the Handicapped.

Mrs. Violet Johnson, the principal at Glenwood, told me that Katherine Robinson added prestige to the school. She said that Katherine went to civic clubs and other city organizations to make speeches and that she could easily talk them into donating money for the special equipment needed for her pupils.

One public official said, with great enthusiasm: "Mrs. Robinson is loved by more people in this town than anyone I know."

She should be. She has helped little children overcome their barrier of blindness. And Katherine Robinson, a Negro, has also overcome the barrier of lingering West Virginia prejudice, to become a trail blazer in education. One of the regular visitors to her classroom was the governor of West Virginia.

* *

I had the unpleasant feeling that I might be persona non grata in Mississippi. I was a member of the hated Northern Press. Fortunately, everyone I met in Greenville, Mississippi, made my visit a happy one.

At that time, Greenville enjoyed the unique distinction of being bypassed by racial disturbances. Not so since. On April 5, 1966, when I rode to the White House with the Teacher of the Year, a group of Negro protesters had thrown up tents in the

139

park across the street, petitioning the President to overcome living and working conditions in the Mississippi Delta. This protest group was from Greenville, and I felt at that moment that something Nell Thomas, the teacher I interviewed there, stood for had been betrayed.

I fell in love with Mrs. Nell Thomas and her family right away. She was a vibrant person, a born teacher, full of charm, femininity, and very easy to talk to. She loved her town of Greenville, a bustling port city on the Mississippi, deep in the delta. It had been dealt with effectively by Hodding Carter's book, *Where Main Street Meets the River*. We had cocktails at the Carters' country home called "Feliciana," set among old cypress trees. Hodding Carter and his wife were in New Orleans, but Hodding III, his wife, and children were there and were gracious hosts. The Carters have long been fond of Nell Thomas. She had taught Hodding III and he was on her winning debate team. He admitted her strong influence on his literary career.

The teaching in Greenville High School, by any standards, was tops. Nell Thomas had some of the school's most brilliant students in her English classes. Here, perhaps, were the new Hodding Carters.

In one of her classes I visited, Nell Thomas discussed Shakespeare's *Macbeth* and Dostoyevsky's *Crime and Punishment*. It took me a few minutes to adjust my ears to the soft and lazy sound of Southern speech, particularly a whole room filled with it. "Are theah een-ny mo-ah questions?" Nell Thomas would ask.

One boy, commenting on the poverty-stricken characters in *Crime and Punishment*, said: "Why does ev-rah charactah haff to be poo-ah? Just for once ad'd luff to read about some charactah as rich as spit!"

Mrs. Thomas emphasized the psychological aspects of the two masterpieces in this class, particularly the words and actions of Macbeth and Raskolnikov. The free-wheeling discussion ranged from references to Milton's *Areopagitica* to Thoreau's *Essay on Civil Disobedience;* from *Peyton Place, Lord of the Flies,* and Bellow's *Herzog* to the theater of the Absurd, Existentialism, Machiavelli's, *The Prince,* the war in Vietnam, discotheques, *One Potato, Two Potato,* Faulkner's *The Sound and the Fury,* Thomas Aquinas and Camus' *The Stranger.* The discussion was brilliant

140

and Nell Thomas adroitly channeled the dialogue back to *Macbeth* and *Crime and Punishment*. The whole performance was a superb adventure of the mind—education at its best.

There were few rules and no formality in Nell Thomas's classes. She did not sit behind a desk, but moved into the circle of chairs used by the students and became one of the group. A seminar atmosphere permeated all of her classes. Free speech was encouraged. No one was inhibited. The disagreement between the liberal and conservative elements in these classes was sharp and witty, but always courteous. Mrs. Thomas knew just when to change the subject and cool down the debate. She quickly detected and challenged false reasoning by skillfully leading her students into amending their own thoughts.

Nell Thomas was chic and attractive, looking almost as young as her daughter Vicki, a practice teacher in Greenville on leave from "Ole Miss" where she studied. Nell's husband, Charles, called "Big Chuck" by everyone to distinguish him from his son called "Little Chuck," had been a college football star and still looked rugged and fit. He had been a teacher in his younger days and now directed regional Boy Scout activities.

Mrs. Thomas had held important posts in regional and national education organizations, and at one time served as president of the Mississippi Education Association. She defended truth with a vengeance outside—as well as inside—the classroom. When the Daughters of the American Revolution tried to alter Mississippi textbooks, Nell Thomas stood up in a meeting and said, "No." The Daughters retreated. Mrs. Thomas holds a BS degree from Delta State college and an MA from the University of Mississippi.

Greenville High has won national awards for its school annual, and it published when I was there a literary magazine, *The Laureate*. Nell's classes edited these fine publications, proving once again that a good teacher sheds creative influence upon every school activity.

Nell Thomas, in her soft Southern manner, upheld this influence.

* *

Richard E. Klinck was a new pioneer in the Old West.

Klinck, a sixth grade teacher in the Reed Street Elementary School in Wheat Ridge, Colorado, was the highest type of American citizen, family man, and teacher. Pioneers into the West had triumphed over all adversity. They were tough. Dick Klinck wanted to preserve those qualities and pass them on to a new generation.

I have never met another family like the Klincks. It was such a refreshing experience to spend a few hours with perfectly natural people still embracing the ideals and traditions of their forefathers. Their response to the evidence of God's work in the beauty surrounding them was an unequivocal "Amen."

Klinck was a tall, athletic-looking man with a crew cut and a healthy outdoor tan. He had a quick, stingless humor. In repartee, he could fence with the best wordsmen. He loved to talk, and could hold your interest for an hour without ever repeating himself.

The Klincks never had much money, and they would never give up the way of life they liked best in order to earn more. When Dick got out of the Navy in World War II, he worked his way through Coe College at Cedar Rapids, Iowa, as a postal clerk. Lois Luckel trained as a nurse, fell in love with and married Dick, and, when I visited the Klincks, worked two or three days a week in a Wheat Ridge hospital. She was an excellent cook, and could prepare the spicy Mexican dishes Dick loved almost too much. The Klinck home was a house of love and laughter, and shared jobs. Dick and Lois had one daughter, Jeannine.

Lois learned to like the outdoors early. When she married Dick in 1950, they honeymooned in a plywood structure Dick had built on top of a Jeepster pickup truck. For nine weeks they explored Mesa Verde, the Grand Canyon and the Southwest. They roughed it, with scarcely enough money to pay for the gas and oil. Lois passed the test. She was included on all nomadic wanderings after that.

On camping vacations, the Klincks picked up shells, fossils, gems, arrowheads, driftwood, bits of flora and bleached bones of fauna from desert floor and mesa, mountain trail and seashore. They got the feel of America for Dick's classes by traveling to its different sections every summer. He, Lois, and daughter Jeannine traveled by car, prepared their own food, slept out. By 1965, they had visited 48 states, camped in 26 of the 32 national parks and 178 of the 204 national park areas. Not once did they sleep in a motel or hotel.

Dick's love of nature made him one of the country's leading conservationists. He wrote extensively for *National Parks Magazine* and other publications, and his book *Land of Room Enough and Time Enough* caught the poetry and history of remote Monument Valley on the Arizona-Utah borderland. He and Lois ventured into lonely and uninhabited wilderness seen by few people during the past century. He recalled: "Once Lois and I were deep in an uninhabited corner of the Southwest, so remote from civilization we neither saw nor heard a plane overhead, nor caught sight of another living being the day and night we spent there. It was as though we were the first persons ever to set foot there since the dawn of creation, and quite possibly we were. Many people would have been frightened and overcome by this loneliness, this vast stillness, so far from human habitation, but Lois and I found beauty and peace and mutual understanding there—even a deep spirituality—such as we have never known before. It was the most inspiring experience of our lives. We can never forget it."

Dick shot hundreds of color slides for his classes. He also made pencil, pen and ink sketches on these nature trips. He collected commemorative stamps dealing with our national parks and natural history. When I visited him, Dick had just built an extra room to house all his books, slides, stamps, and memorabilia, a collection so large he maintained a card catalogue of its contents. He used all of this material in his sixth grade classes.

I was incognito during my visit to the Reed Street Elementary School in Wheat Ridge, part of suburban Denver. Dick Klinck kept my mission secret. I even missed the usual luncheon with the local civic club. The superintendent of schools didn't know I was in town. It was peaceful. Dick made one concession, eating his lunch (brought from home) with me in the school cafeteria instead of his office, where he usually ate. We talked.

"I am proud to be a teacher," he asserted. "As a teacher I have a classroom—a miniature world—where every day a group of students comes. Some come willingly, openly curious and anxious to know and to learn. Others come for conformity, by necessity, with a certain reluctance to learn and a deep unawareness of the

143

magic of knowledge that is all around them. They come from a variety of homes, from a variety of pasts, to the present. And I for a while am their future. They have come together and they are my class and I am a teacher—their teacher."

Dick was informal in attire. He wore a red woolen outer shirt picked up from a Hudson Bay trading post, and sneakers. At Christmas time, as a gag, he came to class wearing white socks with little green Christmas trees woven into them. His pupils adored him and they worked hard for him. He teased them and shared in their fun, but he also knew the split second in which to assume authority. He was a formidable person they listened to and obeyed.

I had never seen classes so well drilled in fundamentals. I have also never seen so much paper work. Dick believed that boys and girls should get the idea early that their professional careers were going to involve a lot of paper work.

Klinck also made these little sixth graders think and act like junior writers and executives. His instruction carried journalistic overtones. He required his pupils to edit constantly and revise what they put down on paper. As a result, his word-conscious pupils were remarkably articulate for their age.

Klinck also gave some of his daily lessons in Spanish. He had a mastery of it, and in Colorado and the Southwest Spanish is a necessary second language for educated people.

Dick Klinck had never taught in any other school, he had never taught anything but the sixth grade. "I want to master the sixth grade psyche," he said. It was his 13th year at Reed Street Elementary. "I teach sixth grade because these are children you can talk to in an adult manner, and yet they are still young enough to accept discipline. It is the age of intellectual transition—just at the borderline of independent thinking. It is the last age in which you can play father and mother to them. They still need security and guidance. They are not old enough to be ill-mannered in a brash rebellious way. They are still sensitive to rebuke or praise."

"I teach the pleasure of working hard," he said. "And we laugh. Every day it is my responsibility to teach how to laugh, as well as how to be serious. We must look at ourselves, see our foibles, laugh at ourselves, and sometimes go about repairing that which

144

we laughed at. I must arm each of my boys and girls with a sense of humor to be better prepared to face the world in the years beyond my time with them.

"Teaching is a link to the future. In a way it offers immortality, and each of us has the innate desire for that. By teaching in the broadest sense—of ideals and understandings—I have the opportunity of being active in the fate of my country. I am not determining its destiny, but I am producing men and women who will decide that destiny wisely and well.

"And on the other hand I can, in part, determine that destiny as well, for by teaching what is right and proper—the preservation of our wilderness and the love of our parks, for example—I am helping to shape the future."

Each year, Dick Klinck took all of the sixth graders in his district to a spot high up in the Rocky Mountains where they lived in cabins for a full week. They studied weather, geology, natural history, botany, conservation and other related subjects. Parents were not allowed. It was also a week's experience in communal living away from home with discipline and control. The sheer enjoyment of outdoor life and the appreciation of nature were the keynotes. It was laboratory of good citizenship, social cooperation and knowledge-gathering.

Before breaking camp, Klinck assigned all the pupils to a cleanup project. Every empty can, carton, bottle cluttering the ground in or near the camp was removed.

Klinck's week-long camp-out is now being copied by many other schools. Unfortunately, such an outing is usually a day at the zoo, rather than a week in the woods and the true self-discovery that Dick Klinck sought for his students.

* *

John McManus had a farm on Route 2, just outside McMinnville, Oregon, the county seat of Yamhill County. The 15-acre setting was beautiful, past a lane lined with pear trees and a grove of English walnut trees. Tall Douglas firs grew up from a dell below the house, and the muddy waters of Yamhill Creek wound through the cow pasture. John fed about 15 Hereford cows, partly to supplement his salary, partly as a hobby. Everyone works at extra jobs in this part of our country. During school vacations,

145

McMinnville boys and girls pick strawberries and Blue Lake beans that help pay for their high school and college educations.

One of the worst floods in Oregon's history had almost paralyzed parts of the state before I arrived, and the earth was still sodden and oozy. The day I visited John McManus in McMinnville High School, the sun came out and everyone rejoiced. My appearance received second billing.

Everyone greeted me. "If John wins," warned the president of the board of education, "we will raise the money to send the high school band to Washington!" I tried to imagine squeezing 100 musicians into the White House Rose Garden.

John McManus was a small man, weighing about 135 pounds, and shy. In our first meeting, I did most of the talking. Gradually we got acquainted. I had dinner with John and his wife and three children the day I arrived by bus from Portland. I took some photographs, the children brought me a sack of shelled English walnuts. Their fingers were stained black from walnut shelling.

John McManus was not a farmer, really. He was a music teacher, one of the best. The moment he stepped to the podium, raised his baton and took charge, he was no longer shy. He was poised, dynamic, sure of himself—a small, coiled spring of a man about to release tremendous energy.

The McMinnville High School band, John's band, could really play. It was one of the best in the entire Northwest. To give his students an idea of expert playing, McManus brought to McMinnville virtuosi like Bill Page, Raphael Mendez, Sigurd Rascher, Wayne Mercer, Warren Baker and Amy Arney. These visiting artists would instruct band members on how to master their instruments. It paid off. I heard these boys and girls play excerpts from Tchaikovsky's *Symphony No. 6*, Ravel's *Bolero*, Percy Grainger's *Lincolnshire Posy*, Aaron Copland's *A Lincoln Portrait*, Rimsky-Korsakov's *Flight of the Bumblebee*, *The Roman Carnival Overture* by Berlioz, *An Original Suite* by Gordon Jacob, *Coronation of the Muse* by Charpentier, and other selections familiar to symphony orchestras but not to many high school bands.

Composer and conductor Meredith Willson, who went to McMinnville to direct the band in one of the special musical programs arranged by McManus, said that he had never heard a finer high school band.

146

Who are today's great teachers?

Musical directors from all the colleges in the Northwest, searching for recruits for their bands, competed with one another in persuading McManus-trained seniors to enroll with them. They were as eagerly sought as football players.

McManus directed the musical program for the entire McMinnville school system. One of his assistants told me: "We were doing team teaching in music years ahead of most schools, even before the term came into vogue." I went with John to the Junior High School. In a small room, he gave a few moments of private instruction to various band members, pointing out faulty techniques, poor breathing, psychological blocks. He improved their finger movements, their lip exercises, their reading of notes. It was done in a fatherly, relaxed manner, and there was no trace of harsh criticism. He was quick to praise each sign of improvement, no matter how slight.

John devoted 10 minutes of private teaching to 55 junior high school students each week, in addition to his other duties as head of the music department. By the time the students reached high school age and enrolled in the band, John knew what each could do musically, and he could assemble the best combination of talent.

Each school day, and often beyond, he instructed more than 300 music students. The high school band, with 100 musicians, was the largest. Since no one pupil could toot the other's horn, and since members of a band couldn't cover up another sour note, John had to work closely with each of these students. McManus had the perfect temperament for the painstaking development of each pupil's skill and potentiality.

In the McMinnville High School band, the girls usually piped the woodwinds and the boys blew on the brasses. Most high school bands seem too loud and too brassy in their unimaginative renditions of familiar themes. Not McManus' band. Here few bells rang, no cymbals clanged, and when the drums played away, they did so gently. John kept saying at rehearsals, "Softer . . . softer . . ." To him, as to most adults, a loud sound was a conspicuous disharmony. He taught the band to play with conscious restraint and moderation. This was the secret of his success as a conductor and leader. He achieved symphonic coloring, delicate nuances, by this velvety approach.

Some pieces were played to the end. But McManus, the perfectionist, stopped others if he detected errors. He didn't strike terror into his students, but smiled, groaned perhaps, and made a few constructive suggestions. The students appreciated this. They, too, were pleased when the right sounds came out.

McManus also encouraged them to listen to experimental music. He played a record of avant-garde Edgar Varese, which had been popularized at the Brussels World's Fair. His pupils discussed this type of music. Most liked it but found Varese a bit of a strain. "You can't listen to this kind of sound very long at one time," one student confessed. McManus replied: "We can always be taken in by something new. We get our leg pulled now and then, but we must learn to accept new things—with a bit of humor at the outset. We must never reject a musical composition because of its strangeness and novelty. We must always be willing to experiment with new sound combinations. I would hate to see Leonard Bernstein lose his job with the New York Philharmonic Orchestra just because he introduces avant-garde music from time to time. We must constantly re-educate ourselves musically, retaining the best of the past, learning to live with the new."

All the people of McMinnville, about 9,000, knew and liked John McManus. I kept finding out good things about him from townspeople, students, teachers, and well-wishers from other parts of Oregon.

John McManus had hitch-hiked the 2,000 miles between LaGrange, Oregon, and Northwestern University in Evanston, Illinois, as a student. For three years in World War II he was a pilot of a B-24 bomber in Italy. Later, while he attended Columbia University in New York, he and his wife lived at old Camp Shanks near Nyack because he could not afford an apartment in the city.

He took his Master of Arts degree in music at Columbia. When I interviewed him, he was president of the Oregon Music Educator's Association. He was a clarinet player with professional talent, but long ago gave up the idea of a musical career of his own. He preferred to develop the talents of others.

* *

I drove to Laconia, New Hampshire, through the winterset hills and valleys of chilly, old, gray New England. As I neared the town, I saw a sign for the "Peyton Place Motel," reminding me

148

that this is the locale of the sex-filled best seller by the late Grace Metalious. As it turned out, I could never find in Laconia the characters Metalious sketched into Gilmanton, N.H.

I passed up the Peyton Place Motel, and stopped for the night at the Laconia Tavern, an aging hostelry. It boasted that President Eisenhower had slept there while conferring with Sherman Adams. Laconia, one of the most picturesque towns in America, had gotten its share, and more, of bad publicity. No sooner had Peyton Place cooled off, and the Adams-Goldfine scandal simmered, than hordes of motorcycle-riding kids roared into Laconia at summer's end to wreck and riot at Weirs Beach.

The teacher I was in town to interview won her nomination because of hot controversy. Local bigots threatened to remove from the high school reading list the book, *To Kill a Mockingbird*. Eleanor Parker defended the book and said she would resign if it were taken from the list. Once again Laconia grabbed headlines it didn't seek.

Laconia High School was housed in an old building, and some classrooms were in the basement, called "The Dungeon" by the students. When the school secretary called Miss Parker in her classroom to announce that I was waiting to meet her in the super-intendent's office, she replied: "I'm too busy." She would not walk out of a class until the bell rang. With her, pupils came first. I liked this attitude. I went down into "The Dungeon" to visit Miss Parker's classroom, which was also her office. She had written my name on the blackboard, and I knew that I had been discussed in advance. Miss Eleanor Parker, a sweet, gentle and effective English teacher, was anything but a Barbara Frietchie. A firebrand she was not. She had an utterly disarming New England composure and a dedication to her job.

Miss Parker did a lot of good without being a do-gooder. She got to school early, taught well and long, played the organ after school hours and directed a choir. She was active in church work. In the evenings, she devoted time to teaching the retarded children of church members, without pay. She went back to college every summer, to improve her skills. She had studied linguistics at Boston University, and then added this course to her program at Laconia High School.

The day I was there, Miss Parker's class discussed Emerson.

149

Each student played the part of Emerson and drew a question from a box. He or he would rise, read the question addressed to Emerson and answer it, identifying the essay on which the question was based. Some typical questions: "Mr. Emerson, why did you leave the Unitarian ministry?" or "Please explain the philosophy of Transcendentalism" or "What do you mean by Nature and how should we regard it?" Miss Parker did not superimpose her own interpretations of Emerson on the students, even when they seemed vague in their answers.

Eleanor Parker wanted her students to draw their own conclusions and do their own thinking. "Of course," she said, "if I see them straying into avenues of thought not consistent with truth, I try to lead them back on the right path."

The right path has always been clear to Eleanor Parker. When Laconia's right wing pressured the high school English department to ban the use of Harper Lee's *To Kill a Mockingbird*, Eleanor Parker appeared before the school board at an open meeting and opposed the censorship. She was eloquent. Her defense revealed her wide knowledge of literature, and her deep understanding of the book. It also gave me insight into her work as a teacher, and her respect and trust for her students.

It has been widely quoted. Here are the highlights of Eleanor Parker's defense of the freedom to read:

"First, I should like to give you a bit of background about the use of the book. It has been on our outside reading lists for free reading since 1960. Last year, it was taught in all the general English XII classes under our expanded reading program. This year, in my class, it was listed with the other books for class reading on a sheet of the year's program handed to all the students the first week of school in September. Last October 9 the book was given to the class, as previously announced. On Tuesday, the 13th, I received an anonymous call stating objections to the book, and although I asked the gentleman several times if he would not come to the school to discuss the problem with me in order that we might reach a better understanding of each other's viewpoints, he refused to do this.

"On Wednesday, I announced to the class that anyone not wishing to read the book should return it to me and would be given another book more acceptable to him or her. No books were returned. Yesterday, I announced that we would not discuss the book yesterday or today because of this meeting. I also urged the class to remember the words of Voltaire: 'Although I disagree with everything you say, I will fight to the death your right to say it.' I asked them to remember that in this country everyone had a right to express his opinion, and that, therefore, anyone was free to object to the book. . . . I also urged them to think about the point emphasized so strongly by Harper Lee in the book, that it is vital for people to try to understand the viewpoints of others.

"I had not expected any discussion following this announcement, but these are alert and intelligent 18-year-olds. They had things to say, and since I had just spoken up for free speech, I could not ask them to keep silent. They commented that they had found the book a wonderful one; that if one bans books, there is no place to stop; that they have only eight more months in which to learn maturity of judgment and understanding, of how to meet life's problems and choices; and over and over they asked me: 'Miss Parker, what is wrong with this book?' I tried to present the other viewpoints as I have heard them, but really answered only one question. One student said, 'What happens if we are told on Monday that we cannot continue to discuss this book?' This question I had to answer, and wish to make clear now what my answer is. If my class and I (and thus, of course, ultimately other classes and other teachers) are not allowed to continue to discuss this book, I shall have to ask the Laconia School Board to accept my resignation.

"From my conversation with Mr. S. and from what I have heard reported, I gather that there are two main objections to the book. One is the supposed event which leads to the trial. Of course, no act of rape was committed, and the point of that part of the book is not the event at all but the injustice of condemning an innocent man because of his race.

"Mr. S.'s other objection is, I believe, to some of the words used in the book. Frankly, outside of the word rape, I could not remember any others, although I have read the book probably a dozen times in order to teach it. He read some of the words to me, and I have since tried to find them because I did not copy down the pages at that time. I have found five after some hunting. It had never occurred to me that they were important since they have no connection with the point of the book and have, of course, never been mentioned or discussed in class. As a matter of fact, at one point in the book, Atticus mentions that all children go through a stage of using bad language, but if parents do not focus attention on it, the children stop soon since they are only doing it to attract attention. Perhaps I might add that since finding these words, I have discovered that one of them, with its derivatives, is mentioned 52 times in the Bible. Of course, as in the Bible, this vocabulary is used either to state a fact or for the sake of realism and has no importance in the purpose of the book.

"What, then, is the purpose of the book and my reason for teaching it? I love to teach. I have spent over half my life working with young people in school and in church and working with language, the miracle that makes us human. It is through language that we think, communicate, express our ideas, and transmit them down the years. Why study literature? Because it is one of the humanities—one of the ways by which man expresses his beliefs, his hopes, his understandings. The study of literature helps us to develop responsibility as individuals, members of families, citizens. It helps us to develop values, ideals, a sense of purpose, an understanding of what life is all about. I consider this book, *To Kill a Mockingbird*, a superior resource for such development because the basic idea of the book is that prejudice poisons the mind, and that the only cure is understanding.

"One of the key sentences in the book is said by the hero, Atticus Finch, a wise and good man: 'You never really understand a person until you climb into his skin and walk around in it.' This, I tell my classes, is what we mean by empathy, actually trying to feel what another feels. The book is often thought of as a novel of race problems, but actually there are many prejudices in the book: one section of town against another; old families against newcomers; educated against uneducated; ignorant against wise; white against Negro, Negro against white; religiosity against real religion; and nearly everyone against the unknown—the root of all prejudice.

"The lesson of this book is the lesson great men like Dr. Martin Luther King, Jr., recent winner of the Nobel Prize, have tried to teach. Dr. King said:

" 'The Negro must work passionately for full stature as a citizen, but he must not use inferior methods to gain it . . . without

152

dependence on God our efforts turn to ashes and our sunrises into darkest nights . . . The Negro must never come to terms with falsehood, malice, hate, or destruction.'

"Above all, this book, unlike so many other modern novels, is full of hope. It does tell us there is evil in the world, and we cannot hide from it or refuse to admit its existence. We must be able to identify it as evil, but then we must give our lives to overcoming it, not by stooping to its level, but by meeting it with good. We have to choose what kind of people we are going to be: those who are overcome by evil, or those who overcome evil with good. Miss Maudie said: 'We're so rarely called on to be Christians, but when we are, we've got men like Atticus to go for us.' When I teach this book, I look at my students and hope that they and I myself will learn to be like Atticus, to meet ignorance, hatred, prejudice, not with more ignorance, hatred, prejudice, but with understanding, goodness, love.

"This is my purpose in reading and teaching Harper Lee's *To Kill a Mockingbird*."

She sat down. Eleanor Parker easily won the fight, and the town. A few months later she received a warm letter from Harper Lee.

* *

When Richard Klinck, the sixth grade teacher from Wheat Ridge, Colorado, won the National Teacher of the Year Award for 1965, he and his family stayed in the Hotel Madison in Washington, D.C. It was a novel and shattering experience for this camping family.

"Heated towel racks!" Dick exclaimed in disbelief.

That wasn't the first shock. We unsettled Dick Klinck from the start. His annual outdoor school in the Rocky Mountains was to take place a week after my visit. In the event he won the National Teacher of the Year Award, Klinck ought to be photographed for LOOK in the mountain school, we decided. But if we waited until the committee met and chose the winner, it would be too late to get pictures as exciting as these. I still hadn't met two other candidates. I was in a quandary. I called my office in New York, and they dispatched a writer and photographer to Colorado immediately to do a story and hold it until the committee met. If

153

Klinck won, they said, LOOK would be ready. If he lost, the picture story was good enough to stand on its own. With the Rocky Mountain backdrop it seemed a shame not to take pictures of an unusual grade school experiment which might be used as a model by other teachers. Not until the committee had selected Klinck as the winner did I tell them about the LOOK preparation. That story was reprinted in many languages all over the world.

Dick was pleased to find so many people from the Department of the Interior at the reception for him in Washington. Secretary of the Interior Stewart Udall was there. Prominent persons from the National Park Services and the Fish and Wildlife Service, familiar with Dick's writing, were anxious to meet him. Secretary Udall was tremendously impressed with Klinck's knowledge of our national parks, and later appeared on television with him.

The camping Klincks were a hit in the Capitol, especially nine-year-old Jeannine. This darling child captured the heart of President Lyndon B. Johnson and won the laughter of a national television audience.

Maybe the Klincks' beagle, "Crackers," had something to do with it. During the award ceremony in the Cabinet Room of the White House, Jeannine suddenly asked the President if she could see "Him," the President's beagle. "Bring in the dog!" LBJ ordered to a press aide, and while cameras clicked Jeannine stole the show from her daddy. The picture of her holding the famous dog made the feature pages of nearly every major newspaper.

No sooner had the humor of the dog incident quieted, than Jeannine burst into tears through sheer awe and happiness over standing with her mother and father before the President of the United States. It was so genuine, so touching, that even President Johnson was visibly moved by it.

During the ceremony, I remembered something Dick Klinck had written: "As a teacher, I know a curious blend of emotions day by day: despair and elation, frustration and contentment, impatience and realization, sadness and happiness, fulfillment and defeat. I know the soaring spirit that comes from hearing of one of my students who went on to be honored and acclaimed and I take a bit of the credit for having caused him to succeed. And I know also the sorrow when I hear of a youngster of mine who has failed and acted against society—and I will take a bit of the blame

154

for not having helped him to avoid that deed, that defeat."

As National Teacher of the Year, Dick Klinck's influence and philosophy spread across the nation. Perhaps, through other teachers, he helped youngsters he never knew, in classes he never taught, go on to be honored and acclaimed.

CHAPTER SIX

"... For students to learn to be useful as unique and different individuals, and yet relate as human beings, we need to organize schools and classrooms horizontally rather than vertically. Children are people. They grow tomorrow only as they live today...."

MONA DAYTON

1966 NATIONAL TEACHER OF THE YEAR

MRS. MONA DAYTON
First Grade
Walter Douglas School
Tucson, Arizona

RUNNERS-UP

ROBERT ARNOLD
Sixth Grade
Lincoln Hills
    Elementary School
Richfield, Minnesota

MRS. ELAINE
    LEDBETTER
Chemistry
Pampa High School
Pampa, Texas

MRS. SYBLE HOPP
Principal
Donovan School
Green Bay, Wisconsin

HAROLD LONG
History
Glens Falls High
    School
Glens Falls,
    New York

1966

Arizona is dry as an old bone most of the year. But I arrived in Tucson in the midst of a cloudburst.

It was past midnight. My dream of enjoying two days of sun in mid-December was not going to come true. Tucson has no storm sewers. When a heavy rain comes it has no place to go, and the streets become turbulent rivers. I sloshed to my hotel.

The next morning it was still raining. I headed for the Walter Douglas School, on North Flowing Wells Road. Just before I got to the school the sun broke through, and over the range of mountains called the Catalinas a rainbow appeared.

I expected a conventional school building. Instead, there were four unusual ones. Each was nearly round or octagonal. The first person I met at the school was Mrs. Wanda Adams, the principal. She escorted me to one of the round buildings, opened a classroom door, and there stood Mrs. Mona Dayton. Tall, lithe, she towered over her brood of first graders. She had a thin, tanned, weather-beaten, sunwrinkled face. She moved about effortlessly, like a trained dancer, which she was. She spoke like a poet.

Mona's class was just under way when I entered. In two minutes I was hung up in one of those tiny chairs built for first graders, and "instant" friends gathered around me.

We, all 26 of us boys and girls, did everything Mona asked us to do, and a few things she didn't ask us to do. On a table was a box containing two or three worn, flat stones the size of a half dollar. The Indians call them "Happy Stones." If you wish to be happy you rub one of these stones. Throughout the day several of my classmates walked over to the table quietly and rubbed the stones gently. I managed to sneak in a couple of rubs myself while no one was watching.

159

Mona Dayton was constantly trying to establish a sense of rhythm and the joy of work in her class. She often sang her instructions: "Put your clay away. I want to see you sitting down. Put your clay awaaaay." Soon the whole class was singing, "Put your clay away." She made up any tune that popped into her head, and repeated it over and over.

The room was a jumble, a world in miniature—animal, vegetable and mineral. Here was an aquarium, there was a pet boa constrictor about four feet long named Rosy Jean, which the children put around their necks without the slightest fear. A child asked if I wanted to hold the snake. I begged off. The children also loved pet mice, but when Mrs. Dayton explained that Rosy Jean had to eat mice in order to live, they learned something about survival.

Mona took the children on nature trips around Tucson. Nearly all the pictures the children drew for me had a distinct regional flavor—the animals, the sun, the tall cactus, the desert and the mountains.

One piece of equipment in the classroom was an upended packing case, with one side open. The boys loved to hide in this box and listen to tape recordings.

Mona used many other devices to gain and hold the attention of her pupils. "Everyone put on your thinking caps!" she shouted. All went through the timeless pantomime of putting on thinking caps and adjusting them to fit. When the class got a bit noisier than usual, Mona reduced it several decibels by holding up a purple device made by the Indians and called by them, "God's Eye," which is the symbol of magic. "It is time we had some magic," she said, waving the symbol. There was a solemn hush. Not a hand or lip moved during the moment of the magic spell. Mona whispered to me: "Whatever it is, it works."

Mona showed me a picture of an old Papago witch doctor. In her hand was a purple plum, which she held all day long. "She caressed it gently," Mona explained. "The touch of smooth things induces in the Indians a state of mind bordering on revery." You may wonder why in this advanced age of science a teacher would resort to superstitious holdovers from primitive times. Mrs. Dayton's use of these psychological devices of another century did the work of discipline. At the same time, it awakened in the child's mind a sense of awe and beauty.

160

Who are today's great teachers?

There was a "pupil of the day" ceremony. A little girl was having a birthday, and she stood in front of the class and received honors. I let it be known that it was also my birthday. I was spanked by Johnny Sierra. The children tried to guess my age. They started with 100. The lowest they got down to was 80, and my vanity was deflated.

Among my birthday greetings from the first graders were things like: "The world is big and round. It has lots of lands. I'm glad you came to our land. The land is our home. The land is soft. The world has lots of color and lots of smells to it."

The children were busy sending Christmas cards to pen pals abroad. One little girl had written on a card with a Christmas candle on it: "And there was a candle that everyone loved because it kept the day long. Then one horrible thing happened it blew out and then the people were scared cause they don't like the dark. They like light."

Mona Dayton believed in "experience reading" and "experience writing." She wanted individual response and individual expression, not the same response to the same page, which you get when every child reads the same book. She kept plenty of books around, and she had electronic reading devices. But each day she stimulated original work involving a personal experience of some kind. One favorite method was to distribute reproductions of famous works of ancient and modern art. The pupil looked at the work, and wrote down what he or she thought of it, without any comment or help from the teacher. Mrs. Dayton didn't care about the spelling and grammar at this stage. To correct mistakes might restrict the free play of imagination and discourage further effort.

Between classes, I went to the principal's office and talked to Mrs. Wanda Adams. She told me about Mona Dayton: "We used to think children could not write until they reached the fourth grade. Mona has them writing in the first grade. When you go into Mona's room you feel a warmth. She has a certain magnetism. Children are immediately attracted to her. She comes from a family of teachers. Her father was a professor of physics at the University of Arizona. She has four children. All were outstanding leaders in our local high school. The youngest, Betsy, is a senior in high school—you will meet her later—Kate is at Pembroke College, Eli is studying at Columbia University Medical School, and Paul is at the University of Washington. You will love the whole Dayton family."

When school was out, Mona drove me to her home. In the Dayton yard and all around the garage area were five or six cars and trucks of various ages and previous conditions of servitude. I got the idea that the Daytons never sold or traded a car, but kept it as a member of the family. Later I learned that all these vehicles were in running order and were used for the annual Christmas trek to the Gulf of Lower California in Mexico, made by the Daytons and their friends.

The Dayton home was filled with Indian rugs, blankets, baskets and other handcrafted objects, each with some special story behind it. Mona even had two baskets with rattlesnake designs on them. These are priceless rarities, for Indian taboos forbid the use of the rattlesnake motif.

To describe the Dayton house in its entirety would cover archeology, zoology, musicology and ornithology. Tame wildlife was all over the place. In the kitchen perched a talking parrot, and across the room from it sat a huge horned owl, Uuvick, who sometimes accompanied Mona to school. There were two dogs, the small one called "Che," from the Argentine word of greeting. In a cage outside were two coatimundis, while walking around the yard with a possessive air was "Mayflower," a live Thanksgiving leftover. "Mayflower" had been purchased, squawking, for the big day. But when the time came for beheading, none of the Daytons had the heart of an executioner. A caucus was held, a vote taken. By the middle of December, "Mayflower" still lived, and there was glowing promise of a long and well-fed life.

Mona's husband, Paul, described as "an elegantly whimsical insurance executive," was completely in favor of what his wife and children did, and was sensitive enough to appreciate the rare quality their humanity manifested. Paul Dayton majored in romance languages at Stanford University, and taught for a while. He switched to the insurance business to make enough money to support a growing household.

Mona's daughter, Betsy, came home from high school with several classmates, including an exchange student from South Africa. A young student from Oregon, Robert McCready, a permanent guest, kept the coffee pot boiling at all hours. The Daytons

162

had known him in Oregon and since he was now enrolled in the University of Arizona, it would be ridiculous to have him live anywhere else except with them. Right?

When the rain let up, Mona and Bob McCready took me for a drive out to the mountains to show me the groves of giant cacti called Saguaro, which have grown in those foothills since time began. Mona was disturbed because thoughtless persons had shot holes in some of them. These plants live to be hundreds of years old. The Indians use the ribs of the Saguaro for their house building, and make preserves from the fruit of the plant.

It began to rain again and we ran for the car. When we got back to the Dayton "estancia" a fire was blazing in the fireplace, Paul was home from work, and Betsy and her friends were casting their youthful spell upon the place. Quietly, without much visible activity, cocktails were served and dinner was on the table. I told about the children singing "Happy Birthday" to me at the school. A few moments later, as we ate fried chicken and hot biscuits and honey, the parrot in the kitchen sang clearly, "Happy Birthday to you," and we all laughed.

Mona Dayton's philosophy is not a verbal thing. Her pupils and the members of her family are the benefactors of her joyful and creative wisdom. She writes: "An autobiography of me is one of the family. My physicist father had time to impart to us the wonder of the world we lived in. I was raised feeling the forces of centrifugal force pulling on energy curves; sound and light, and magnetism touching my ears and eyes and mind with the excitement, and beauty, and wonder of life. This I have tried to impart to my children, always blanketed with the security of love, so that as they grow old their understanding would engulf all others."

Her family lived by this. Mona's daughters Betsy and Kate went among the Papagos and lived and worked with them, teaching them and being taught by them. As Mona said: "Other Anglos don't enter Hogans, but our children did. Sheep herding, gathering and shaping stone, singing together, made peoples see together their sameness."

Other students who have lived with the Daytons in the past included Sandy Lookstwice, a Sioux Indian; Josefina, a Mexican girl; China, a girl from Argentina; and Christine, from France. "They gave us a new perspective, widened our culture," said Mona.

163

"Adequate persons are well informed. To be an adequate learning person one must discover oneself as a person of dignity and integrity. For students to learn to be useful as unique and different individuals, and yet relate as human beings, we need to organize schools and classrooms horizontally rather than vertically. Children are people. They grow into tomorrow only as they live today."

Mona made sure her students grew well.

* *

The winds blow across the Texas Panhandle day and night in a ceaseless dirge. You feel that they have been blowing since the dawn of creation, the cry of the cosmos. Elaine Ledbetter had attuned her lyre to this lonesome whine. She would live nowhere else. The Texas landscape left me with a sense of desolation, and I viewed it with melancholy detachment.

The high plains of Gray County in the heart of the panhandle, dotted with oil and gas rigs, and murky with a cloud cover of carbon black, have lost their old time wildness. Bat Masterson, Billy the Kid, Charlie Siringo and Kit Carson once rode this-a-way, south to the old Tascosa or north to Dodge City, Kansas. On June 27, 1874, a handful of buffalo hunters armed with Sharps rifles repulsed more than a thousand attacking Kiowa, Comanche and Cheyenne Indians, headed by a half-breed, Quanah Parker, in the Battle of Adobe Walls. In December, 1965, all seemed peaceful. There were no signs of war.

It was Sunday morning. I had taken a bus in Amarillo, and on the journey north to Pampa I was the only passenger. The names of passing towns amused me: "White Deer," and a sign pointing toward "Goodnight." I noticed many mobile homes along the way. Amarillo is filled with trailers. Many are manufactured or sold there, and I am sure old ones, like elephants, returned home to die.

Elaine Ledbetter was born Elaine Walker in Tonkawa, Oklahoma, May 28, 1917. As a little girl in Blackwell, Okla., she rode a pony to school. Later, her parents drove her to high school in a Model T Ford. Elaine graduated from the University of Oklahoma in 1939. She took her Master's at North Texas State College in 1954. She had attended summer sessions at the University of Arizona, the University of California, and the Oak Ridge Institute

164

of Nuclear Studies. She had been teaching chemistry at Pampa High School, Pampa, Texas, since 1940.

Like Lawana Trout, who was born in the same part of Oklahoma, Elaine had a favorite tree she visited for deep thoughts and urgent prayers. Disciplined by the harsh demands of a rough country, among older people who still remembered the dangers and hardships of frontier life, Elaine Walker developed the kind of character that faced up to all challenges of life. As she grew, the scant but poignant beauty of the lonely land stirred something within her. Out of this was born *Triumphant Moment*, a book of poems Elaine wrote and illustrated with her own photographs. She had her own photographic studio.

She published her second book of poetry after I visited her. She was also co-author with John H. Marean, of a book, *Matter and Energy, the Fabric of the Universe*, published in 1966. It was her poetry that impressed me at first, filled with anguish, regrets and bitter ashes—quite different from her daily activities and thoughts. The sadness in her life, it seemed, was contained between the covers of her two books of poetry.

Elaine Walker Ledbetter was also one of the top chemistry teachers in the Southwest, and had been much honored as such. I like to think of her as a poet. All teachers are not poets. Those who are have added a medium of expression and communication between their world and the world of youth. Sometimes, this is the strongest link of all.

Elaine Ledbetter had poise and sophistication. She believed in good grooming. The day I was there she wore a red dress and gold slippers and gold beads. She was tall, strikingly blonde, with a broad smile that played about rather full lips the moment you engaged her attention. Bill Ledbetter was an engineer with the Skelly Oil Company. He and Elaine lived in a somewhat paternalistic company-owned development called Skellytown, a few miles out of Pampa, near White Deer Creek, a branch of the Canadian River. Skellytown is a cluster of silvery, aluminum-coated refinery structures behind a high wire fence. The product is gasoline. You can smell it. A row or two of company-owned houses run close to the refinery structures. From the outside, they are unpretentious, and the lawns are small, but inside they are modern and attractive. The Ledbetters lived in one of the better houses.

It had a sizable library. These books were in three main categories: religion, science and poetry. Elaine was active in church work, and taught Sunday School. She bought a great many inspirational books for themes. She was such a deeply religious person there was really no separation of the spiritual life and the daily classroom involvement. She was a moral force seven days of the week. Her disciplined spirituality derived from exemplary conduct and quiet conviction rather than Bible-thumping oral expression. And with all this, she had a fine sense of humor.

Elaine and Bill had no children, and did not need extra rooms. They converted one room into her photographic studio. I saw there almost every piece of modern equipment needed for creative photography. Elaine was a fine photographer, and many of her friends had sat for portraits. The American landscape also appealed to her. She had a good file of black and white negatives, kodachromes and transparencies. She used much of this material for classroom work in school and church.

Pampa High School was in a large school district embracing 450 square miles. There were 1,250 students in the high school and 68 teachers. Even with recent new additions, the long-corridored, multi-storied building seemed overcrowded to me. Elaine Ledbetter's chemistry lab needed more space, more equipment and more supplies.

Elaine Ledbetter took a great interest in Texas and national science fairs, and always had a number of students preparing exhibits and papers. Her experience with one of these fairs inspired her to remake the science department at Pampa. She had accompanied one of her brilliant students, Malcolm Brown, to a science fair held in Los Angeles. She and Malcolm were amazed at some of the exhibits. Other schools in other parts of the country were far ahead of Pampa High School in programs and facilities. Elaine came back from Los Angeles determined to upgrade Pampa's chemistry department. She appealed for funds and equipment. The school board and the school officers gave her full support. Within a few years Pampa students, trained under Elaine Ledbetter, were winning high honors in statewide and national science fair competition. Her first prize pupil, Malcolm Brown, is now an assistant professor of botany at the University of Texas. Many other students of hers hold important jobs in industry and education.

166

Who are today's great teachers?

There were no lectures the day I was in class. Elaine had assigned some laboratory experiments. Everyone donned aprons and protective eyeglasses. The problem of the day dealt with extreme temperatures of certain chemical solutions. The class was to pool its findings. Elaine Ledbetter walked among the students, giving advice, answering questions, pointing out possible errors of procedure. She wanted the students to know what was happening, and why it was happening. She asked them to explain to her why certain changes were taking place. Her goal was to get them to do independent thinking and reasoning.

There was quiet concentration. Everyone seemed serious and inquisitive. When the bell rang, they did not rush out the door. They seemed reluctant to put away their equipment just on the verge of making new discoveries of old truths. I liked the deportment of these young people. They considered it a privilege to study chemistry under Elaine Ledbetter. She had a way of handing on to them the excitement of research.

"I believe students are lamps to be lighted, not cups to be filled," Elaine told me. "This has helped shape my teaching philosophy. I try to kindle a real desire to 'know' and then guide the student as he finds out. Helping him without telling him what to see is important, but not easy. I believe students want firm teachers, teachers who demand all the students can give them and then some. What a teacher demands should be made clear. Students like a teacher who is fair, and who can, on occasion, relax a rule. I try to teach and test for understanding and comprehension, not for facts alone. I try to show my students how to attack and solve their problems with the tools at hand. Their experiences establish confidence in their ability to meet a new situation and conquer it. The teacher must constantly increase the complexity of the experiences."

She continued later: "Students today are knowledgeable and receptive. If you can meet their steady gaze and know in your heart you are what they think you are, and that you are giving them the best instruction possible, that you are not deceiving them, then you need have no concern about your value as a teacher in our modern society. But if you are putting up a front, preaching one set of standards and living another, if you are concerned with petty detail while overlooking the broader field of concept develop-

167

ment, then it is time to take a second look at yourself as a teacher."

To unlock the mysteries all around us we need to have a few keys. Chemistry is a key. Poetry is a key. Elaine Ledbetter used them both well.

* *

Robert Arnold, 37, and his family, lived in a modest home a few blocks from the Lincoln Hills Elementary School in Richfield, Minn. As you entered the house you were greeted by a friendly hound named "Fritz," who wore a perpetual look of sadness. He was actually a very happy dog; he belonged to a hunting family.

In two rooms of the Arnold home hung an assortment of rifles and shotguns, alongside bows and arrows. Quivers of arrows were everywhere—each arrow tipped with a lethal steel point strong and sharp enough to sever the arteries of a deer. Bob's wife, Diane, and their three sons were experts in the use of bow and arrow. So was Bob. They could kill a cottontail on the run. Bob was an amateur taxidermist, and in one room of the house was the head of a deer he killed with bow and arrow.

In spite of a roomful of weaponry, Bob Arnold was also a conservationist, and wished to protect our wildlife. In the summertime, the Arnolds went to their cabin at Detroit Lakes, Minn. They fished for pike and did a lot of canoeing. They loved the wilderness.

Bob was born on a 440-acre farm near Hawley, Minn., in June, 1929, at the very beginning of the Great Depression. He won 4-H honors and became a leader of youth. He went to Moorhead State Teachers College, and part of his college expenses were paid from money he made on a herd of prize Herefords he had started back in his 4-H days. He married his hometown sweetheart, Diane Swenson, in 1950. He hoped to get a Ph.D. someday and teach in college. He had his MA from Moorhead State.

Schools, like teachers, accept whatever money they can get. Richfield, Minn., is geographically a part of the Minneapolis sprawl, but has a separate municipal government. It is an independent enclave. The part of Minneapolis immediately north of Richfield is zoned to prohibit the granting of liquor store licenses. Richfield has no such restrictions, and the neighboring residents of Minneapolis buy their liquor from friendly Richfield. The town government controls the sale of liquor and gets the proceeds: a net profit of half a million dollars a year. The money is used to build and maintain schools and parks.

Arnold's classroom was filled with books, assorted charts and wall decorations that are the standard equipment wherever I go. Current news clipped by the pupils filled one bulletin board. There was a telescope pointed, as Bob kiddingly remarked, not at the heavens, but at the girls in the playground of the parochial schools just across the street. A section of a cottonwood tree, reluctantly cut down to make way for a new hospital, leaned on one wall. It was 13½ feet in circumference. The pupils counted its rings to determine its age.

As part of the arithmetic lesson, Arnold had one boy read a report on the moon, its distance from earth. Bob took the chance to describe the work of Michigan scientists who spent several days listening in day and night shifts, for intelligent sounds from a distant planet. They had the most sensitive instruments for this experiment. Arnold told of efforts to formulate a simple code by which we could transmit or receive messages from outer space. Suppose we sent back sound impulses in even groups such as 00 0000 000000, and got back bleeps in odd units such as 0 000 00000? This might show intelligence and would be proof of life on other planets. Sixth graders got excited about the ways of reaching other beings.

Training for citizenship on this planet was an important part of Bob Arnold's teaching. The day I listened in on his teaching, he was instructing the pupils in local, state and federal government. Each child had a chart giving the names of chief executives in the state and the names of Minnesota members of Congress. These had to be memorized. Arnold gave a short quiz on government. He wanted his pupils to appreciate the meaning of "community," "state" and "nation," not in abstract terms, but in their daily lives. He chose a novel way of dramatizing a public meeting, and of teaching parliamentary procedures. He selected three boys and three girls and placed them in chairs forming a circle at the front of the room. Each had a rubber ball of a different color. One boy bounced his ball in the center of the floor and another boy caught it (anyone can pick up an idea that is tossed into the discussion); one girl kept catching all the balls and holding them (too much hogging of discussion by one person); everyone tossed the balls

169

back and forth at random (free exchange of ideas). The teacher would stop the play to explain what was good and what was bad. Everyone got the point.

Later, groups of pupils went to the school library to draw up bills for an imaginary session of the Minnesota legislature. Arnold had given careful instructions on the wording of bills and how to present them. The bills covered auto safety, taxes, education, state parks and other things pupils and parents should take active interest in. The judicial system was a subject of classroom discussion. Arnold cited violation of laws and ordinances and asked the class to tell him whether they should be tried in a municipal court, district court or supreme court. The pupils soon began to understand the degrees of guilt and innocence, crime, punishment and legal jurisdiction.

Arnold dominated his classroom. He stood tall and commanding like an army officer in civilian clothes. With his crew cut, his glasses, his scholarly manner, he looked like a university man doing a bit of practice teaching in an elementary school. He was not soft. He had a vein of steel. Arnold worried about the development in small schools of materials and supplies for good teaching, and the growing improvement in the quality of the teachers themselves. He saw a lack of communication between elementary and junior high schools, and between junior and senior high schools. "Sectioning off education is not possible, and it's not always obvious we are working together," he insisted. Arnold wanted more cooperation on every level. He also thought counseling should begin on the elementary level. He said to me: "If today we know everything there is to know about teaching children, tomorrow we will be ten years behind. All too often children are thrown on the educational conveyor belt, presently traveling at a tremendous rate of speed, lucky just to hang on, let alone acquire knowledge. Yet, by some miracle, they do learn. They are screened, sorted, graded and grouped like so many potatoes and dumped into so many social bins. Some will bring a top price, most will stabilize the market and others will perish where they are."

The day I was in Lincoln Hills Elementary, I had several talks with John Bleedorn, the principal, a down-to-earth educator. He didn't agree with all of Bob Arnold's ideas (including counseling), but confided that he had hand-picked him for the job and had

170

worked closely with him for 11 years. "I'd like to see more men like Bob teaching in our elementary schools," Bleedorn said. "Fathers are no longer leaders as they once were and as they still should be. They have defaulted. Children too often make decisions in the home. This is ridiculous. Many children find in a strong masculine teacher like Bob Arnold the father image they have lost at home. The teacher, in a way, replaces the father as a moral and intellectual leader. Personally, I incline toward strict discipline and a more formal and traditional classroom atmosphere. Bob is all for a more informal, relaxed intellectual climate. He runs a loose class, but not a permissive one, and he gets results. I cannot quarrel with the results. His pupils respect him. His 'no' is a father's 'no' and you can imagine what this means to children from unhappy, or broken homes, who need love and guidance and who want to know right from wrong."

Bleedorn and Arnold sharpened their ideas on one another. They respected one another's views. There was a strong bond of friendship between them, which allowed healthy disagreement from time to time. Neither would have respected a "yes" man.

Bleedorn was full of quips and questions on education. "We need educators and not businessmen for our top school planning. Some school officials could stand a bit more knowledge of humanities. The public is way ahead of educators most of the time. School board members and superintendents around the country are older people for the most part and are thinking of education as they once knew it, maybe forty or fifty years ago. They have to fight constantly the conservatism and tradition they find in themselves. If school boards had been more aggressive we would not have needed federal aid."

I spent some time with the Arnold family after school was out. Bob, a restless man off campus, discussed with me quite seriously the war in Vietnam. It worried him. He was in the U.S. Air Force during the Korean War. How are teachers going to explain the Vietnam impasse to school children? Teachers like Bob Arnold have the intelligence and perception to do it.

* *

Brain damage causes the mind to shrivel before blossoming. The tree has life, but bears no fruit. If you are an educator work-

171

ing with hopelessly retarded children, you have to develop new insights, new frames of reference. What we consider the normal classroom situation does not prevail in schools created for the care and instruction of mentally retarded children. In such a school, in such an atmosphere, pedagogy has to be raised to a high level of spirituality, for where the mind cannot be reached the soul must be sought.

I found such a teacher. I found such a school. This encounter was a memorable and chastening experience. I write about Mrs. Syble Hopp, principal of the Donovan School, Green Bay, Wis., with deep humility. I hope to convey some of the character and compassion of Joseph Donovan, the founder of the school, the humanitarian who discovered Syble Hopp and gave her a lifetime's challenge.

For many years, Joseph Donovan was superintendent of schools of Brown County, Wis. He knew every teacher in the county, hired most of them, watched their progress. He spent 45 years of his life as an active school administrator, and for many of those years he was appalled by the lack of a program, and by the lack of facilities, for educating mentally retarded children. He was also appalled by the parents of such children, who sometimes kept them chained to their beds or hid them in institutions.

In those days, few parents agreed with Joe Donovan that there ought to be special classrooms for these neglected children.

Before his retirement, Joe Donovan made other plans. He rented a room off the school grounds and persuaded two teachers in Green Bay to devote a few hours a week to children who might otherwise receive no education at all. A demand for such instruction developed rapidly. Some of the best known families in Brown County came to Joe Donovan and asked: "What can we do? Is there someone who can help us? What will happen to our children who cannot read or write or tie their shoes?"

Joe Donovan was thinking about his little program the day Syble Hopp, who had been teaching in the rural and small town elementary schools for a number of years, dropped into his office for a chat. She had an outgoing personality, a deep love for children. "I knew she was the teacher I had been looking for the moment she walked in," Joe Donovan recalled. Mrs. Hopp told the story this way: "After spending three hours in Mr. Donovan's

172

office discussing mental retardation and the need of a proper school for children of low mentality, I told him I would like an opportunity to teach in such a school. I also told him I had no special training in the field, but would like to take some instruction somewhere. He reached for the telephone and put through a call to the St. Coletta School for Exceptional Children in Jefferson, Wis. This is where President Kennedy's sister was sent, and where she remains to this day. It is one of the best schools in the country. Mr. Donovan arranged that I spend the summer there, working with mentally defective children. I learned a great deal, and in the fall I returned to Green Bay to become the first teacher of the mentally retarded in the Brown County school system."

She continued: "A room was rented in the Howe School, and 12 children enrolled, some educable, some trainable. Except for the training and the confidence I gained from the Sisters of St. Coletta's, I could not have handled these children, nor could I have met the challenge they presented. Before the year was out, three more children came to class, and soon there was a long waiting list. Many parents, instead of keeping their mentally retarded children from us, now willingly placed them in our hands. Our little school was a success. They were the happiest children I ever taught. For the first time in their lives they were getting love, attention and understanding in the classroom. They no longer had to compete with children far above their mental level. They said: 'I love it here. No one laughs at me.' After this first year, I knew I wanted to devote the rest of my teaching career to helping these unfortunate, but lovable, children."

As I walked through the Donovan School, I could see visible evidence of a dream come true. The school was housed in a large, modern building in spacious acreage just at the edge of Green Bay, where city ends and farmland begins, and the Fox River winds its way. There were nine teachers and two aides. Ninety children were brought here each day in buses driven by carefully selected men who knew how to handle children of low mentality. These men often remained at the school building and helped out with maintenance, food procurement, custodial and other services. I never saw a school like this one. It was love-powered from top to bottom.

The Donovan School was part of the county school system, and was not a private school, even though it appeared to be one

173

at first. It was Joe Donovan's creation. Syble Hopp had the tools to help build it.

Syble took her pupils to the bowling alleys, to a new swimming pool, to weekend campouts. Once a year, she invited about 20 of her older students to a pajama party at her home. Some of the other teachers acted as chaperones and counselors, and Syble's husband, Harley Hopp, helped out. None of these social gatherings was ever a part of the lives of these children until Syble Hopp took over. "I feel social skills are of utmost importance in their lives," she said. "Learning by doing is the most effective way of teaching these children. I hold annual parties for them at Christmas and at Easter in the dining room of one of our leading stores. This gives the children a chance to learn social graces. The public knows about these parties, and there is a wider and wider acceptance of the fact that mentally retarded children are among us in greater and greater numbers and that we must absorb them into our life as human beings with souls like our own. My exposure of these children in public places has produced a climate of understanding and sympathy, and where the desire to help is expressed, the means to help is always found."

Syble Hopp had a splendid group of teachers working for her. She had known all of them for years. The whole school ran smoothly. It was tidy, immaculate, sweet-smelling. It didn't have that institutional odor of disinfectants and poorly ventilated kitchens.

I spent a soul-searching day among these unfortunate children. Most of those in Syble's classes were in their teens, two or three were 20 years old or more. One or two boys were big enough and strong enough to play football in a city that made football famous. But they couldn't write their names on a piece of paper, and they spent hours rubbing their hands together with no apparent reason. They cut pieces of colored paper into strips and pasted them together. Good-natured smiles came easily. They loved being together, away from homes that were lonely prisons to them and they loved being with Syble Hopp and with Joe Donovan, the quiet man who dropped in to see them every day.

The day I visited, the Donovan School planned a trip to one of the local lunchrooms. Syble Hopp thought it would be a break in the routine to take all the kids to a public eating place once a

174

week, give them a few cents to spend, let them place their own orders, talk to the waitresses and learn simple manners other children learn. Syble and I and several pupils rode in the school bus to the restaurant. We were the first to arrive. Different bus drivers brought in other pupils from more distant areas of the county. Cheers and greetings went up as new arrivals came in, bundled up in their winter clothes. Each child went to his or her particular booth or seat, for these weekly visits had established a sort of "seating order" among them. Joe Donovan joined us. Coca-cola and ice cream sticks were the popular items ordered. Since each student was spending less than a quarter, there was a limit to what he could order. The kind woman who was in charge of the lunchroom knew all the retarded children by name, and had a few friendly words for each as bills got paid. The customers who had dropped in for coffee seemed to understand the situation and did not stare at the children or show any resentment over their takeover of the premises.

Syble Hopp's method was to keep these children busy and keep them together. The retarded cannot stand more than two or three hours of instruction a day. Companionship, equality, love, attention—these are things the retarded need most of all. To Syble, who had a deep religious conviction, these young people were God's creatures. Believing this, everything she did fell neatly into place.

One thing that surprised me was the dancing. Syble stopped all activity for a few minutes each day, played a record of soft music, and everyone danced. The pupils paired off haphazardly, youngest with oldest. All wished to dance with Syble. There was no boy with boy, girl with girl, sometimes boy with girl, tall with short, shyness. Big boys who had been stroking their hands or cutting out paper strips suddenly came to life and started dancing. They showed surprising grace and agility. Music seemed to unfreeze their inhibitions.

Later that day I went to the gym and watched some of Syble's students performing on the trampoline. Adding the "tramp" to the gym equipment was a fortunate stroke. Syble got it by her persuasiveness. She made speeches, and the money and equipment poured in. She also got an old-fashioned, four-wheeled popcorn machine the school used. The Green Bay civic clubs found it and

175

donated it. Joe Donovan told me that Syble spent much of her free time bringing the message of the school to local clubs. She often showed colored slides of the work being done, and her description of the students and their needs and fears often brought tears to the eyes of her audience.

"I have children in my class who are 20 years old, and they cannot read or write," she told me. "I spent one year just trying to teach a boy to remove his shoes and socks and put them back on, a miracle his parents could not teach him to perform. I have worked with some of my pupils for 11 years. I do not want to turn them loose in a world that does not understand them."

You cannot let the physical aspects of retardation get under your skin if you plan to work in this field. Some of the children are marred with the traits of mongolism—the flat face, stubby nose, slanted eyes, fat and soft skin, open mouths and stubby fingers. I noticed that several of Syble Hopp's pupils had these characteristics, the girls more than the boys. One or two of these girls were in their late teens, but seemed more like 12-year-olds. They took quite a fancy to me, becoming coy and flirtatious, much to Syble's amusement, and she later said this was good for them, for I brought them out of their shells and overcame their shyness. Accepting a stranger as one of the group made their day more enjoyable.

Consciousness of making a hit with the out-of-town visitor was not absent with the boys either, and many sought my smile of approbation or the friendly touch of my hand on their shoulder. One unforgettable exchange went this way:

"I'm Jim," said a boy with an engaging smile. He held out his hand to me. The ritual of shaking hands brought him great joy. "I'll tell Uncle Will I saw you." Many times that day Jim reintroduced himself to me, and repeated the ritual. Later, I watched him shave himself with an electric razor. He was old enough to have whiskers. He wanted me to run my hand over his face.

"All gone," I said. "Nice and smooth."

"I'll tell Uncle Will I saw you."

A big boy who did nothing but put plastic rings on a peg for an hour at a time stood in front of Joe Donovan when the school day ended. It was as though the boy, a big hulking fellow, was trying to look through the window of the soul. Joe Donovan never twitched a muscle. The boy saw something he liked. This was a

176

ritual between them. I knew it for what is was—wordless understanding, mental therapy, something deeper than pedagogy. Joe Donovan's nod to me seemed to say as much.

Syble Hopp, as principal of the school, had many administrative duties, but she took time to teach about 30 trainables, those with IQs of about 30. Other teachers handled 60 educables, those who can read and write and progress to a point where they will be able to earn a living. Syble's pupils will never fit into society. She was teaching some of the girls to sew, make beds, iron shirts, and do simple cooking. Some of the boys were being taught to wash dishes and help with other chores in the school's big, modern kitchen. With supervision and kindness, two or three boys might be taught to mow lawns or rake leaves or carry wood.

Syble Hopp was born October 5, 1918, one of 12 children. She always wanted to be a teacher. She attended the State University of Oshkosh, where she got her BS degree, and then went to Eastern Michigan University for her MS in special education. When it became clear that the Donovan School would have to have a psychometrist to test each new student, Syble went to the University of Minnesota and obtained a psychometrist's license. She was qualified to give each child at Donovan the individual evaluation so necessary to program planning for a child-centered curriculum.

Syble talked of school and the children: "I believe every child has a right to an education regardless of mental capacity, rate of maturation or ability to adjust socially. Until a few short years ago, the trainable child was forgotten because he could not compete with his normal brothers and sisters in school. Society must recognize the trainable child's hidden potentialities. These potentialities must be developed to the fullest extent. Each child, regardless of mentality, can make a contribution to the common welfare and to his own happiness. Parents have the right to expect some type of education for each child born to them. The public school should be informed of the needs of the mentally retarded child. Visitors should be wholeheartedly welcomed to view activities and learning situations in the classroom. The teacher must know the child's home environment. That means frequent visits and consultations. Most parents realize in situations involving the mentally retarded that the teacher knows best because of intensive training."

Are these almost helpless children to be abandoned by a society

177

that places a premium on personal success? The late Albert Giacometti, a Swiss sculptor who was always testing life's values, gives the answer: "In a burning house I would save a cat before a Rembrandt. Life has more value than art."

* *

Heavy snows had fallen during the winter and Glens Falls, N.Y., was like a Currier & Ives print the January night Harold Long drove me and Mrs. Burke from the Queensbury Inn to his home on Monroe Street. The Longs had a house in a neighborhood of white clapboard, two-story, turn-of-the-century houses built for large families. This would have made an ideal setting for Eugene O'Neill's Ah! Wilderness or Thornton Wilder's Our Town. Any one of the streets could have been renamed, "Nostalgia Lane." As we drove to his home, he gave a running historical commentary on the civic monuments, old homes, important families.

The Longs lived in a gracious New England tradition. Their Monroe Street home had just the right amount of heirlooms, and the comfortable lived-in look of an old house. Books and magazines were much in evidence, not neatly arranged, but left where last read. A steep stairway took you to Harold's den, piled high with books and manuscripts and the trappings of scholarships. Strong-smelling pipes were there to reveal Harold's worst habit, a habit Carolyn, his wife, deplored but could do nothing about. On his desk was an article he was writing about India's poet, Rabindrinath Tagore. Everything about Harold Long—his office, his home, his loose-fitting clothes, his mannerisms, his mind—suggested the college professor. He had the professorial touch, even to the seeming inner compulsion to guide conversation towards worthwhile subjects. He was so absorbed in his work he never quite found time enough or words enough to explain it to you as he walked back and forth.

A fire was blazing in the fireplace in the Long's living room. The logs were renewed and poked by Mrs. Long, a native of Peachem, Vt., and a fireplace tender by habit. Her 92-year-old mother, Mrs. Martin, stooped but beautiful, brewed tea for us. Harold and Carolyn Long went to Peachem every summer to enjoy with Mrs. Martin her ancestral home filled with many memories. Harold Long had the instincts of a historian when it came to delving into the ancestry of any place he loved. The editor of the Glens Falls *Post Star* wrote in commemoration of "Harold Long Day" (Oct. 19, 1964): "We also wish that Harold Long will one day do the definitive history of Peachem, Vt. It simply has to be a best seller."

Harold Long was a teacher of history at Glens Falls High School, a post he had held since 1930. That was a remarkable tenure, but other teachers have taught as long. What catapulted Harold Long to fame and a nomination was his outstanding work as director of the ITWA program in the Glens Falls public school system. "ITWA," as Harold called it, was an educational experiment of vast potential known as Improving the Teaching of World Affairs. (For the best account of this program, see the booklet, *Improving the Teaching of World Affairs, the Glens Falls Story, Bulletin No. 35*. National Council for the Social Studies, 1964.)

Harold Long initiated this program in the Glens Falls schools. It was a unique experiment. It served as a pilot study for other schools at home and abroad. Since 1957, Harold pointed out to me, 225 foreign observers have come to Glens Falls to see how the program works and to participate in it. ITWA was so well known, many United Nations delegates, arriving in New York City for the first time, would ask, "How do you get to Glens Falls, New York?"

The ITWA program featured integrated teaching units. The elementary school as well as the high school was oriented towards world understanding. The art classes arranged to have children's art of other countries sent to Glens Falls for exhibition. Foreign language classes often had lessons from foreign visitors. Machine shops used tools manufactured in other countries, and the students studied the engines of imported automobiles. Business classes learned about foreign currencies, foreign business terms and forms. Social studies classes made trips to the UN and invited UN delegates to visit Glens Falls. Biology classes familiarized themselves with the World Health Organization. Journalism students subscribed to the Manchester *Guardian* and London *Times* and several French and German newspapers and magazines. Harold Long, as director of ITWA, coordinated all this study, and had committees working on a world-centered curriculum. The traditional American subjects and interests were not overlooked, but each student was constantly reminded that fellow students in other lands have equal

179

NOT FOR GLORY

problems and equal rights and the same desire for freedom and the good life. Putting oneself in the other fellow's shoes was the core of ITWA.

You may ask the question: "So, don't all American high schools strive to promote world understanding? What's so special about Glens Falls?" The basic difference, as I saw it, was that Glens Falls High had a full-time director of its ITWA program, and had deliberately integrated each teacher, each classroom and each level of the public school system into the ITWA concept. An unfriendly school board, a reactionary principal, a rebellious faculty could undermine and destroy an ITWA program elsewhere. There had to be a unanimous and coordinated drive towards an idealistic goal to make something like ITWA come off.

I attended two of Harold Long's classes. He got right down to business. He threw questions at his students on current affairs, the day's newspaper headlines. He tried his best to get them to think clearly, express themselves correctly. Fuzzy answers got turned aside. He gave quick written tests. He knew instantly which students were doing their homework, and which ones were not. All in all, his classroom performance was traditional, competent, serious, but in no way spectacularly brilliant or different. His true leadership was displayed in his almost day-long involvement in the work of the other teachers. They beat a path to his office; he was in a position of power and prestige. The younger teachers regarded him as "professor."

I toured the high school with him. "The teachers designed this building," he said. "That is why it is so functional. We have our library on the second floor next to the English department and the humanities. We have the music department at the opposite end of the building, and separated from the other departments by the gymnasium and the auditorium. This deadens sound. Our auditorium seats 1,500 persons. We made it larger than any other auditorium in town so that plays and concerts would have to be held here, and that would bring people to the school, which their tax money helped to build. We have more than 8,000 books in our library, and that does not include textbooks. I maintain my own library of material on foreign countries. I also keep on file hundreds of pamphlets on the United States, and I get requests for them from people all over the world. Part of the function of ITWA is to

180

disseminate information about any given country to all other countries in need of such information. The printed word is a bridge between peoples."

Harold Marshall Long was born in Utica, N.Y., on August 30, 1905. He attended the Utica public schools and took a BA from Colgate University in 1930; he got his MA in 1934 from Columbia University. Harold was of medium height, with a graying crew cut, and glasses. He liked loose-fitting sports jackets of the tweedy sort, and the smell of the pipe was upon him. He was full of energy, preferring to stand than sit, even while teaching, and would rather walk than stand still.

Among other academic exploits, Harold had been a John Hay Fellow in 1961 at Williams College, and a participant in the White House Conference on Education. He had given summer teacher training lessons at Harvard, Syracuse, Colgate, and Boston Universities.

William L. Bitner, III, superintendent of schools in Glens Falls, had a large office, insulated against the intruder. To see him, I had to get past a battery of secretaries and administrative aides and assistants in a separate building across the street from the high school. Once I got inside Bitner's executive suite, he was most generous with his time. His desk had no paper work on it. All I saw was a rack of pipes. "I have other teachers," he said, "who can do as good a job in the classroom as Harold Long. He isn't the kind of teacher students get chummy with. He's too serious for that. But they respect him. Harold is a genius at organization. When I am looking for someone to carry through a program, I call on Harold. If I ask him for advice, he speaks his mind, even when he does not agree with me. He is absolutely honest. He is so much a part of the ITWA program I worry about our being able to carry it on successfully after he retires. Without him, it would never have got off the ground. In the beginning, it almost died for lack of funds, but Harold went downtown and coaxed bankers and heads of foundations to lend financial aid. They had faith in Harold and they put up the money."

It took bold imagination, raw courage and an unrelaxing follow-through to create and maintain an ITWA program. It was so much easier to abort a project like this and let it die.

Because of Harold Long, Glens Falls, with a population of

18,000, bustles with visitors from foreign countries studying the ITWA program, and a turban or sari, fez or ceremonial robe causes hardly a ripple on the streets. How much did this city admire Harold Long? When "Harold Long Day" was proclaimed, Oct. 19, 1964, by Mayor James E. Wallace, it was not something the school officials had promoted or even thought of, but a spontaneous outpouring of love and esteem by the citizens themselves.

That's a lot of esteem.

* *

Mona Dayton was selected by the committee as Teacher of the Year, and I was given the happy privilege of calling her on the phone and breaking the good news to her, but swearing her to secrecy. LOOK photographer Charlotte Brooks and LOOK writer Dan Chapman flew out to Tucson to do the story, and they spent almost a week with the Daytons.

At the White House ceremony at noon, April 5, the Cabinet Room was packed. Only Mona and Paul and Betsy had been cleared originally as the members of the family authorized to attend, but at the last minute the whole family was admitted. Paul, Jr., had flown in from the University of Washington, Eli and his wife, Dena, had come down from New York, Kate and her boyfriend had come in from Providence, R.I., where she was a student at Pembroke College. Even the boy, Robert McCready from Oregon, who lived with the Daytons was at the White House. The newly nominated Commissioner of Indian Affairs, Robert L. Bennett, was present, along with John W. Gardner, Secretary of Health, Education and Welfare, Harold Howe II, U.S. Commissioner of Education, Mrs. Sarah Folsom, Arizona's Superintendent of Public Instruction, and others. Our party filled three black limousines.

Mona presented President Johnson with a beautifully bound scrapbook of greetings addressed to him from her first grade pupils. The first one showed the President riding a bucking horse at his ranch. This gave the President, visibly worried about the worsening situation in Vietnam, his biggest laugh of the day. One little boy had written: "Mr. President, what do you do with all that money?"

In his presentation talk, President Johnson said, among other things: "We are here to honor a woman who makes democracy work. She is a soldier in the greatest and the most glorious battle that man has ever fought—the battle for truth and the understanding that alone has set man free ... She has taken the great outdoors of Tucson as her classroom, and the great desert as her desk. She has taken the animals as her teaching assistants, and she has taken nature and beauty by one hand, and boys and girls by the other, and she has made them dance together in a happy circle of understanding and respect."

At the luncheon given for Mona, she told members of the press how she taught first graders. It was a speech that brought tears to some listeners. In it was some of the magic that had impressed me so much the day I visited her classroom.

John W. Gardner, Secretary of Health, Education and Welfare, and Harold Howe II, U.S. Commissioner of Education, were present at the White House ceremony. They continued to lend moral support to the National Teacher of the Year Award, even though the U.S. Office of Education no longer co-sponsored it. Missing from the scene was John Lloyd of the U.S. Office of Education, who had set up the White House appointment for us for many years. This important function now fell to Dr. Edgar Fuller, Executive Secretary of the Council of Chief State School Officers, and to Miss Blanche E. Crippen, the council's Assistant Executive Secretary.

CHAPTER SEVEN

"... I am mainly concerned with helping boys and girls discover the power and beauty of their own voices with all the life enrichment that means. The purpose of my professional life is to give the students' lives direction and purpose. I want my students to avoid the blunders of ignorance, hatred and injustice. In the mobile society in which we now exist, a teacher's influence on the lives of his students may be felt someday in any area on earth. Thought of in this light, teaching is almost a frightening responsibility...."

ROGER TENNEY

1967 NATIONAL TEACHER OF THE YEAR

ROGER TENNEY
Music
Owatonna, Junior-Senior High School
Owatonna, Minnesota

RUNNERS-UP

GENE DOTY
Science
Hillsboro Union
  High School
Hillsboro, Oregon

MRS JAMES
  HERLONG
English
Saluda High School
Saluda,
  South Carolina

JOHN K.
  MOULTON
Mathematics
Brookline High
  School
Brookline,
  Massachusetts

PAUL G.
  PLANTICO
History
West High School
Green Bay, Wisconsin

1967

There was an added significance to my meeting with mathematics teacher John K. Moulton, in Brookline, Massachusetts, just before the Christmas holidays in 1966. He was the fiftieth teacher I had interviewed in the seven years I had been associated with the National Teacher of the Year Award.

Naturally I wanted my landmark interview with Moulton to stand out, and he more than came up to my expectations. The setting was just right, too, for the Boston area is an educational shrine in itself. Here was founded the first public school in America, April 13, 1635. The statue of Horace Mann stands in front of the State House on Beacon Hill, facing Boston Common. It has been said that nearly 100,000 students are currently attending colleges within a radius of three miles from Boston's Copley Square.

Brookline is a wealthy, independent enclave surrounded by urban Boston. It broke away from Boston in 1705 and still has annual town meetings, although its population is more than 53,000. John F. Kennedy was born in Brookline, and his influence is felt everywhere, including the high school, which named a room after him. Brookline High School is operated on the house system in order to arrange its 2,277 students into four manageable house groups of about 600 students each. It enjoys the reputation of being one of the best high schools in the United States.

Tall, thin, sports-jacketed and bow-tied John Moulton looked for all the world like a Harvard professor as he explained the intricacies of modern mathematics to keen-minded seniors who would have intimidated with their brilliance any teacher lacking Moulton's background and competence. He was a master teacher in every sense of the word. He and Martha Zelinka had co-authored with

187

George B. Thomas, Jr., professor of mathematics at M.I.T., one of the best manuals of recent years, *Elementary Calculus From An Advanced Viewpoint*. Professor Thomas is regarded as the top authority in his field in New England.

Moulton won and held the respect of all his students. With his thinning hair, rimless glasses and professorial bearing he created a classroom atmosphere of authority tempered with kindness and human dignity. His artist's hands were thin and long-fingered and he handled chalk like a painter. When he addressed a student he looked him straight in the eye, but always with a gentle smile breaking or about to break and his words were freighted with encouragement and approbation, never with ridicule or depreciation or impatience. He had a little speech habit of tossing in a quizzical *n'est-ce pas?* when he made a point or validated a theorem.

I told John Moulton that I knew little about math. "Feel free to walk out of my classroom when you have had enough," he said sympathetically. I did not walk out and I was never bored. It was sheer delight to watch a master at work, to scan the faces of students caught up in the excitement of revelation as new ways to solve old problems were discovered and tested. The intellectual byplay between teacher and students was easy to follow even when not fully understood, as in my case. You saw the bold student advance when he spotted something vulnerable in the teacher's statement, ready to cross swords with him; then you saw the feint, the rapier-like thrust of the teacher as he exposed some lack of logic in the student's thinking, and then you saw the good-natured retreat of the presumptuous neophyte—a little battle of wits enjoyed by the whole class. Sometimes the challenger won a victory which Moulton encouraged. He did not wish to crush the spirit of challenge and inquiry so necessary for mental growth.

Sometimes he would ask a student to share the spotlight. One boy walked to the blackboard and demonstrated, step by step, a rather complicated problem in calculus, stopping to explain everything with the aplomb and skill of a full fledged teacher. It was a virtuoso performance in mathematical artistry and I saw John Moulton's face light up when the lad put down the chalk and walked back to his seat. A Moulton-trained student usually found college a little easier for in a real sense he received college-level instruction, and the attitudes that went with it.

188

Who are today's great teachers?

Moulton's greatest contribution, according to Brookline High School's headmaster, Dr. Bertram H. Holland, was his pioneering efforts in setting up Advance Placement Mathematics programs in high schools in close cooperation with the New England colleges and universities most of his students later attended. A New Englander by birth and temperament (he was born in Hartford, Conn., July 8, 1914), Moulton graduated from Harvard University in 1936. He took his Ed.M. degree there in 1940 and his A.M. degree at Bowdoin College in 1962. He told me that his father was a mathematics teacher, the best he had ever studied under. His grandfathers on both sides of the family were teachers, so he grew up in a genteel atmosphere of learning. In June, 1937, John Moulton married a Brookline music teacher, Miriam Hoagland, and they had two grown daughters and two grandchildren. Miriam was a warm, outgoing person with a lively wit. John was more reserved, but his gentlemanly manners and quiet charm, and above all his intellectual integrity, soon revealed the inner man. He wore well. He was solid.

He and Miriam looked forward to their summers at Chebeague Island in Maine where they lived the simple life. In your mind's eye you saw John scraping the hull of his beloved boat, tinkering with a kerosene-fueled "fridge," fetching water from an old well, or picking wild berries for dinner.

Moulton, like all other good math teachers, had to make rapid adjustments to the new science which had sprung up during the 1960's as a result of space exploration and a preoccupation with nuclear energy. "I knew that I would have to go back to school and tool up for the new science," Moulton said to me. "I had to learn new methods and test new theories. To survive, I had to keep on growing. I decided to keep abreast of my times. What I have learned I feel obligated to pass on to others. The classroom is still the best forum. I could make more money by doing research for big industry, but I would miss the rewards and challenges of classroom teaching." To make ends meet, John taught several evenings at Lincoln College, Northeastern University. In the summer following my visit he was scheduled to teach mathematics at the Portland branch of the University of Maine, not too far from his retreat at Chebeague Island.

As Moulton put it: "Teaching, like mathematics, is an open-ended field. You never know all the answers, or indeed, all the problems. Much of the material we are teaching now will be out of date in the next decade. Thus we are as much learners of mathematics as we are teachers of mathematics. The medium through which the teacher approaches his task is his subject matter. If he does not know his subject well, and present it with genuine enthusiasm, he will be ineffective. One also teaches by precept and by example. The teacher is transmitting to the next generation his attitudes towards his country, the arts, learning, and towards his fellow man. In this respect his value to our country far transcends whatever subject matter he may impart. But still the subject matter is basic; unless it is taught effectively, the rest is lost." This, it seemed to me, got to the very heart and core of education. A lot of John Moulton's character was compressed into those few short sentences. To quote reams of testimonials from his admiring colleagues and pupils would only obscure this sharply drawn portrait. He was simply a monumental reality in the crowded halls of Brookline High School, a school that sends 80 percent of its seniors to college.

Moulton was training some of his pupils to program material for a computer system operated by the Massachusetts General Hospital. Experts in data processing came over to the high school to explain the use of the computers. The instruction was informal and no credit was given, but a few exceptionally bright math students got a headstart on college courses in space age electronics by familiarizing themselves with computers. Moulton was the most eager learner of all. With his experience and sensitivity and perception he could instinctively set greater and lesser areas of difficulty for each of his classes, ranging from a seminar of 8 to a class of 32 pupils. I watched him adjust the tempo of his teaching to class levels and individual levels. Many of his students were exceptionally bright. Here, I knew, were students and teacher worthy of each other.

* *

Shortly after my arrival in Saluda, South Carolina, Mrs. James Herlong and her husband picked me up at my hotel and drove me to the annual Christmas party held by the members of the local school board. This enabled me to meet the whole educational establishment in an informal way, but since religion was the underlying theme of the evening's program, I felt almost as if I were sharing an experience I had not earned. I was blanketed with the warm hospitality South Carolina traditionally bestows upon its guests, and when I met many of the same people at the high school the next day I felt at home.

Mrs. Herlong, "Bela" to all her friends and associates, sat next to me at the dinner table and to my left sat high school principal, Boyce Todd. My presence brought everyone to the happy realization that this pretty woman was South Carolina's Teacher of the Year nominee. I have learned to distinguish between the "love" instantly generated for a teacher by a community for my express benefit and the genuine affection which needs no priming. Bela Herlong was genuinely loved.

Find a good teacher and you turn up a success story. Ruby Euela Padgette was born July 29, 1931, and on the lips of children "Euela" became "Bela," and so it had been ever since. Her father owned a cotton farm near Saluda and her mother taught in a country school. Bela had to help with the farm chores. Her family had a tough time during the Great Depression, and the state had to pay her mother in bonds instead of cash. When Bela's sister Madaline enrolled in Winthrop College these bonds were accepted as tuition money. Bela also attended Winthrop College, earning her way by tutoring. In the summers she worked in a factory. She was always at the top of her classes but found time to be active in athletics, campus social life and church work. She graduated from Winthrop College in 1951, *magna cum laude*, winning the Sylvan and Tillman awards for highest academic average and most extra-curricular achievements. Bela took her master's degree in English at the University of South Carolina in 1965, doing her thesis on one of the South's great novelists, Ellen Glasgow.

In 1951 Bela Padgette married James E. Herlong of Saluda who had been a pilot in the U.S. Air Force during World War II. By 1952 Jimmie was back in the service because of the Korean War and Bela came back to Saluda to await the birth of her first child, James Edmund, Jr. Later, there was a daughter Madaline and another son, William. After the war Jimmie bought a dairy farm near Saluda, and Bela devoted all her time to teaching and going to school.

191

I enjoyed my day at school, sitting in Bela's English classes, watching her at work. To my surprise she opened the school day with a prayer—her own and somehow it did not seem as "unconstitutional" as I had been led to believe. From her it sounded just right. The first class was taken up with readings from Shakespeare's *Macbeth*. The second class was absorbed in a masterful interpretation of Thornton Wilder's *Our Town*. As Bela read lines from these plays South Carolina suddenly seemed a part of Macbeth's castle in Scotland and Grover's Corners in New Hampshire. The transfiguration of a standard school assignment into a sublime work of imagination is teaching at its best. You recognize this artistry when you see it. Like Lawana Trout, Bela Herlong had a sense of mission. It was a deeply spiritual motivation, never fully defined as such but something subtly apprehended.

You can't visit a South Carolina school without thinking of other people and other dreams. Principal Boyce Todd put it this way: "We are offering our Negro students in Saluda freedom of choice. They can attend any school they like, the only stipulation being that Negro boys and girls who enroll in the high school originally built for white students must meet our high academic requirements. We will not lower our scholastic standards. There's a lot of good will in this town, and we are determined to give every boy and girl the best education possible." Bela Herlong would subscribe to that last statement.

Bela Herlong expressed her teaching philosophy in these words: "Life is all around me in the four walls of my classroom— throbbing humanity—each child an individual looking for his place in the world . . . I want my classroom to be an exciting adventure where each child feels free to share his experience, where he can grow by helping to plan the work, where he reaches forward ever grasping a new idea or a challenging assignment, where learning is a search and where he feels the fulfillment that comes through accomplishment.

"I look upon the tragedy, comedy, valor and truth, the courage, constancy, heroism and failure which blend into the pattern that is the teacher's life. There is the tragedy of a child closed to the world, shut up in a box of his own making but rebelling and seeing a way out. There is the comedy of a classroom incident. Then there is the palpable valor of a boy crippled by cerebral

192

palsy, a boy struggling to live in a school designed for people who walk and run. Not so evident is the quiet valor of the boy who has worked hard to win the prized position, but who says with sincerity, 'I'm glad you won the award; you deserve it.' I see the heroism of the girl who dares to say, 'I will not go; I will not be a part of something I know is wrong just because everyone else is doing it.'

"Then when I see the hard thin line of truth emerge; I see students grasping for the first time what truth means and knowing for the first time that in the final analysis each individual must discover truth for himself. I wonder at the courage of the lone Negro boy who dares to face an alien environment because he wants a better chance; I see his look of thankfulness when I speak to him—a voice breaking through his world of silence.

"Sometimes students come to me from unlovely homes where they are unloved. Because I teach English, the broadest course in the whole curriculum, I can open to them a whole world of loveliness in books—the world of man's search for truth. And because I love and respect these students, I can open up another world for them—a world in which they can respect themselves for what they are.

"Literature, drama, poetry, language itself—these are my tools; with these I try to show these developing human beings how man has recorded his fears and his sorrows and that they are not unique in feeling that life is too much for them at times. I can show them that all men have been interested, delighted, scared and puzzled by life and that literature is one form into which man has translated his thought.... I must help my students to live in the real world; no society is ideal and no individual is ideal. I must help each learner to accept himself, both his limitations and his potentialities, while at the same time I am helping him to accept his society—its greatness and its faults. If I do these two things, I have helped him to become a better citizen because he is a more aware person. I teach not so much appreciation as understanding because I believe that appreciation which may come with understanding can never come without understanding.

"I feel that I must live what I teach ... I hope that my life and my actions demonstrate the things that I believe."

Bela Herlong with her black hair and lovely face, her disciplined dynamism, her neat figure and her genius for being dressed just right for every occasion, was the epitome of charm. It was her total personality that cast such a spell over you.

I got the impression that her students knew that they were getting something extra out of her teaching. The golden years pass quickly. Bela Herlong knew this. She wasted no time. She carefully rehearsed in her own mind the messages she wished to convey and she related her instruction to life in ways so vivid and meaningful there was never a moment of boredom in any of her classes. The bells rang all too soon. The breathless quality of the shared experience is education's finest hour.

Because of Bela Herlong, English was the most popular course in Saluda High School. The proficiency of her teaching, in ways that can be measured, was much higher than the state average.

She identified with her students. Many of them came from lower income groups and had to work on farms and in factories. She had done this kind of work. She knew the price one must pay for a college education. She knew the cultural pull of large cities far from home and the nostalgic pull of the little corner of America where one grew up. The "Ridge" country of South Carolina, where peach blossoms and loblolly pine scent the air, was her inheritance. When her retired father bagged a quail he sent word: "Come out and share a bird with me." She knew much more than that would be shared. His wisdom had been a never-ending source of strength and inspiration to her. Teachers dip into many wells, and are themselves fountains.

Mrs. Nell Taylor, student counselor, told me: "College students come back to Saluda and tell Bela they got more out of her classes than they got in college classes. She made them feel more important in the scheme of things."

* *

On the plane from Chicago to Green Bay, Wisconsin, sat big Jim Taylor, one of the star football players of the Green Bay Packers. Everyone recognized him and asked for his autograph. The thought came to me that any teacher in this football-minded town who could make the newspaper headlines along with Jim Taylor and Bart Starr would have to be truly outstanding. I was about to visit such a teacher, Paul Plantico.

194

Who are today's great teachers?

No city in the United States had come up with Teacher of the Year finalists two years in a row, but Green Bay had just achieved that distinction. I had fond memories of my visit with Mrs. Syble Hopp, principal of the Donovan School who was doing such a tremendous job with retarded children. One year later, I was awaiting my first meeting with finalist Paul Plantico, teacher of social problems, Russian and world history at West High School.

I was joined in Green Bay by Jay Laurence Taylor, LOOK's manager of education services, who wanted to sit in on one of my interviews and actually see a Teacher of the Year finalist at work. A former college teacher himself, Jay turned out to be an excellent observer and we combined our notes for a joint report.

Jay and I drove out to West High School, crossing the frozen Fox River. The air at eight degrees below zero was exhilarating, and the streets lay blanketed under a new layer of snow. There was a hubbub in the high school as an urgent call to Mr. Plantico went out over the intercom. This was the first day back after the long Christmas holidays, the toughest teaching situation for a man under observation. We told Paul Plantico this and pretty soon he was teaching in high gear as usual. Good teachers inspire that extra effort. The first class was in economics and Paul presented the basic economic theories of the Soviet Union and compared them with theories of the capitalistic countries of the West. A few years ago many communities would have fought the introduction of one or two of Plantico's courses on the grounds that they were "un-American." "Why should anyone go to school to learn about Communism?" The Green Bay school authorities, to their great credit, recognized the fact that one of the prime goals of education is an informed citizenry. An objective look at what was going on in the Soviet Union, Red China, Latin America and Southeast Asia had to be taken at the high school level. To tell a boy that he need not bother to learn about Communism and then send him to Viet Nam to fight a war involving Communist forces didn't make sense.

West High School used the "modular" system of class scheduling that combined a maximum degree of individual instruction with the greatest possible flexibility of program. It did away with the so-called "study hall." There were three, hour-long sessions, one 90-minute and one 30-minute each week rather than five equal blocks of one hour each. Seminars were conducted in Plantico's courses under a rotating student chairmanship. Debate was encouraged and basic parliamentary rules were politely observed under the watchful eye of the teacher.

Paul Plantico attended Marquette University in Milwaukee, Wisconsin, from 1944 to 1948, earning his bachelor of philosophy degree there and he took his MA degree at the University of Wisconsin in 1949. From 1962 to 1963 he attended the University of Chicago on a John Hay Fellowship. For himself, his wife Lois and their four children (there were later five) the year in Chicago was the most rewarding one of their lives. They took full advantage of the cultural opportunities Chicago afforded and lived in one of the poorer districts with several Negro families as neighbors. The evening Jay Taylor and I spent in the Plantico home in Green Bay, a home reflecting the good taste of its occupants, will remain in our memory as a place of love and laughter. The well-behaved children captivated us.

Paul Plantico met and married a teacher, Lois Belonger, in his home town, Two Rivers, Wisconsin. He was born there on January 10, 1925. The Planticos were a close family, and his closeness was reflected in Paul's teaching. Principal George Dauplaise put it this way: "It seems Paul always treats each of his students as if they were his own sons and daughters, and they respond to this quickly."

Among other things, Plantico coached debate. His teams had competed four times in state finals at Madison. The value of debate was quite clearly demonstrated in Plantico's seminars. The boys and girls who carried the burden of the discussion, who phrased their questions and answers the best, who pronounced words correctly in the firmest manner, were members of the debate team. They had learned to overcome self-consciousness and they did not mumble their words in tones so low as to be indistinct.

In Paul Plantico's classes, the half-hour period each week (called the "cultural thirty") was spent listening to musical and literary recordings. The day we visited him he played a record of Tchaikovsky's *1812 Overture*, after presenting a fine analysis of its historical background and musical content. Mr. Plantico also supervised the audio-visual program at West High School. Films were delivered to his office, thirty or forty a week as a rule, most of
196

them on a free rental basis from the University of Wisconsin. He pointed out that teachers were completely free to choose film subjects as often as they liked. Films and other devices got flicked on as part of cultural aids used during the shorter periods of the modular system. Listening to good music was a change of pace enjoyed by teacher and pupil alike, but in Plantico's case the music tied in with curricular subject matter.

Paul Plantico always wanted to be a teacher. He stated his philosophy in these words: "Each of us, each generation, has the responsibility to preserve and perpetuate the knowledge and wisdom we have inherited from those who lived before us. Man has now reached the stage where nuclear war threatens the human race. Equally terrifying is the fact that technology threatens to strip man of his humanity, to draw from him all tenderness and love and compassion, the very qualities that through the ages have made him human. History is one of the guides into this uncertain future. A knowledge of the past can provide us with perspectives on the future, an understanding and appreciation of the noble heritage of free men, and a vision of the kind of world it lies within man's power to create."

* *

The first big snow of the season fell upon Owatonna, Minnesota, the day I arrived. But no schools closed. In Minnesota, in January, snow is a way of life. I walked through drifts of it in a pair of galoshes I had borrowed from Teacher of the Year candidate, Roger Tenney, a strapping six-footer who wore size 12 shoes.

Roger Tenney was director of vocal music at the Owatonna Junior-Senior High School. It would be difficult to imagine a teacher being any better at this job than Tenney. He had the perfect training for it as well as the perfect temperament. When he was a student at nearby St. Olaf College in Northfield, Minnesota, he studied under a leading choir director, Olaf Christiansen, and sang for two years in the famous choir which has made this relatively small college known throughout the world. Tenney told me of his debt to his great teacher Christiansen, but he also said this: "Each choral director must have his own style, and he must fit his teaching to the needs and talents of his students. To produce a choir good enough to travel around the country and appear before

197

critical audiences it is necessary to be highly selective. In the old days we admitted everyone to the choir. We do not discourage anyone who wishes to sing and I may give individual singing lessons to a hundred students a week, but to put together a senior choir of eighty singers of concert caliber, I may have to select them from one hundred and fifty students. A good choir is a delicately tuned instrument, requiring coordination of many trained voices."

From the moment his first class began I knew I was watching a great teacher at work. In his case I did not have to wait until the day was over before making an appraisal. Certain qualities manifested themselves the moment he took charge of the classroom situation. Poise, competence, confidence and leadership—you sensed all these things immediately. Tenney was a born actor—he had had leading roles in several musical comedies in summer theater —and his total personality hits you suddenly and movingly like the opening of a Beethoven symphony. "I am mainly concerned with helping boys and girls discover the power and beauty of their own voices with all the life enrichment that means," he said to me. "The purpose of my professional life is to give the students' lives direction and purpose. I want my students to avoid the blunders of ignorance, hatred and injustice. In the mobile society in which we now exist, a teacher's influence on the lives of his students may be felt someday in any area on earth. Thought of in this light, teaching is almost a frightening responsibility."

Roger Tenney was born in Litchfield, Minnesota, July 7, 1930. When he was sixteen he was asked to direct a local choir, and from that day on he knew that he was going to become a music teacher. Roger graduated from St. Olaf College in 1952 with a Bachelor of Music degree. It was not until 1959 that he took his Master of Music Education degree at the University of Colorado. When he left St. Olaf College he went into the U.S. Army and was stationed at Fort Riley, Kansas. The camp needed an organist for religious services, so Roger kept busy playing for Jewish, Protestant and Catholic servicemen. As chaplain's assistant he found himelf writing letters for the illiterate members of the Fort Riley detachment. The realization that these men could not write the simplest letters to parents and sweethearts and wives affected Roger Tenney deeply, and he was more determined than ever to take up teaching. He took his first teaching job at Mountain Lake, Minnesota.

198

Who are today's great teachers?

While there he conducted a two-hundred voice choir and fifty-piece orchestra in an annual production of Handel's "The Messiah."

In 1956 at the University of Colorado, he met an Oklahoma girl, Ethel Humphrey, who was also a teacher. They had leading parts in the play "Carousel." Roger told Ethel about his teaching job at Mountain Lake. The principal at Mountain Lake had once promised him: "Find the girl you want to marry and I'll see that she gets a job in my school." After meeting Ethel, Roger wired back: "I've found the girl."

They were married, went to Mountain Lake and Ethel was hired as school librarian. Later she got a job teaching. The Tenneys had three daughters, Diane, 7, Christine, 6, and Sharon, 4, and they completely won my heart the two days I was in Owatonna. Both Roger and Ethel were active in the Trinity Lutheran Church. Roger directed the church choir which had several of his students in it, and Ethel was active in teaching and building-fund activities.

I learned a lot of details about choral work the day I spent in Tenney's classroom. The middle of the floor was kept clear, for the teacher needed lots of room. Tenney was tall, athletic and extremely agile (in spite of those big feet of his), and he moved back and forth, rocking now on his toes, now on his heels, sliding, bending, gesturing, sometimes with fiery emphasis, sometime with gentle pleading, his eye movements eloquent, his nods crisp and final, his hands alive with nuance and instruction, his verbal punctuation perfectly timed.

Tenney put his senior choir through a muscle-relaxing set of exercises before a single note was struck. Each singer massaged the neck and shoulder muscles of the person in front of him. They breathed deeply. Everyone jumped up and down to get the blood circulating from head to toes. Tenney was always saying, "Sing from your toes on up. Put your whole body and soul into it, like a Negro choir singing those wonderful spirituals. You ought to take more gut exercises. Exercise your diaphragm as you walk along the street. Breath through your nose. Warm air relaxes tension, and nose breathing is warmer. Support the tone! Support the tone! No choir singer has ever broken a lung."

After a weak response Tenney would drop his head and shoulders to imitate a state of lassitude or weak effort: "That was a supreme example of blah!" he would say. "Get with it. Remember,

199

sing from the toes on up. Sing as though you were marching in a victory parade of some kind. But loudness is not enough. Quality. That's what we're after. Quality."

Sometimes he would run back to the back row and place his ear next to the face of a singer giving a lukewarm performance. "Let me hear that again!" There was immediate improvement. When one of the members of the choral group practiced directing, and everyone in a Tenney group got to practice leading the others, Tenney went back and joined the choir and sang along, following the directions of the student leader. The whole class then criticized the student director's poise, choice of music, hand and eye movements. Sometimes a whole hour was devoted to playing records, with Tenney stopping the disk from time to time for discussion and interpretation. The day I was there I heard selections from Smetana's *The Moldau*, Schoenberg's *Transfigured Night*, Respighi's *Pines of Rome*, and Grofé's *Grand Canyon Suite*.

"With a thirty-hour week coming we have to be able to fill our leisure hours with something that will satisfy our cultural needs," Tenney told his pupils. "Why not music? Music is omnipresent. We spend one quarter of each day listening to it one way or another if we include TV commercials. It is necessary to cultivate your taste. You ought to be able to get beyond 'Twinkle, twinkle, little star' and 'Batman.' Cultivating your own voice enlarges your capacity to appreciate music. With a little time and patience I can teach anyone to sing. The human voice is an unsurpassed instrument, and most people never learn to use it properly. That's why all of us are here today. We want to discover our own voices."

Tenney-directed choral groups were much in demand throughout the year. Fame came quickly. The Governor of Minnesota had requested that Tenney's entire senior choir from Owatonna High School be flown to Seattle for the World's Fair in 1962. Tenney herded the choir to Seattle, and it performed brilliantly. Each December a group of choral singers from Tenney's classes, calling themselves "The Carolers," and dressed in authentic Elizabethan robes, sang for two or three weeks before Christmas, in the public park, in homes and hospitals. They made a special point of visiting shut-ins, an emotional experience which broadened their sympathies.

The Tenneys lived in a very comfortable home in the most

desirable new section of Owatonna, and their house was open to members of the high school choral groups. Students often dropped by to play games and sing with Roger at the piano. Sometimes they met at the house to work out plans for an out-of-town concert, or some school event.

After school hours Roger Tenney's office was also open to any of his students who had personal problems. Most of these problems had nothing to do with music, but these boys and girls respected Roger Tenney and knew that they could talk to him about anything that bothered them. He was one of those rare human beings who could absorb the other person's burdens without seeming to add to his own, and his kindness and understanding had a therapeutic effect on teenagers in trouble. The moral force of a teacher like this is incalculable.

Roger Tenney had the character to take everything in stride. He was quite humble about the whole thing as we talked on the long ride to the airport, and he told me about some of his own problems, goals and setbacks. That very day his wife Ethel had taken the last of the cobalt treatments that had cured her of a rare disease, cancer of the vocal chords. Sometimes in this life it takes a lot of courage to sing!

* *

On a bright Sunday morning, January 8, 1967, I was driven from Portland, Oregon to Hillsboro, through the lush Tualatin Valley, perpetually green. After the blizzard in Minnesota the sunlight seemed warm and relaxing, and I was beginning to feel kindly toward teacher Gene Doty even before I met him. My night flight out to Portland had been rather spectacular, for around midnight I saw the Northern Lights from my plane window. All my life I had wanted to see this phenomenon, and there it was, the whole show, and I had a front row seat!

Hillsboro, Oregon, is a small town, and I explored all of it that lazy Sunday afternoon. The stores were closed, no people stirred, the streets were empty. A banner was stretched across the main stem of the downtown area and on it, in huge letters, were these words: "CONGRATULATIONS! GENE DOTY TEACHER OF THE YEAR." I knew I was in the right town. I have a recurring nightmare in which I show up at the wrong school, in the wrong town in the wrong state. To zero in on the right target after thousands of miles of jet travel always strikes me as being a miracle.

Monday morning I was at the high school bright and early, and I recognized Gene Doty right away from a photograph I carried in my attache case. He was short, plump and gave me the impression he was slightly stooped, perhaps from bad posture induced by years of slumping over examination papers, typewriters and writing desks. He shuffled along like Tennessee Ernie Ford with a casual air the very opposite of the stiff professional stance affected by some pedagogues. He added the impression of being completely at ease and having fun, even when working. We got along together from the start.

Gene taught chemistry mostly, but other science subjects when necessary. As head of the science department of Hillsboro High School, he liked to keep abreast of new ideas not only in chemistry, his special field, but also in physics and related subjects.

Nebraska-born Gene Doty liked the outdoor life. He and I walked briskly from the high school to his home, car distance to most people. We stopped to admire a giant redwood tree that I was surprised to see growing so far north. He and his wife Mary Helen and their two sons, Richard (13) and Steven (10), loved to go on camping trips to the sea and mountains every summer. They just piled everything into the station wagon and took off, and they seemed to be a happy-go-lucky family, one for all and all for one. Gene wrote a lot, even on vacations, in order to supplement his meager income. "I barely have time to keep the winter dandelions off my lawn," he said.

Gene Doty was a weekend journalist. When he was not teaching he was writing a column called "Chalk Dust" for the Hillsboro *Argus* (this local newspaper had a full page of pictures of Doty in his school laboratory the day I was there), and he edited a science teacher's sheet called "Hear Now," and "The Oregon Science Teacher," the official organ of the Oregon Science Teachers Association. He also wrote chemistry manuals and was planning a chemistry textbook, which he outlined for me. His articles for learned science journals were "straight" with none of the humor he loved so well, but in his more relaxed compositions, he delighted in "corn" and faculty lounge banter. He had a slight touch of Mark Twain, Will Rogers and Ring Lardner in him, and had he gone into jour-

202

nalism as a profession, he might have become a syndicated humorist.

He had written more than half a hundred magazine articles, popular as well as scholarly, and most of them had to do with chemistry.

"What's the best textbook in chemistry?" I asked him.

"Mine, if I ever get around to writing it," he said with a smile. "There is a great need for a simplified chemistry textbook, one with phonetic devices to reduce all those long and unpronounceable chemical terms to short and sensible ones. It is utter nonsense to foist all this jaw-breaking jargon upon high school kids."

I had never run across a teacher who used as much classroom humor as Gene Doty. Everything he said had a pun, a quip or some other humorous turn to it. It was a deliberate attempt to use humor as a teaching device. I asked him about this. Here is his defense of the method: "It seems to me there is an incongruity about almost everything, given time to find it, and if a student can appreciate the humor in something he has demonstrated an awareness of the situation's basic content. The funny statement or incident is remembered longer than the duller expression and the more stereotyped situation. That's my theory at least. I like puns, for they require a maximum of mental agility to appreciate. Jokes, parodies, burlesques—all can be fused into a course to provide relief from drudgery. Why separate work from fun?"

Gene Doty was born in Omaha, Nebraska, October 8, 1928, and after his family moved to Oregon in 1943 he went to Lewis and Clark College where he took his B.S. degree in 1951. He earned his M.Ed. degree there in 1954. He did graduate work at Syracuse University, Reed College and the University of Redlands. When he got out of the Army in 1951 he began his teaching career at Canby, Oregon. He was there for seven years and when I met him he had been teaching at Hillsboro Union High School for seven years. He felt he might have to go into college teaching or into the research department of some big industry eventually because he needed money for a new home. He and his wife had been living in a rented house, and Mrs. Doty had been working as a secretary in the local hardware store. When the Chamber of Commerce held a luncheon for Gene Doty after the mayor had proclaimed January 6, 1967 as Gene Doty Day in Hillsboro, he was presented with $300 in cash. A teacher's lot is not an easy one. It is always heartening to go into a town and see it solidly behind a favorite teacher.

There were 1,435 students in Hillsboro Union High School, and eighty percent of them came to school in regular school buses. Doty said it cost thirty-seven cents a mile to operate the buses, and since many students live 24 miles away the transportation costs eat into the budget. In his column, "Chalk Dust," in the Hillsboro *Argus*, Doty liked to cite statistics of this kind in an effort to make the citizens aware of what they are paying for with their school tax dollars. He had set out singlehandedly to educate the public as to what schools were for and how they could be best used. He deserved much credit for this.

Gene Doty believed that students should be taught to investigate for themselves the interesting things in life and education which lie a little to the right or the left of the beaten path and the textbook. Independent thinking comes from making one's own opinions, not from waiting for them to be handed down by a teacher.

"I want to be fair to my students," Doty said. "I believe each child is worthwhile in his own right. But I want my students to recognize that I am a person a community of adults has chosen to impart education to their children. The decision as to what is to be studied in the class is mine, not theirs. My employment is a reflection of the community's confidence in my judgment, and for me to abdicate this to the 'democratic' whims of a class population is tantamount to encouraging anarchy. A classroom should be a teacher-dominated situation, and permissiveness has its limitations. I believe that children want guidance. It seems my prime function, as a teacher, is to build up a set of attitudes towards learning which will persist after the facts have changed."

In a lighter vein he said at the town luncheon in his honor: "A teacher is one who spends all day helping other people's kids grow up, and then comes home and can't understand his own children. He spends his life helping kids get more knowledge than any generation in history, but can't remember to bring home a loaf of bread. He teaches his students to romp through set theory, cellular metabolism, the intricacies of the economic theory, chemical bonding, but can't balance his own check book. He spends hours meticulously planning his classwork, and then goes on a camping trip

204

Who are today's great teachers?

with his family and leaves the tent at home. He spends hours marking papers, and then tries to avoid crying openly when he sees the fruits of his labors used as scratch pads for a game of tic-tac-toe."

* *

April 19, 1967 was a cool day in Washington, D.C., but the sun broke through the clouds at high noon for the Teacher of the Year Award ceremony in the Rose Garden of the White House. For Roger Tenney of Owatonna, Minn., this had to be the brightest moment of his teaching career. On this day he was given national recognition for his achievements.

The day before the ceremony began there was an impressive send-off in Owatonna. When it had been announced that the Owatonna High School Choir was going to Washington at the request of President Johnson, parents raised almost $10,000 in three days to charter a plane to carry these eighty boys and girls to and from the nation's capital. Ninety percent of them had never been on a plane before.

Tenney and his choir were constantly busy in Washington. Tenney was asked to direct a performance of the Howard University Choir, which he did with great aplomb, even without benefit of rehearsal. On the day before the ceremony, he and his choir gave an evensong concert at the Washington Cathedral. Last year's winner of the National Teacher of the Year Award, Mrs. Mona Dayton, of Tucson, Arizona, sat beside me during their performance of Bach's *Jesu Priceless Treasure.*

The climax, of course, was the presentation at the White House. The top-ranking Minnesotan, Vice-President Hubert H. Humphrey was there, in good humor and looking fit after his trip to European capitals. Several members of Congress from Minnesota were on the portico steps facing the Rose Garden when President Johnson emerged from his office and strode briskly to the podium. Facing him on risers were the 80 robed members of Roger Tenney's Choir who sang with great enthusiasm for their President and their teacher.

When the first song was ended, President Johnson walked across the narrow strip of lawn and shook hands with some of the girls in the choir who were standing in the first row. Two or three girls wept, and the President blessed them with a fatherly smile.

Both Johnson and Humphrey were moved by the young singers. When they sang "Let There Be Peace on Earth," arranged by Tenney, which contained the injunction "And Let it begin with you," President Johnson praised the performance but added with a grin, "And thanks for the message." Obviously no political overtones had been intended, but the President's remark brought a ripple of laughter.

Before the ceremony the guests mingled in the Rose Garden. Roger Tenney's wife Ethel and their three children, Dianne, Christine and Sharon, made an instant hit with everyone. Vice President Humphrey walked over to chat, complimenting them on their pretty dresses and white gloves. Later, President Johnson asked that the children be brought up to the portico steps to be near him. He leaned down and asked them questions, and this was the newsworthy moment the television cameramen had been waiting for. You could hear them grinding out footage. This was the human interest picture the newspapers carried.

That day, and all during his visit, Roger Tenney felt the gravitational pull of instant celebrity. After the whirlwind of activities in Washington he was received graciously at City Hall by Mayor John Lindsay of New York who invited Roger and Ethel to visit Gracie Mansion and meet Mrs. Lindsay. On Sunday night Roger was introduced on the Ed Sullivan Show. A large reception greeted him when he returned home to Owatonna.

As I shared with Roger Tenney the excitement generated by the National Teacher of the Year Award I thought of the long road I had traveled and the many excellent teachers I had met since that day in November, 1960, when I interviewed the first of the fifty-four teachers whose lives were to be forever linked with mine. Marietta, Georgia, where it all began in the office of Mrs. Sherman Lee, was now seven years and over 100,000 air miles behind me. I could close my eyes and re-create the sights and sounds, the words, faces and atmosphere of those adventures in friendship. My microscopic examination of fifty-four separate school systems encouraged me to believe that nothing in American life can match the vigor and importance of the classroom confrontation of minds. Therein lies our future. There is no turning back. The kinds of teachers I met are not content to look upon education as something finished. No teacher, no American, can afford that luxury.

Catechism
of the
Catholic Church

MODIFICATIONS
from the *Editio Typica*

Libreria Editrice Vaticana

First printing, January 1998

ISBN 1-57455-166-3

INTRODUCTION

On September 8, 1997, Pope John Paul II formally promulgated the *editio typica* (the definitive Latin language edition) of the *Catechism of the Catholic Church*. The next day the modifications to the original editions, published in the various modern languages, were made public. The modifications are intended to bring the texts of the modern language editions into conformity with the Latin text. This booklet contains the modifications to the English language text published in the United States in 1994 in trade editions and in 1995 in mass market editions. The numbers in bold preceding each of the modifications correspond to paragraph numbers in the original editions of the *Catechism*.

MODIFICATIONS

NOTE: The insertion of new footnotes is indicated in the text with the symbol ^{NT}, or when there is a series of such, with the symbols ^{NT1, NT2} etc.

Par. No.

57   Eliminate the phrase in the first sentence which reads "entrusted by divine providence to the guardianship of angels" as well as the reference in footnote 10 to Dt 4:19 and 32:8.

Thus, the sentence will read:

This state of division into many nations is at once cosmic, social, and religious.

10 Cf. *Acts* 17:26-27.

88   Add the words "or also when it proposes, in a definitive way, truths having a necessary connection with these."

Thus the paragraph will read as follows:

The Church's Magisterium exercises the authority it holds from Christ to the fullest extent when it defines dogmas, that is, when it proposes, in a form obliging the Christian people to an irrevocable adherence of faith, truths contained in divine Revelation or also when it proposes, in a definitive way, truths having a necessary connection with these.

Also add cross-references: 888-892, 2032-2040.

108   The first part of this paragraph is to be changed to read as follows:

Still, the Christian faith is not a "religion of the book." Christianity is the religion of the "Word" of God, a word which is "not a written and mute word, but the Word which is incarnate and living."

116   Add a cross-reference to paragraphs 110-114.

118   In footnote 87, after giving the Latin text of the couplet, add the reference:

Augustine of Dacia, *Rotulus pugillaris,* I: ed. A. Walz: Angelicum 6 (1929) 256.

134   This paragraph will appear as follows:

All Sacred Scripture is but one book, and this one book is Christ, "because all divine Scripture speaks of Christ, and all divine Scripture is fulfilled in Christ" (Hugh of St. Victor, *De arca Noe* 2, 8: PL 176, 642: cf. ibid. 2, 9: PL 176, 642-643).

240   This paragraph will appear as follows:

Jesus revealed that God is Father in an unheard-of sense: he is Father not only in being Creator; he is eternally Father in relation to his only Son, who is eternally Son only in relation to his Father: "No one knows the Son except the Father, and no one knows the Father except the Son and any one to whom the Son chooses to reveal him."

335   Cancel the reference in this paragraph to the Roman Canon: that is, the words "in the Roman Canon's *Supplices te rogamus* . . . ['Almighty God, we pray that your angel . . .']."

Thus the first two sentences of the paragraph will read:

In her liturgy, the Church joins with the angels to adore the thrice-holy God. She invokes their assistance (in the funeral liturgy's *In Paradisum deducant te angeli* . . . ["May the angels lead you into Paradise . . . "]).

336   Change the reference to "From infancy" to "From its beginning until death."

Thus the first sentence will read:

From its beginning until death, human life is surrounded by their watchful care and intercession.

398   Change the third sentence from "Created in a state of holiness" to "Constituted in a state of holiness."

Thus the third sentence will read:

Constituted in a state of holiness, man was destined to be fully "divinized" by God in glory.

627   The second sentence of the paragraph is to be modified to read:

But because of the union which the person of the Son retained with his body, his was not a mortal corpse like others, for "it was not possible for death to hold him" and therefore . . .

The final sentence of the paragraph is to be modified to read:

Jesus' Resurrection "on the third day" was the sign of this, also because bodily decay was held to begin on the fourth day after death.

So the entire paragraph will appear as follows:

Christ's death was a real death in that it put an end to his earthy human existence. But because of the union which the person of the Son retained with his body, his was not a mortal corpse like others, for "it was not

possible for death to hold him"ᴺᵀ and therefore "divine power preserved Christ's body from corruption." Both of these statements can be said of Christ: "He was cut off out of the land of the living," and "My flesh will dwell in hope. For you will not abandon my soul to Hades, nor let your Holy One see corruption." Jesus' Resurrection "on the third day" was the sign of this, also because bodily decay was held to begin on the fourth day after death.

NT *Acts* 2:24.

702   The second part of the paragraph is to be added to in the following way:

By "prophets" the faith of the Church here understands all whom the Holy Spirit inspired in living proclamation and in the composition of the sacred books. . . .

708   In the second sentence cancel the words "the letter of the."

Thus the first two sentences will read:

This divine pedagogy appears especially in the gift of the Law. God gave the Law as a "pedagogue" to lead his people towards Christ.

723   In the second sentence, cancel the words "With and. "

So that the second sentence will read:

Through the Holy Spirit, the Virgin conceives and gives birth to the Son of God.

833   Add to the first sentence the words "first of all" before the word "the diocese."

Thus, the first sentence will read:

The phrase "particular Church," which is first of all the diocese (or eparchy), refers to a community of the Christian faithful. . . .

And add to footnote 313 the canons of the CCEO 177, 1; 178; 311, 1; 312.

So that footnote 313 will appear:
Cf. CD 11; CIC, cann. 368-369; CCEO, cann. 177, 1; 178; 311, 1; 312.

875   Change the sentence which presently reads:

"From him, they receive the mission and faculty ('the sacred power') to act *in persona Christi Capitis.*"

This sentence will read:

From him, bishops and priests receive the mission and faculty ("the sacred power") to act *in persona Christi Capitis;* deacons receive the strength to serve the people of God in the *diaconia* of liturgy, word, and charity, in communion with the bishop and his presbyterate.

879   Expand the first sentence of the paragraph to read as follows:

Sacramental ministry in the Church, then, is a service exercised in the name of Christ. It has a personal character and a collegial form.

911   Cancel the words *"in solidum."*

916   Change the opening words of the paragraph from "The religious state" to read:

The state of consecrated life . . .

921-
922   The title which appears between paragraph 921 and 922 is to be changed to read:

Consecrated virgins and widows

922   Change the paragraph to read:

From apostolic times Christian virgins[NT1] and widows,[NT2] called by the Lord to cling only to him with greater freedom of heart, body, and spirit, have decided with the Church's approval to live in the respective states of virginity or perpetual chastity "for the sake of the kingdom of heaven."[461]

The footnotes are as follows:

NT1 Cf. 1 *Cor* 7:34-36.
NT2 Cf. John Paul II, *Vita consecrata* 7.
461 *Mt* 19:12.

1014   Add the word "ancient" before "litany of the saints" so that the paragraph begins as follows:

The Church encourages us to prepare ourselves for the hour of our death. In the ancient litany of the saints, for instance, she has us pray:

1141   In this paragraph the text from *Lumen Gentium* 10 in the first sentence is to be given completely, so that it reads:

The celebrating assembly is the community of the baptized who, "by regeneration and the anointing of the Holy Spirit, are consecrated to be a spiritual house and a holy priesthood, that through all the works of Christian men they may offer spiritual sacrifices."

1170   Change the sentence which begins "The reform of the Western calendar . . ." to read as follows:

Because of different methods of calculating the 14th day of the month of Nisan, the date of Easter in the Western and Eastern Churches is not always the same. For this reason, the Churches are currently seeking an agreement in order once again to celebrate the day of the Lord's Resurrection on a common date.

1184   Change the first part of this paragraph to read:

The *chair* of the bishop *(cathedra)* or that of the priest "should express . . .

Add a cross-reference to paragraph 1348.

1256   Change the second sentence which reads "In case of necessity, any person, even someone not baptized, can baptize, if he has the required intention" and omit the phrase in the third sentence which reads "and to apply the Trinitarian baptismal formula."

These sentences will be changed and a footnote added:

In case of necessity, anyone, even a non-baptized person, with the required intention, can baptize,[NT] by using the Trinitarian baptismal formula. The intention required is to will to do what the Church does when she baptizes.

The footnote to be added will read:

NT CIC, can. 861 § 2.

Also add cross-references to paragraphs 1239 and 1240.

1261   Add a cross-reference to paragraph 1257.

1281   Change the final part of the paragraph which presently reads: ". . . seek God sincerely and strive to fulfill his will, are saved even if they have not been baptized. . . ."

The phrase should read:

. . . seek God sincerely and strive to fulfill his will, can be saved even if they have not been baptized. . . ."

1289   Substitute the final sentence which presently reads:

"In the West, *Confirmation* suggests both the ratification of Baptism, thus completing Christian initiation, and the strengthening of baptismal grace — both fruits of the Holy Spirit."

This sentence should read:

In the West, the term *Confirmation* suggests that this sacrament both confirms baptism and strengthens baptismal grace.

1297   Cancel the word "Syriac" so the text reads:

The liturgy of Antioch expresses the epiclesis for the consecration. . . .

1300   The second half of this paragraph, referring to the Eastern Churches, is to be modified and a new footnote added:

The second half of the paragraph will read:

In the Eastern Churches of Byzantine rite, after a prayer of epiclesis, the more significant parts of the body are anointed with myron: forehead, eyes, nose, ears, lips, chest, back, hands, and feet. Each anointing is accompanied by the formula Σφραγὶς δωρεᾶς Πνεύματος Ἁγίου (*Signaculum doni Spiritus Sancti*): "the seal of the gift of the Holy Spirit."[NT]

NT *Rituale per le Chiese orientali di rito bizantino in lingua greca,* Pars Prima (Libreria Editrice Vaticana, 1954) 36.

1302   Change the word "full" to "special" in the sentence which presently reads:

"It is evident from its celebration that the effect of the sacrament of Confirmation is the full outpouring of the

Holy Spirit as once granted to the apostles on the day of Pentecost."

So that the paragraph will read:

It is evident from its celebration that the effect of the sacrament of Confirmation is the special outpouring of the Holy Spirit as once granted to the apostles on the day of Pentecost.

1307   Change the first sentence of the paragraph which presently reads: "The Latin tradition gives the 'age of discretion' as the reference point for receiving Confirmation."

The paragraph will read:

For centuries, Latin custom has indicated "the age of discretion" as the reference point for receiving Confirmation.

1313   Change the first part of the paragraph from:

"In the Latin rite, the ordinary minister of Confirmation is the bishop. Although the bishop may for grave reasons concede to priests the faculty of administering Confirmation, it is appropriate from the very meaning of the sacrament that he should confer it himself, mindful that the celebration . . ."

The new formulation is:

In the Latin rite, **the ordinary minister of Confirmation is the bishop. If the need arises, the bishop may grant the faculty of administering Confirmation to priests, although it is fitting that he confer it himself, mindful that the celebration . . .**

1314   Change the first sentence which reads "If a Christian is in danger of death, any priest should give him Confirmation."

The sentence should read:

If a Christian is in danger of death, any priest can give him Confirmation.

1320   The final phrase of the paragraph which presently reads: "... in the Roman rite, or 'The seal of the gift that is the Holy Spirit' in the Byzantine rite."

Should be changed to read as follows:

in the Roman rite, or: *Signaculum doni Spiritus Sancti* **[the seal of the gift of the Holy Spirit] in the Byzantine rite.**

1367   This paragraph and the corresponding footnote 188 should be modified to appear as follows:

The sacrifice of Christ and the sacrifice of the Eucharist are *one single sacrifice:* **"The victim is one and the same: the same now offers through the ministry of priests, who then offered himself on the cross; only the manner of offering is different." "And since in this divine sacrifice which is celebrated in the Mass, the same Christ who offered himself once in a bloody manner on the altar of the cross is contained and offered in an unbloody manner ... this sacrifice is truly propitiatory."[188]**

188 Council of Trent (1562) *Doctrina de ss. Missae sacrificio,* **c. 2: DS 1743; cf.** *Heb* **9:14, 27.**

1388   The first part of this paragraph and footnote 219 are to be changed as follows and a new footnote added.

It is in keeping with the very meaning of the Eucharist that the faithful, if they have the required dispositions,[NT] *receive communion when* **they participate in the Mass.[219]**

NT Cf. CIC, can. 916.

219 Cf. CIC, can. 917; *The faithful may receive the Holy Eucharist only a second time on the same day* [Cf. Pontificia Commissio Codici Iuris Canonici Authentice Intrepretando, *Responsa ad proposita dubia*, 1: AAS 76 (1984) 746].

1389   In this paragraph cancel the quotation marks around the phrase "to take part in the Divine Liturgy on Sundays and feast days" and change footnote 221. Thus, the initial phrase of this paragraph and the corresponding footnote will appear:

The Church obliges the faithful to take part in the Divine Liturgy on Sundays and feast days and, prepared by the sacrament of Reconciliation, to receive the Eucharist at least once a year, if possible during the Easter season. [221]

221 Cf. *OE* **15; CIC, can. 920.**

1400   Change the second sentence which presently reads:

"It is for this reason that Eucharistic intercommunion with these communities is not possible for the Catholic Church."

This sentence should read:

It is for this reason that, for the Catholic Church, Eucharistic intercommunion with these communities is not possible.

1417   This paragraph is to be changed to read:

The Church warmly recommends that the faithful receive Holy Communion when they participate in the celebration of the Eucharist; she obliges them to do so at least once a year.

1454   The second sentence of this paragraph is to be changed to read:

The passages best suited to this can be found in the Ten Commandments, the moral catechesis of the Gospels and the apostolic Letters, such as the Sermon on the Mount and the apostolic teachings.

1471   The final sentence of this paragraph should be changed and a new footnote added:

The faithful can gain indulgences for themselves or apply them to the dead.[NT]

NT CIC, can. 994.

1481   In the middle of this paragraph, the reference to "the Pharisee" is to be changed to:

the publican

1483   The sentence which reads:

"In this case, for the absolution to be valid the faithful must have the intention of individually confessing their sins in the time required."

Is to be changed to:

In this case, for the absolution to be valid the faithful must have the intention of individually confessing their grave sins in the time required.

1537   Add a cross-reference to paragraph 922.

1583   Change the first part of the first sentence of the paragraph which presently reads:

"It is true that someone validly ordained can, for a just reason, be discharged from the obligations and functions linked to ordination. . . ."

The phrase will read:

It is true that someone validly ordained can, for grave reasons, be discharged from the obligations and functions linked to ordination. . . .

1605   In the second sentence of this paragraph cancel the words "i.e., his counterpart" so that the sentence reads:

The woman, "flesh of his flesh," his equal, his nearest in all things, is given to him by God as a "helpmate";

1611   Change the last sentence of this paragraph which presently reads:

"Tradition has always seen in the *Song of Solomon* a unique expression of human love, a pure reflection of God's love — a love 'strong as death' that 'many waters cannot quench.'"

This sentence will read:

Tradition has always seen in the *Song of Solomon* a unique expression of human love, insofar as it is a reflection of God's love — a love "strong as death" that "many waters cannot quench."

1623   Change this paragraph to read as follows, with the addition of two footnotes:

According to the Latin tradition, the spouses as ministers of Christ's grace mutually confer upon each other the sacrament of Matrimony by expressing their consent before the Church. In the traditions of the Eastern Churches, the priests (bishops or presbyters) are witnesses to the mutual consent given by the spouses,[NT1] but for the validity of the sacrament their blessing is also necessary.[NT2]

NT1 Cf. CCEO, can. 817.
NT2 Cf. CCEO, can. 828.

1635   The second half of this paragraph is to be changed to read:

This permission or dispensation presupposes that both parties know and do not exclude the essential ends and properties of marriage; and furthermore that the Catholic party confirms the obligations, which have been made known to the non-Catholic party, of preserving his or her own faith and ensuring the baptism and education of the children in the Catholic Church.

1672   Change the reference from "the consecration of virgins" in the second sentence to:

the consecration of virgins and widows,

1684   This paragraph will be changed to read as follows and footnote 15 (Cf. SC 81-82) is to be canceled.

The Christian funeral is a liturgical celebration of the Church. The ministry of the Church in this instance aims at expressing efficacious communion with *the deceased,* at the participation in that communion of *the community* gathered for the funeral, and at the proclamation of eternal life to the community.

1687   In the final sentence of the paragraph, change the reference to the "fortieth day after death" to:

thirtieth day after death

1702   Change the word "union" to "unity" in the second sentence so that it reads:

It shines forth in the communion of persons, in the likeness of the unity of the divine persons among themselves (cf. *chapter two).*

1863   Change the sentence which presently reads:

"However venial sin does not set us in direct opposition
to the will and friendship of God; it does not break the
covenant with God."

This sentence should read:

**However venial sin does not break the covenant with
God.**

1864 Change the biblical citation which introduces this
paragraph:

The paragraph will begin:

**"Therefore I tell you, every sin and blasphemy will be
forgiven men, but the blasphemy against the Spirit
will not be forgiven."[136]**

Footnote 136 is to be changed to read:

136 *Mt* **12:31; cf.** *Mk* **3:29;** *Lk* **12:10.**

1878 In the second sentence the word "union" is to be
replaced by "unity." This sentence should read:

**There is a certain resemblance between the unity of
the divine persons and the fraternity that men are to
establish among themselves in truth and love.**

1890 Again the word "union" is to be replaced by "unity."
The paragraph will read:

**There is a certain resemblance between the unity of
the divine persons and the fraternity that men ought
to establish among themselves.**

2041 In the second sentence the word "indispensable" is to be
replaced by "very necessary" so that it reads:

**The obligatory character of these positive laws
decreed by the pastoral authorities is meant to**

guarantee to the faithful the very necessary minimum in the spirit of prayer and moral effort, in the growth in love of God and neighbor:

2042   The description of the first precept of the Church is to be changed and footnote 82 is to be expanded to read as follows:

The first precept ("You shall attend Mass on Sundays and on holy days of obligation and rest from servile labor") requires the faithful to sanctify the day commemorating the Resurrection of the Lord as well as the principal liturgical feasts honoring the mysteries of the Lord, the Blessed Virgin Mary, and the saints; in the first place, by participating in the Eucharistic celebration, in which the Christian community is gathered, and by resting from those works and activities which could impede such a sanctification of these days.[82]

82 Cf. CIC, cann. 1246-1248; CCEO, cann. 880 § 3, 881 §§ 1, 2, 4.

The initial part of the description of the third precept is to be changed as follows:

The third precept ("You shall receive the sacrament of the Eucharist at least during the Easter season") guarantees as a minimum the reception of the Lord's Body and Blood. . . .

2043   The fourth and fifth precepts are to be changed to read as follows:

The fourth precept ("You shall observe the days of fasting and abstinence established by the Church") ensures the times of ascesis and penance which prepare us for the liturgical feasts and help us acquire mastery over our instincts and freedom of heart.[NT1]

The fifth precept ("You shall help to provide for the

needs of the Church") means that the faithful are obliged to assist with the material needs of the Church, each according to his own ability.[NT2]

NT1 Cf. CIC, cann. 1249-1251: CCEO can. 882.
NT2 Cf. CIC, can. 222; CCEO can. 25; *Furthermore, episcopal conferences can establish other ecclesiastical precepts for their own territories* (Cf. CIC, can. 455).

2265   This paragraph will be changed to read:

Legitimate defense can be not only a right but a grave duty for one who is responsible for the lives of others. The defense of the common good requires that an unjust aggressor be rendered unable to cause harm. For this reason, those who legitimately hold authority also have the right to use arms to repel aggressors against the civil community entrusted to their responsibility.

2266   This paragraph will be changed to read:

The efforts of the state to curb the spread of behavior harmful to people's rights and to the basic rules of civil society correspond to the requirement of safeguarding the common good. Legitimate public authority has the right and the duty to inflict punishment proportionate to the gravity of the offense. Punishment has the primary aim of redressing the disorder introduced by the offense. When it is willingly accepted by the guilty party, it assumes the value of expiation. Punishment then, in addition to defending public order and protecting people's safety, has a medicinal purpose: as far as possible, it must contribute to the correction of the guilty party.

2267   This paragraph will be changed to read:

Assuming that the guilty party's identity and responsibility have been fully determined, the

traditional teaching of the Church does not exclude recourse to the death penalty, if this is the only possible way of effectively defending human lives against the unjust aggressor.

If, however, non-lethal means are sufficient to defend and protect people's safety from the aggressor, authority will limit itself to such means, as these are more in keeping with the concrete conditions of the common good and more in conformity with the dignity of the human person.

Today, in fact, as a consequence of the possibilities which the state has for effectively preventing crime, by rendering one who has committed an offense incapable of doing harm — without definitively taking away from him the possibility of redeeming himself — the cases in which the execution of the offender is an absolute necessity "are very rare, if not practically non-existent."NT

NT John Paul II, *Evangelium vitae* 56.

2296   This paragraph will be changed to read:

Organ transplants are in conformity with the moral law if the physical and psychological dangers and risks to the donor are proportionate to the good that is sought for the recipient. Organ donation after death is a noble and meritorious act and is to be encouraged as an expression of generous solidarity. It is not morally acceptable if the donor or his proxy has not given explicit consent. Moreover, it is not morally admissible directly to bring about the disabling mutilation or death of a human being, even in order to delay the death of other persons.

Add a cross-reference to paragraph 2301.

2297   In the third sentence which presently reads:

"*Terrorism* which threatens, wounds, and kills indiscriminately is gravely against justice and charity."

The word "which" is to be omitted so that the sentence reads:

Terrorism **threatens, wounds, and kills indiscriminately; it is gravely against justice and charity.**

2326 The word "gravely" is to be added to this paragraph so that it reads as follows:

Scandal is a grave offense when by deed or omission it deliberately leads others to sin gravely.

2337 Add a cross-reference to paragraph 2349.

2351 Add a cross-reference to paragraph 2528.

2352 The final phrase of this paragraph which presently reads:

". . . force of acquired habit, conditions of anxiety, or other psychological or social factors that lessen or even extenuate moral culpability."

This phase will be changed to read:

force of acquired habit, conditions of anxiety, or other psychological or social factors that can lessen, if not even reduce to a minimum, moral culpability.

2358 The second sentence of this paragraph is to be changed to read as follows:

This inclination, which is objectively disordered, constitutes for most of them a trial.

2366 The sentence in the middle of the paragraph in which chapter 11 of *Humanae vitae* is cited is to be changed to read as follows:

So the Church, which is "on the side of life," teaches that "it is necessary that each and every marriage act remain ordered *per se* to the procreation of human life."

2368   The first sentence which presently reads:

"A particular aspect of this responsibility concerns the *regulation of births.*"

This will be changed to read:

A particular aspect of this responsibility concerns the *regulation of procreation.*

2372   The final sentence of this paragraph which reads:

"It is not authorized to promote demographic regulation by means contrary to the natural law."

This will be changed to read:

In this area, it is not authorized to employ means contrary to the moral law.

2403   The first sentence presently reads:

"The *right to private property,* acquired by work or received from others by inheritance or gift, does not do away with the original gift of the earth to the whole of mankind."

This sentence will be changed to read:

The *right to private property,* acquired or received in a just way, does not do away with the original gift of the earth to the whole of mankind.

2411   The words "and between institutions" are to be added to this paragraph so that the first sentence reads as follows:

Contracts are subject to *commutative justice* which regulates exchanges between persons and between institutions in accordance with a strict respect for their rights.

2417   The final sentence of this paragraph presently reads:

"Medical and scientific experimentation on animals, if it remains within reasonable limits, is a morally acceptable practice since it contributes to caring for or saving human lives."

This sentence will be changed to read:

Medical and scientific experimentation on animals is a morally acceptable practice if it remains within reasonable limits and contributes to caring for or saving human lives.

2483   The second sentence of this paragraph presently reads:

"To lie is to speak or act against the truth in order to lead into error someone who has the right to know the truth."

This sentence will be modified to read:

To lie is to speak or act against the truth in order to lead someone into error.

2508   This paragraph will be changed to simply read:

Lying consists in saying what is false with the intention of deceiving one's neighbor.

2599   The first part of this paragraph is to be changed to read:

The Son of God who became Son of the Virgin also learned to pray according to his human heart. He learns the formulas of prayer from his mother, who kept in her heart and meditated upon all the "great things" done by the Almighty.

Add a cross-reference to paragraphs 470-473.

2715   The second sentence of this paragraph is to be changed to read as follows:

"I look at him and he looks at me": this is what a certain peasant of Ars in the time of his holy curé used to say while praying before the tabernacle.

2834   The sentence which reads:

"Even when we have done our work, the food we receive is still a gift from our Father; it is good to ask him for it with thanksgiving, as Christian families do when saying grace at meals."

This phrase is to be changed to read:

Even when we have done our work, the food we receive is still a gift from our Father; it is good to ask him for it and to thank him, as Christian families do when saying grace at meals.